P9-AGF-795

THE DRAMA OF MEDIEVAL ENGLAND

THE DRAMA
OF MEDIEVAL
ENGLAND

by
ARNOLD WILLIAMS

MICHIGAN STATE UNIVERSITY PRESS

1961

LIBRARY

OCT 2 2 1963

UNIVERSITY OF THE PACIFIC

122801

Copyright © 1961

Michigan State University Press
Library of Congress Catalog Card Number: 60-16415

Manufactured in the United States of America

★ ★
★
★
★

CONTENTS

PREFACE

THIS BRIEF ACCCOUNT of the liturgical drama of Western Europe and of the vernacular drama of England from the late tenth century to about 1500 is addressed to the general reader, not to the literary scholar. The latter has an abundance of resources more definitive and more authoritative than I can provide.

But the lover of the theater, the playgoer, or the tourist who has seen the magnificent production of the old plays at York and would like to know more about the sort of drama they represent is not so well served. If he lacks the technical tools of scholarship, a knowledge of Latin and of Middle English, for example, or if he is unfamiliar with the interests and techniques of literary scholarship, five hundred years of a drama which he might learn to love is pretty well closed to him.

It is my hope to provide the sort of introduction such a reader can use. To that end I have tried to do much of the specialized work for him, and to transfer the result of specialized scholarship into the terms of a living theater. The Latin I have translated, except for a few terms (*quem quaeritis*, for example) which baffle my efforts. I have likewise modernized the English, which is generally not only medieval but also dialectal, as much as I could without losing the rime or upsetting the meter. When it was necessary to keep an archaic word or expression I have glossed it.

The sole purpose of all of this is to get at the dramatic essentials, which are likely to be obscured by unfamiliar language, stage conventions, and social usages. Once these are understood, the remarkable vitality of the drama of the later middle ages can work its own way with the reader.

If any of my more learned colleagues condemn such procedures as vulgarization I can only reply as Professor Coghill did to those who accused him of "surrendering the castle" when he modernized Chaucer. "I never thought of Chaucer," he said, "as a castle, but as a garden."

The bibliography at the end is intended for the more curious reader who may want to venture a bit further into the drama of the Middle Ages. Though it provides a reference for every work specifically cited in the text, it does not record my indebtedness to the host of scholars whose results I have used, much less to many friends, colleagues, and students on whom I have tried out my opinions. Dr. W. L. Smoldon and Professor Hans Nathan helped me with the music, and Professor Nevill Coghill called my attention to the van Alsloot paintings.

Chapter 1. PROLOGUE

OF ALL THE LITERARY ARTS drama is the most social and the most popular, in every sense of that word. Alone among the literary arts drama requires a cooperation of several people for its being. A novel may be written in solitude and read in solitude; so may an epic or a lyric poem or an essay. True, in earlier times poetry was generally sung or recited to an audience, and a folk story is normally told to a group. But they need not be. As the written and then the printed word has replaced the spoken, literature becomes more and more a solitary enjoyment—all kinds but the drama.

In its very essence a community of people is required for the production of a play. Today there is commonly an author, a producer, a director, a group of actors, and numerous specialists in costume, lighting, scenery, perhaps even music and choreography. Next time you go to the cinema, note how many credit titles there are: "technical direction by so-and-so, Miss Star's gowns designed by so-and-so," and the rest of them. This is testimony to the community of talents necessary to produce the favorite kind of drama of our age. The millions of people who see the picture are witnesses to the popularity of this sort of drama.

In simpler ages, of course, not so many people were required in the production of a play. But by the utmost economy—"nine may play it at ease" reads the note to an early play—you need a group of actors. A play read is not a real play any more than a blueprint is a house. A play must be acted, and therefore you must have actors. It is also common, and before radio and television it was necessary, to have an audience. That means that to enjoy drama you must become one of a group. People buy and read novels individually, but they must witness plays or the cinema, collectively.

This is perhaps the most distinguishing mark between drama and the other literary arts. Drama is social, communal, and popular. Its rise and flourishing is always associated with some sort of group consciousness. Its great periods have invariably coincided with periods when a special solidarity was felt among large groups of people, whether the citizens of fifth century Athens, the burghers of medieval York, or the populace of Elizabethan London.

The great dramatists of the world have appealed to a wide public. Aeschylus aimed at the whole population of Athens and Shakespeare at a considerable part of that of London. Milton wrote his *Paradise Lost* for a fit audience though few, and so have numbers of novelists, Proust for instance. But so far as I can discover no great dramatist ever wrote for

I

a select coterie. Doubtless the very nature of drama prohibits such limitations, for it is a notorious fact that when you put people in groups, you rub off much of their individuality and level down their intellectual differences. Great dramatists, no matter how serious their message or how profound their philosophy, have always contrived to put into their works enough blood and thunder, suspense and pageantry to appeal to the lowest common denominator of their audience.

If, then, we call drama the most social and the most popular of the literary arts, we shall accurately describe it, but of course we shall not define it. What is drama? One thinks of certain elements which all or most dramas have in common. One is dialogue. The play tells its story by an interchange of speeches between its characters. But unless we wish to exclude both pantomime and the silent cinema, dialogue is not necessary. It is also true that many works using dialogue as the exclusive method of presentation are not dramas, the Dialogues of Plato for instance. Drama also usually tells its story in action, instead of narrative, but this does not apply to the radio play.

We have, however, assumed two elements which are the very heart of drama, story and impersonation. The former is really the genus and the latter the differentia of a definition of drama. Aristotle noted this when he defined tragedy as "an imitation of an action." A drama may not have dialogue, it may not have action, its presentation may be in a theater, it may not use costumes, scenery, lighting, or any other of the effects we are used to. But it must tell a story, and it must have actors (in the plural, unless we are to regard a monologue as drama), who pretend, for the time being, that they are someone else. Make-believe is of the essence of drama.

It should be noted, however, that it is enough for a portion of the story to be presented by impersonated characters for the work to qualify as drama. The Greek drama had its chorus, the medieval drama its expositors and doctors, later English drama used choruses, prologues, epilogues up until the latter part of the nineteenth century. Under the influence of Ibsen and other naturalistic dramatists, critics began to condemn such devices as "non-dramatic," and one will find such attitudes in much that has been written on the medieval drama. But, though banished from the stage in the first decade or so of this century, the chorus, the commentator, the narrator have made a strong comeback in the last twenty years, and if we disallowed such devices, we would exile from dramatic literature not only Sophocles and Shakespeare, but also Thornton Wilder.

The fact is that many kinds of drama need the assistance of someone standing, as it were, outside the action and providing the background for it or explaining or commenting on it. Radio, cinema, and more recently television have found the commentator or the narrator invaluable. Of

2

course, the chorus may necessitate impersonation, as when Aeschuylus has one of Spartan elders in *Agamemnon*—the audience knew that the men in the chorus were actually Athenians, hence impersonation is involved— but again it may not. In some early medieval plays, narrative and comment are provided by the choir, which does not pretend to be anything but what it is. So we can hardly require that all parts of a play be represented in impersonation; it suffices that some are.

Another important fact about drama is that it originates in religious ritual. At least all drama whose origins have been studied turns out to have arisen out of ritual. Students of myth and ritual suggest, with strong supporting evidence, that drama goes back to some sort of ceremony in which a king-god was killed, and a new one inaugurated in his place. This ceremony they view as an obvious imitation of the death of vegetation in the fall and its rebirth in the spring. In the earliest ceremonies of this sort the king-god was actually killed, often by his successor, who then became the new god, for a reign of one year. The time came when the more foreseeing members of the tribe rejected the actual killing as wasteful, and the more tender hearted as too bloody.

Still the necessity for the ritual remained. If man did not imitate nature, nature might fail to imitate man, and the vegetation would not revive in the spring. The solution was some sort of imitation or substitution. Instead of killing a man, one could kill a beast, pretending that it was a man. Something like this lies behind the story of Abraham's sacrifice of Isaac. Or the ceremony could be performed in make-believe. The killing could be only pretended; the king-god pretended to die, then to rise again. This is a story, and it is told in something like impersonation. Still another possibility is that the killing may be actual, but the person killed is not the real king, but only a substitute, pretending to be the king for the purposes of the ceremony. This version qualifies in every respect as a drama.

Doubtless this account is over-simplified. It is conceivable that somewhere a play rose from a ceremony of a very different type, but this death-and-rebirth ritual is extraordinarily widespread among agricultural peoples, and it certainly gave birth to dramatic rituals. Perhaps it does not strictly apply to the origin of Greek drama. The exact details of the development of tragedy and comedy among the Greeks is still a matter of dispute among classical scholars and mythologists. Beyond dispute is the fact that both forms rose out of some sort of religious rites, most probably of the god Dionysius.

Most of us think of Dionysius as the god of wine, but his province was much wider, including pretty nearly all aspects of fertility, reproduction, and growth. As such, he must have been more important to the common folk, who labored in field and vineyard, than were the Olympians, even Zeus himself. It seems certain that out of his ceremonies came the combination of dance, song, and story told in imitative action which we call tragedy. The word means merely "goat song," apparently because the worshippers who acted the first tragedies were dressed as goats—the imitative principle again—and the goat was specially sacred to Dionysius.

Greek comedy has a similar, though even more obscure, origin. The "old comedy" of Aristophanes was an exercise of personal abuse and general scurrility. It reflects probably the more obscene and vulgar side of the Dionysian festivities, and its name derives from a word, *komos*, meaning merely "revelry," the sort of merriment characteristic of uninhibited peasants at harvest time. The fantastic in both situation and character, still observable in the mardi gras of Latin peoples, played a great part. This old comedy was reformed into the "new comedy" which kept and refined the merry spirit of the old but adopted the tragic method of telling a story, and became somewhat more dramatic in the change.

The tragedy and comedy of the Greeks, imitated by the Romans, might have furnished models for the earliest playwrights of the modern European vernaculars. The epic of Greece, in the Latin form of Virgil, certainly influenced the poets of medieval Europe, as did classical lyric poetry, classical history, and classical philosophy. But it did not happen so with drama. Tragedy and comedy on the Greek model had little if any impact on Western Europe until the fifteenth and sixteenth centuries, when another sort of drama had been in existence for five hundred years.

Drama has had two births in Europe, once from the rites of pagan Greece, the second time from those of Christian Rome. How this came about is a fascinating story, conjectural in parts but sufficiently clear in broad outline to afford perhaps the best account anywhere of the rise of a literary form.

The drama of classical times died with the Roman empire—it was probably moribund even before Vandal and Goth extinguished Roman political power in the West. Scholars have tended to blame Christianity too exclusively for the demise of drama. No doubt the Church was hostile to plays. But when Christianity became the official religion of Rome in 378, plays did not immediately cease. St. Augustine, who died in 430, was, judging by the many allusions to plays and actors, an ardent theatergoer. Actually a combination of causes killed the classical theater. The drama was never a particularly strong art form in Rome, whence Western Europe received its introduction to classical culture. The theater seems to have been commercialized and (perhaps therefore) degraded in Rome; Roman law takes a rather severe attitude towards players both before and after the triumph of Christianity. Persistent attendance at theaters is named as a reason for divorce, for instance. In many respects, the Church merely echoes the sentiments of the stricter moralists among the pagans.

4

The chief cause of the death of the Roman theater lies, I believe, in the very nature of drama, the fact that it is the most popular and social of the literary arts. The social structure of Roman society was so changed both by the disintegration of the empire and by barbarian invasion that an art form weak to begin with and utterly dependent on social consciousness, did not survive the double blow. Epic and lyric, philosophical dialogue and didactic essay could survive, because it was necessary only that the manuscripts survive which contained the *Aeneid* or Horace's *Odes*. So long as they were about and so long as men could read, they could survive. But drama is not a matter of manuscript—it is a tradition and a social phenomenon.

In fact, the manuscripts of Roman drama did survive. Terence was read, copied, and quoted all through the Middle Ages, and of course Plautus and Seneca survived, else we would not have them today. The words *tragedy*, *comedy*, and *theater* continue in usage throughout the time. In the tenth century a German nun, Hroswitha, even wrote some "plays" modeled on Terence. But here is a revealing note on the nature of drama. Hroswitha, though she wrote six pieces in imitation of Terence, never seems to have realized that a play is designed to be presented on a stage by actors. She apparently thought they were only to be read, or perhaps declaimed. In medieval authors a "theater" is a particular kind of edifice. Chaucer makes his Monk define tragedy as a story of someone that stood in great prosperity, falls into misery, and ends wretchedly. Comedy is the opposite. To Dante a poem of epic proportions which starts with the author lost in a dark woods, carries him through hell, purgatory, and heaven, and ends with an instant of the beatific vision is a "divine comedy."

So although the texts of some Roman plays lived, drama itself died in Western Europe. Or perhaps we should say that it was reduced to the simplest form in which it could retain dormant life, like a spore. For as long as the texts existed, it was possible that they could come to life when people regained the dramatic vision. Perhaps also drama lived on in some form in the activities of the hosts of popular entertainers, minstrels, scops, jugglers, acrobats, troubadours and troveres. Perhaps some of them kept alive the arts of the Roman *histrio* and on occasion to heighten the effect of their story or performance did a bit of impersonation. If so, their activity lies outside the province of documentary history.

Scholars have sought drama in another place, also: in the rites of Germanic or Celtic paganism, living on, after the introduction of Christianity, as folk customs. Pagan rites suitable for dramatization existed in plenty—both Celts and Teutons had myths of dying and resurrected gods. Folk customs which seem to go back to these rites lived through the Middle Ages into modern times, the morris dance for instance. Sir E. K. Chambers was able to assemble a whole volume of such material, and the German scholar Stumpfl added a great deal to the bulk. The mummer's play of St. George, which involves a death and a miraculous restoration to life, and the Robin Hood plays are thought by most scholars to go back to pagan ceremonial rites. It is quite possible that plays existed among the folk—true plays because they required impersonation and told a story.

It is possible, but there is no proof. The trouble is that the earliest mention of such plays comes from the fifteenth century. In one of the Paston letters, dated 1473, Sir John Paston laments the departure of a servant who played "Saint George and Robin Hood and the Sheriff of Nottingham." A scrap of paper, probably also from the Paston collection, gives a part of a Robin Hood play. But by 1473 a drama based on the Bible had been in existence half a millenium and had reached maturity in form. So the case of folk drama as the origin of the drama of the Middle Ages is unproved and unprovable.

One must not, however, in ruling out folk drama as an origin deny that the broken-down rituals of paganism greatly contributed to the religious drama of the Middle Ages. In fact, as we shall see, hardly any source contributed more to great cycle plays and the moralities except the Bible and the liturgy of the Roman Church.

To understand the exact mechanics of the origin of drama in the early Middle Ages we must review some centuries of liturgical development. As with the folk custom, the liturgy of the Roman Church abounded in materials easily dramatized. Anyone who has ever attended a Catholic mass knows that it teems with elements of drama: the dialogue of antiphon and response, the movements of the priest, the elaborate costuming of the vestments, the symbolic actions of the priest, such as the elevation of the host—all is the finest kind of material for the dramatist. Only impersonation is lacking. If only the priest were impersonating Christ when he pronounces the words of consecration: "This is indeed my body." But he isn't. The canon of the mass makes it clear that he is quoting, not impersonating: "Who before he suffered took bread in his holy and venerable hands . . . blessed it, broke it, and gave it to his disciples saying: Accept and eat of this all of you. This is indeed my body."

Some additions to the liturgy, however, came near, or may even have become, drama. One of these is the dedication of a new church. As the dedicating bishop approaches, he strikes the door three times singing "Lift up your heads, o ye gates" (Psalm 24). In some versions, two subdeacons run out of the side or back door of the church as the bishop enters. Obviously they are devils being exorcised by the dedication ceremonies. The dramatic possibilities of this rite are later realized in the plays of the harrowing of hell, almost all of which use this psalm.

The most interesting of such liturgical additions are two related observances of the Easter season. On Good Friday from twelve to three in the afternoon Catholic Churches today display a cross, usually on the steps leading to the sanctuary. The faithful come to pray and to kiss the cross. Many medieval churches carried this observance much further. The cross, after the adoration was over, was taken to a "sepulchre," some sort of coffer, and deposited there. An alternative was to deposit a host consecrated on Maundy Thursday in the sepulchre instead of a cross. Then on Easter morning the cross or host was taken out of the sepulchre, a clear representation of the burial and resurrection.

This ceremony may at times have been an actual drama. It is hard to tell from the extant texts, and even harder to know whether the deposition and elevation of the host or cross antedates the first extant liturgical play. If the deposition and elevation did come first, then it was certainly one element that contributed to the first recognizable drama. That is uncertain. It cannot, however, be doubted that another liturgical development is entirely or chiefly responsible for the rebirth of drama in Western Europe.

In the Merovingian age several liturgies were in use in Western Europe, the Ambrosian, the Gallican, probably an Irish one, and the Roman. The reign of Charlemagne saw a strong effort to unify liturgical practice on the Roman model. This might be called a stifling of creative impulse, since the Roman liturgy was more standardized and offered less opportunities for elaboration than the Ambrosian or the Gallican.

The creative impulse, or perhaps only the desire to be different, stopped at one point, broke through at another. One imagines that monks, required to sing the same words over and over again to the same melody, became so bored that they were driven to improvise variations—choirs today will do that unless restrained by a firm hand. One variation was to prolong the vowel sounds of certain important words. The product of such prolongation you can hear even today, when towards the end of the mass the priest sings the words of dismissal, *Ite missa est*, "go the mass is over." In even the plainest sung mass the *e* of the *ite* will be prolonged: iteeeeeeeee and so on. Many vowel sounds in the service were so treated, producing what is technically known as a "sequence." The one in which we are particularly interested is the *alleluia* of the introit to the Easter mass.

According to Notker Babulus, writing before 912, remembering these long wordless sequences imposed a burden on the memory of the singers. When he was a boy in the great Swiss monastery of St. Gall, he tells us, he found it very difficult to remember the music. And well he might! For there was but one service book for the whole choir, which was too far away for many to see—probably only the leader. And in any case

7

musical notation, where it was used at all, was very rudimentary in those days.

When in 851 a monk came to the monastery of St. Gall from Jumièges in Normandy, then under attack from the Northmen, he brought with him a service book which solved Notker's problem. In the book, Notker says, he saw that words were written to the long sequences. Notker liked neither the words nor the music in the stranger's book, but the idea was invaluable. So Notker tried his hand at writing new words and new music. He showed the result to his master Yvo, who made some correctional comments and encouraged the boy to perfect the new style. This Notker did, producing perhaps fifty "tropes," as these words to sequences were called.

Scholars do not all agree to accept this as the true account of the invention of tropes. Some doubt that tropes were invented at a particular time and place, but suppose that, as the next logical step in the evolution of liturgical music, the trope may have been invented severally at different monasteries. Notker's story, however, must be at least symbolically true. Certain it is that the first tropes appear in France, and that in the early tenth century the monks of St. Gall excel in their composition.

Be that as it may, a tenth-century manuscript from St. Gall contains a trope designed for the introit of the Easter Mass, which runs thus:

QUESTION: Whom seek ye in the sepulchre, followers of Christ.
RESPONSE: Jesus of Nazareth who was crucified, O heavenly beings. He is not here, He has risen as he had foretold. Go, announce it, because he has risen from the tomb.

Then follows the regular introit of the Easter mass, beginning, *Resurrexi*, "He has risen."

This trope called from the first two words in Latin, "quem quaeritis," is already a dialogue, and it strongly suggests the setting and action of a playlet. The three Marys approach the tomb on Easter morning, bringing spices to anoint the body of the Lord. At the tomb they find an angel who asks them whom they seek. They reply and he tells them the news of the resurrection. All we need for a true, though brief, play is impersonation. If instead of merely dividing the text between two halves of the choir, or between the leader and the rest of the choir, one member of the choir sings the question and three others the answer, and if these four people try in some manner to give the impression that they are the angel and the three Marys, respectively, then we have a play. As soon as that happens we are safely on the road that leads to the York cycle and *Everyman*, Shakespeare and Shaw, and the latest Hollywood epic.

Before this could happen, the trope had to be shifted from its place in the mass to a freer locality. As long as it was part of the mass, development was inhibited, for you can't be perpetually interrupting the central rite of the Church for side issues. A little extra singing is all right for a special feast like Easter, but not the introduction of long ceremonies.

So many tropes were moved, including the quem quaeritis. A half century or so later we meet it as part of the monastic service of the hours. St. Benedict had divided the time of his followers among work, rest, and prayer. The prayer had been organized into services at regular intervals during the day. The first of these, matins, preceded daybreak, and was divided into three nocturnes, each containing antiphons, verses, prayers, and lessons and responsories. It is here, often at the end of the third lesson, that we begin to find the quem quaeritis trope.

This was a good location for it. It was free to develop. The time of its presentation, early Easter morning, was symbolically appropriate. Moreover, its development was in the hands of perhaps the strongest social community of the age, the monastery, which held moreover almost all the learning and more than a moderate share of the intelligence of the age.

And here it developed into a real play.

Chapter II. THE RESURRECTION PLAY

THE FIRST MEDIEVAL DRAMA comes from England in the third quarter of the tenth century. That is not quite accurate, either. An accurate statement is that no trope which can be proved to be a drama can be proved to be earlier than the Easter trope contained in the *Regularis Concordia*. We have samples of the quem quaeritis undoubtedly earlier, but we cannot prove that the monks who sang them also impersonated the characters. We likewise have tropes whose presentation certainly involved impersonation, but we cannot date them before the English one.

The *Regularis Concordia*, "harmony of the rule," was compiled by St. Æthelwold, probably between 965 and 975, in an attempt to get some uniformity in the liturgical observances of the Benedictine monasteries of England. The preface says that King Ædgar (d. 975) suggested the project, and Ælfrida, who became Ædgar's queen in 965, is mentioned. Other persons mentioned in the work, St. Æthelwold and St. Dunstan, have corroborating dates. This definiteness of date is unusual in medieval liturgical manuscripts, most of which can be dated only roughly by the handwriting.

Unusual also are the comprehensive rubrics, here used as the first stage directions, which put the matter of impersonation beyond doubt. The author, if that is the correct title for him, reminds us of Shaw in the length of his stage directions. He apparently wanted to take no chances that some lazy or ignorant monk somewhere in England would merely sing, instead of also acting, the lines.

"While the third lesson" of the third nocturne of matins, the rubrics read, "is being chanted, let four brothers dress themselves, of whom let one, clothed in an alb, enter as if to take part in the service. And let him approach the sepulchre unnoticed, and there let him sit quietly with a palm in his hand. While the third responsory is being sung, let the other three follow, all dressed in copes, holding thuribles with incense in their hands. Let them slowly come to the place of the sepulchre in the manner of those seeking something. This is done in imitation of the angel seated at the tomb and the women coming with spices to anoint the body of Jesus. When therefore the one sitting sees the other three wandering about as though they were searching for something, let him begin to sing in a sweet and medium voice."*

---

* Musicologists are still arguing over the meaning of such phrases as "in a *middle*" or *high* or *low* "voice," which are fairly frequent in the liturgical drama. Some scholars think pitch is meant, others volume. So I leave undecided the question of whether the angel sings in the baritone range or somewhere between piano and forte.

There can be no doubt that we have here a play, or perhaps more accurately, an opera. Certainly it is not a recitation, or an oratorio. Even the word *imitation*, the crucial difference between mere recited dialogue and drama, is used, and the author is obviously concerned with getting his actors on stage and even with costuming and properties. The alb, a long white garment, is the nearest thing to the proper garb of an angel which the vestry could furnish. The thurible is a suitable container for the "spices" which the women brought to anoint the Lord's body.

The dialogue which follows is a little fuller than the short quem quaeritis of the last chapter. I have translated the rubrics into stage directions of a modern sort, but I did not invent them or change their intent.

ANGEL. Whom seek ye in the sepulchre, followers of Christ?
WOMEN. Jesus of Nazareth, heavenly being.
ANGEL. He is not here. He has risen as he had foretold. Go announce that he has risen from the dead.
WOMEN. [*to choir*] Alleluia. The Lord has risen. Today has risen the brave lion, Christ, the son of God.
ANGEL. [*recalling them to the tomb*] Come and behold the place where the Lord was laid, alleluia. [*Lifts the veil and shows them the sepulchre, empty except for the grave cloths*]
WOMEN. [*Laying down their thuribles, turning to the clergy, and holding up the grave cloths*] The Lord has risen from the sepulchre, who hung for us on the tree, alleluia. [*They lay the cloths on the altar*]
        [*The Prior begins the hymn*] Te deum laudamus.
        [*As the hymn begins, all the bells chime in unison*]*

Certainly this little Easter play shows a considerable awareness of the dramatic, though probably quite unconscious. The correlation of dialogue and business is of a high order. Even the recalling of the women by the angel, which has been criticized as awkward, adds a certain subtlety. It is as though the women at first think only of their own joy, forgetting their duty of announcing, indeed of proving to the world, the marvelous event of which they are witnesses. Shakespeare uses exactly the same device in Antony's funeral oration. When the citizens prepare to avenge themselves on Brutus and the other assassins of Caesar merely on the word of Antony, he recalls them to hear Caesar's will. They must not only act, but know why they are acting.

Shakespeare was a relatively free agent, at least he wrote his own dialogue. The author of the Easter play in *Regularis Concordia* did not. All he could do was to write the stage directions. But with this limited freedom, he contrived to break through into sound dramatic construction.

* The complete score for this little music-drama, transposed into modern notation by W. L. Smolden, is found on p. 180.

As the first drama of the Middle Ages, this would be a remarkable achievement. But we cannot be sure that it is the first. The conditions of its production suggest that a considerable dramatic development preceded it. One would rather expect a codifier and harmonizer to gather together existing usages than to invent new ones. Moreover, England is not the most likely place to find the first play. The extensive activity in writing tropes and in developing the sung dialogue on which the play is based took place in Switzerland and France rather than in England, and we would rather expect the first real play to come from the continent than from a somewhat isolated island.

In fact, tracing the chronological development of medieval drama is a hazardous business. Most of the scholars, from Marius Sepet, who propounded the first theories about a hundred years ago, to Karl Young, whose *Drama of the Medieval Church* was published in 1933, were too much under the influence of theories of organic evolution. The picture they and their followers give us is too neat. What they had to work with was a mass of documents, mostly liturgical texts, some in manuscript and some printed, dating all the way from the ninth to the seventeenth centuries. That is, the books date from the tenth to the seventeenth centuries. But the fact that a certain trope is found in a manuscript of the eleventh century does not prove that the trope was composed then. All we can say is that it was not composed later. It is entirely possible, to take an extreme example, for a play that occurs in a sixteenth-century printed book to have been composed earlier than one contained in a manuscript written before 1150. My copy of Shakespeare was published in 1942, whereas I have some plays of Shaw printed before 1920.

In dealing with such data scholars have customarily arranged it in a presumed order of composition, supposing that the simpler forms antedate the more complicated. Thus, if we have two plays, one with approximately the text we have above and the other with an added scene at the beginning in which the women sing a lament before they encounter the angel, we would naturally suppose that the longer play is later. But could it not also be that the shorter one represents a cutting of the longer?

How perilous it is to deal with problems of chronology as though they were problems of logic will appear if we take the "evolution" of some familiar device. An archaeologist of 3100 A. D., having dug up several refrigerators might well arrange them in this order: simple wooden boxes for ice, more elaborate metal boxes for ice, metal boxes for mechanical refrigeration. But those who lived through the period when the mechanical refrigerator replaced the ice box know better. The right order is: wooden boxes for ice, mechanical refrigerators, metal boxes for ice. The makers of wooden ice boxes, suffering from the competition of the mechanical boxes, redesigned their product in metal.

May not this sort of thing have happened often in the "evolution" of the liturgical drama? One clear example is available. We have a semi-dramatic singing of the passion story in the gospel according to St. John, in which the text is split up among three cantors, called Petrus, Christus, and Pilatus. We have also a few real liturgical passion plays. Young at first supposed that the plays derived from the sung passion. Later he discovered that all the evidence pointed to the conclusion that the sung passion was actually later than the plays, apparently a partial imitation of them. In our own time, we have seen the stage, certainly the older medium, borrow items of technique from the younger cinema.

So, since the Easter play in the *Regularis Concordia* is virtually unique in giving us firm dates of composition or compilation independent of the date of the manuscript, our efforts at arranging liturgical plays in any order must be tentative. There must be sudden leaps, when a genius reaches in one step a development for which a series of lesser men would require fifty years. The work of such a genius may have been so advanced as to be rejected by his fellows, so that his achievement had to be repeated again half a century later when general taste found it acceptable. All we can do is to reduce the extant documents to a logical order, an ideal line of development, which probably does not represent the true chronological order with its jumps and regressions.

In thinking of the development of liturgical drama, we must also make an effort to recast our minds to medieval times, to free ourselves from the modern prepossession with originality and individuality and novelty. You will no more find a medieval play that is all of one piece, than you will find a medieval church that was built all in one stretch of time. Underneath the Norman Church you will find a Saxon one, and part of the foundation may be that of the old Roman temple; and, of course, someone will have added a porch in the early decorated style. It is the same with medieval drama. No one wrote a new play when he could adapt or augment an old one. In the midst of the York play on the resurrection, which was still playing in Queen Elizabeth's life time, are lines translated, without change, from the quem quaeritis trope.

Our task then is to arrange the plays in an order of simple to complex, presuming that that roughly corresponds to their chronological development, but always prepared to reckon with the fact that some skillful writer may have achieved dramatic effects in an early form which are lacking in a later. A choir somewhere prolongs the vowel sound in the alleluia into a mellismatic sequence. Monks find it hard to remember the music, and someone writes words to the notes. These words tell a story, so St. Æthelwold, or someone earlier, decides the music and the words will make the religious point better if accompanied by mimetic action. Later others add other words and other actions.

Where do the words come from? Usually from the liturgy itself. A hymn or antiphon, another trope, a part of a reading, a psalm would make a suitable introduction or conclusion for a somewhat more elaborate Easter play. Thus the play develops, for a long time within the framework of the liturgy and out of bits and pieces of liturgical material. At first, no one realizes that the product is drama, for no one has a conception of drama. The words they use for the plays are *office, order, procession,* all liturgical entities. Only in the famous *Carmina Burana* manuscript from the Bavarian monastery of Benidictbeuren do we find the title *ludus,* play, and the *Carmina Burana* can hardly antedate the twelfth century.

It is then as part of the liturgy that the drama develops. No one is consciously attempting to produce entertainment, but to perform rites just a bit better than they have been performed before. When the time comes that the liturgy will no longer furnish sufficient materials for dialogues, the newly composed material will be cast in liturgical form. The liturgical drama grows like a snowball or a sedimentary rock.

The Easter play of the *Regularis Concordia* begins with the women wandering about and approaching the sepulchre. The dialogue begins with the angel's question, "Whom seek ye?" An early addition gives the women something to say, or rather sing, as they approach. They wonder how they will get into the tomb: "Who will roll back for us the stone at the door of the sepulchre?" This was an Easter antiphon before it got absorbed into the play. As an antiphon, its text ran, as in Mark 16:13, "And they said to one another: who will roll back," etc. An early play text from Reichenau keeps the antiphon intact:

PRIESTS IN THE ROLE OF WOMEN.   And they said to one another, who . . .

It is an obvious improvement when the play texts drop the speech tag. Thus the realization of proper dramatic construction grows. But one should not think that every addition marks an improvement. Most often it doesn't, for what is added is not a dramatic scene, but some bit of liturgical song, which usually has a speech tag or some similar non-dramatic element. The next step is to drop the non-dramatic part and keep the dramatic. Like as not, the next addition will have to go through a similar process.

Another factor that puts many obstacles in the way of dramatic development is the discrepancies among the gospel accounts of the resurrection. Rather late plays have two angels (as in Luke and John) instead of the *Regularis Concordia's* one (as in Matthew and Mark). Still others have two Marys instead of three. At least one starts with an antiphon based on Matthew 28:1 "In the eve of the sabbath, as it began to dawn toward the first day of the week, came Mary Magdalene and the other Mary to see the sepulchre," and then goes on to the scene with three Marys! In still another, first one angel seated before the tomb tells the Marys that the Lord is risen, and then two angels within the tomb comfort the weeping Magdalen. If we regard one angel and three Marys as the best arrangement, these are clear examples of regression.

Other material, too, was added to the beginning. A version of Sicilian origin, preserved in a manuscript now in Madrid, prefaces the question about the door with a lament, in which each of the Marys sings a part:

FIRST MARY. Alas! Why has it happened so unfortunately that we see the death of the Saviour?
SECOND MARY. Alas! Why did the Redemption of Israel wish to act in such a way?
THIRD MARY. Alas! Why did our consolation undergo death?
THREE MARYS. O God, who will roll back for us the stone at the door of the sepulchre?

The possibilities of addition to the beginning are still not exhausted. The Marys have come to anoint the body of the Lord. So we can have a scene in which they buy the spices. In the simplest form, the choir merely tells us that they bought spices. Fuller versions have them announce their intention of buying the spices, then follow with the purchase in pantomime. Finally, as in a version from Prague, the merchant can be provided with a speech. Liturgical drama ends the development of the scene here, but vernacular drama, probably borrowing from folk materials, enormously elaborates the spice-merchant motif into a comic scene with a sales talk by the merchant, a scuffle between the merchant and his mischievous apprentice, and sometimes even a shrewish wife for the merchant.

The scene at the tomb was not only subject to numerous prefaces, it also accumulated epilogues. After the angel has shown the empty tomb to the Marys he commands them to "Go, announce to the disciples that he is risen." This leads, but not without several false starts, to the race of Peter and John to the Tomb, as told in John 20:4: "So they ran both together: and the other disciple did outrun Peter, and came first to the sepulchre." The development is, as usual, first the gospel words sung by the choir while Peter and John run their race in pantomime, then the provision of speaking parts for the two disciples. They repeat the action of the angel and of the Marys in displaying the cloths and calling attention to the proofs of the resurrection.

Another scene that may be added is the appearance of Jesus to Mary Magdalen, as told in the accounts of Mark and John. In the simplest, though not necessarily the earliest, development of this scene, the appearance of Jesus immediately follows the action at the tomb. It is a bit awkwardly introduced in this Rouen play. After the angel has told the Marys (apparently two) that the Lord is risen, Magdalen begins weeping. Two other angels within the tomb ask her why she weeps:

MAGDALEN. Because they have taken my Lord, and I do not know where they have laid him.

ANGELS. Women, He whom you seek among the dead is alive. He is not here, he has risen. Remember how, when He was still in Galilee, he spoke to you saying that it was necessary for the Son of Man to suffer and be crucified and arise again on the third day. [*Magdalen kisses the place. Afterwards all leave the sepulchre. Jesus, dressed in alb and stole, and carrying a cross, meets them at the left of the altar*]

JESUS. Woman, why do you weep. Whom do you seek?

MAGDALEN. Master, if you took Him away, tell me, and I will take him.

JESUS. [*showing cross*] Mary!

MAGDALEN. [*kneeling and crying in a high voice*] Master!

JESUS. [*forbidding her with his hand*] Touch me not, for I have not ascended to my Father. Go to my brothers and say to them: I ascend to my Father and to your Father, to my God and your God. [*Reappears to right of altar while women cross from left to right*] Hail, be not afraid. Go, tell my brothers to go to Galilee. There they will see me. [*Exit Jesus*]

MARYS. [*in unison*] Alleluia, the Lord is risen, Alleluia.

One interesting feature of the music of this dialogue is that immediately after Magdalen recognizes Jesus, his voice, which has been in the baritone register, climbs up high into the tenor. The liturgical dramatist, when he chose, had an element of dramaturgy which he could add to dialogue and staging—music!

So the Easter play grew. After two hundred years or more of accretion and experiment, it reached a fullness of dramatic elaboration seen in a sample from the Bavarian monastery of Klosterneuberg, preserved in a manuscript of the early thirteenth century and first performed perhaps in 1204.

The Klosterneuberg "Easter Order" begins with the Jewish priests, probably Annas and Caiaphas, asking Pilate for a guard over the tomb of Jesus. They have heard from the populace that He said he would rise again after three days. Pilate must command his soldiers to guard the tomb that night, lest the disciples steal the body and the populace believe Jesus alive. Pilate gives them the guard and instructs the soldiers. The soldiers promise to watch diligently. As they march around the tomb, they sing: "We don't believe Christ will rise, but just so no one can take the body, we keep a night watch, a watch because of plots."*

After five verses in this vein, an angel appears with an unsheathed

* This refrain, "a watch because of plots" is in a mixture of German and Latin: "*Schowa* [*Schaue*] *propter insidias.*"

sword, singing "Alleluia, the Victor has risen from the dead." He strikes one of the soldiers, all fall to the ground stunned, and the Angel sings a hymn, beginning "The Shepherd bringing back the sheep on his shoulders." The soldiers lie on the ground as though dead.

The Klosterneuberg play is not constructed on one line, but by alternating scenes, as in Shakespeare. Probably the next scene is in a different part of the "stage," that is the church. Mary Magdalen and the other Marys come to buy spices. The spice merchant apparently displays his wares, promising to "give them the best ointments to anoint the body of the Saviour, in memory of his burial and in glory to his name." Buying the spices, the Marys proceed to the tomb (the soldiers presumably have risen and cleared the place), repeating three times "Who will roll back for us the stone from the entrance of the tomb?"

An angel comes forth from the tomb, singing a variation of the well-known quem quaeritis: "What living person do you seek among the dead?" When the Marys shrink back from this message, he reassures them. "Be not afraid. You seek Jesus of Nazareth who was crucified. He is not here; he is risen as he said to you in Galilee. But go tell his disciples and Peter that he goes before you into Galilee."

Back to the soldiers. We see them, recovered, returning to the priests.* They want to give back the money. "While we were guarding and keeping the night watch there came to us a heavenly messenger, who said: 'The Lord is risen.' A heavy sight we have suffered, we have seen terrible youths, and with the quaking of the earth, which we felt, we saw the crucified one rise." The priests then bribe the soldiers to keep silent about what they have witnessed: "Keep back these words you bring. Take this reward and carefully guard your knowledge, lest the rumor get out to the populace. Do our will among the people. Say that the body was taken secretly. Say, 'when a heavy sleep overcame us, a thief took him away by night.' " The soldiers carry out the suggestions of the priests, but with a few changes in detail: "The watching overcame everyone. Then we began to sleep a *little*. *Thieves* hastened to the tomb to carry the master away somewhere." After all, it's asking a good bit of professional soldiers to expect them to admit that they were sound asleep while on guard.

Here we "cut," as the movie scenario would say, to the Marys. Magdalen goes to the apostles reporting that she has seen an angel and heard his testimony that the Lord lives. Peter must believe her. The apostles

* Actually, the manuscript is confused here. The scene with the Marys continues through their announcement of the resurrection to the apostles, then follows the scene of the soldiers and the priests, then a repetition of the scene of the Marys and the apostles. I follow Young in supposing that the first scene of the Marys and the apostles is a scribal mistake, which should be deleted. He thinks the deletion is marked on the manuscript.

are dubious. These words sound like delirium (Magdalen's lines are a bit breathless and disorganized); they are not persuasive to men's minds. But they must see for themselves. Peter and John race to the tomb; John returns with the grave cloths, Peter with the linen shroud. The tomb is empty. Either He has risen or someone has taken the body.

Magdalen, who has followed Peter to the tomb and is now alone, when he returns to the other apostles, laments. "Sorrow grows, my heart trembles at the absence of my master, who saved me from many vices, thrusting seven devils from me. Alas, that the Redemption of Israel should suffer such a death!" This inability or refusal to comprehend what has happened has a dramatic point: it adds to the suspense, and it is the natural reaction of even the devoted Magdalen to such a unique event as the Resurrection.

Then Jesus appears in the guise of a gardener. It is a well-prepared entrance, and the dramatist wrings more suspense from the scene than most of his predecessors:

JESUS. [*in guise of a gardener*] Woman, why do you weep?
MAGDALEN. Because they have taken my Lord away, and I know not where they have laid him.
JESUS. [*repeating*] Woman, why do you weep? Whom do you seek?
MAGDALEN. Sir, if you have taken him, tell me where you have laid him, so that I can take him.
JESUS. [*showing himself as Christ*] Mary!
MAGDALEN. Master! [*Tries to touch his feet*]
JESUS. Do not touch me, etc.

This ends the "gardener scene." The play passes on to an episode not usually found in the Easter play, the harrowing of hell. An early Christian belief held that Christ went down to hell and released the souls of the just, who had sojourned there since heaven was closed by the sin of Adam. Though non-biblical, this belief is included in the Apostles' Creed, but not the Nicene.

In the Klosterneuberg representation of the harrowing, two angels go before Jesus, singing, "Alleluia, Christ is risen and shines upon his people, whom he redeemed with his blood." Jesus finds the gates of hell closed. "Lift up your heads, O ye gates," he sings in the words of Psalm 24, "and be ye lift up, ye everlasting doors; and the King of Glory shall come in." The Devil within asks, "Who is this King of Glory?"* Jesus answers, "The Lord strong and mighty, the Lord Mighty in battle." After repeating this response three times, Jesus with a powerful blow

* This question is omitted in the manuscript, but its presence on similar plays of the harrowing, as well as the following lines of Jesus, is proof that the omission was a mere scribal oversight.

18

shatters the gates of Hell, and the captive souls within sing joyously, "You have come, O pleasing one."

Now we pick up the Marys and the Apostles again—we see no more of Jesus in the play. Magdalen, finding the other two Marys, sings, "I have seen the Lord alive." Convinced, the Marys must now convince the apostles. They are murmuring "Jesus, our Redemption," when they see Magdalen from afar.

APOSTLES. Tell us, Mary, what did you see along the way?

MAGDALEN. The sepulchre of the living Christ I saw, and the glory of the risen one, angelic witnesses, the burial cloths and the shroud. Christ is risen, my hope. He goes before his own into Galilee.

APOSTLES. [*in unison*] Mary, ever truthful, is rather to be believed than the lying crowd of Jews. We know that Christ has truly risen from the dead. Have mercy on us, Victor King.

This scene carries the essential religious purpose of the play. The dramatic representation of the events of the resurrection is all for convincing the beholders of the truth of the resurrection. According to the rubrics, the three Marys "now convinced of the resurrection of the Lord, shall announce it to the Apostles." When the apostles are convinced, they display the burial cloths to the "people," that is the congregation who witnessed this performance, possibly as a prelude to Easter mass: "behold the burial cloths, and the body of Jesus was not found in the sepulchre." Unfortunately, the play goes awry at this point. The "chorus," that is the choir, sings an antiphon which, since only three words are given in the manuscript, is not positively identified. Then, by curious misplacement of material, they sing the words of John, "So they ran both together," which we have already seen in their proper position to introduce the race of Peter and John to the tomb.

The conclusion of the play gets back to the main purpose. "The whole people," reads the rubric, "now convinced" of the resurrection sing a German hymn, "Christ is risen."* The play has progressed from the event of the resurrection to understandable doubt and even distress on the part of Magdalen, to conviction on the part of the Marys, to conviction by the apostles, to final conviction of the whole people.

This ample treatment of the resurrection is typical of the liturgical drama in its fullest development. It is not without dramaturgic flaws. There is certainly no justification for the antiphon "So they ran both together" occurring where it does. The play would be better without the harrowing of hell, which, according to all accounts, ought to take place before the resurrection. Critics of two generations ago would doubtless condemn the finale, which violates the naturalistic principle that a play

* The music is that of the familiar Easter sequence, *Victimae paschali.*

is overheard, not directly participated in by the audience. The Klosterneu-berg Easter play certainly includes the audience, that is the congregation, in its action; but so do some modern playwrights.

Against these flaws, some of which may be the fault of the scribe rather than of the play itself, we must put many dramatic virtues. There is plenty of movement and bustle. The Shakespearean technique of build-ing tension by rapidly alternating short scenes has a predecessor here. The scene of the terrified and stunned soldiers at the resurrection and the smashing of the gates of hell are spectacular. A subtle appreciation of the comic appears in the changes which the soldiers make in the story the priests have asked them to tell. The dramatist shows considerable maturity in the manner in which he builds suspense, especially in the scene between Jesus and Magdalen. We can only speculate how the change of Jesus from gardener into Christ was managed, but such dis-coveries are tried-and-sure dramatic expedients. The role of Magdalen affords plenty of opportunities for effective acting. She dominates the action in the scenes where she appears, and the breathless quality of her last report to the apostles, enhanced by the music, is a high spot.

Of course, it is a long way to the superb religious drama of the fifteenth century, but with the Klosterneuberg play we are well em-barked.

Chapter III. THE CHRISTMAS PLAY AND OTHERS

IN FOLLOWING THE LINE of development of the resurrection play, we have, however, got ahead of our story. The resurrection is only one, though the earliest developed and the most central, of the incidents in the complete religious drama. While the quem quaeritis was expanding into a large play, other incidents underwent a similar development. Two such are particularly worth following—the nativity and an Old Testament prologue to the nativity known as the "Prophet Play."

Of these, the nearest to the primitive Easter play is the Nativity play. In its simplest form it seems to be an imitation of the Easter play, with a manger instead of a sepulchre, shepherds instead of the Marys, and midwives instead of angels. An eleventh-century manuscript from Limoges preserves what appears to be an undramatized trope, attached to the introit of the mass, precisely as with the earliest quem quaeritis. The test does not tag the speakers, but we can supply the tags from later versions.

MIDWIVES. Whom seek ye in the manger, Shepherds? Tell us.
SHEPHERDS. The Saviour, Christ the Lord, a baby wrapped in swaddling clothes, according to the message of the angel.
MIDWIVES. Here is the little one with Mary his mother, of whom the prophet Isaiah, foretelling long ago, spoke: "Behold a Virgin shall conceive and bear a child." And now go forth and proclaim that he is born.
SHEPHERDS. Alleluia, Alleluia. Now truly we have seen Christ born in the earth, whom let all sing with the prophet, saying, "A boy is born."

That this nativity trope is a direct imitation of the Easter trope needs no laboring. So far as extant texts indicate, its development into a play seems attended with less trial and error than that of the Easter trope. Doubtless this is because the trail had already been blazed. In fact, it is hardly necessary to suppose any pioneering at all. A particular monastery or church wanting a nativity play need not start at the beginning. It could simply imitate the most developed Easter play procurable. In-between stages could be skipped.

A simple but complete shepherds' play comes from Rouen. Though the manuscript is late, fourteenth century in fact, one supposes that the play is much earlier. A boy, impersonating an angel, announces the nativity to five canons. Other boys "In the roof of the church" sing the angels' song, "Glory to God in the highest, and on earth peace to men of good will." The shepherds, that is the five canons, sing a hymn on their way to the manger. And thenceforward as in the trope.

Even with its palpable imitation, the Christmas trope and even more the shepherds' play contain one element we have not seen hitherto—the use of material from the New Testament Apocrypha. There are shepherds, but no midwives, in the nativity story of Luke. Older scholars thought the midwives invented just to provide someone to answer the shepherds' question. They did not need inventing, any more than Voltaire's God. They already existed in a popular apocryphon, the Proto-Gospel of Matthew, a fantastic compound of romance and devotion, where they testified to the virginity of Mary. Their use in the nativity trope opened up a well-stocked storehouse of dramatic motifs much raided by later medieval dramatists.

Though there are several texts, the shepherds' play did not have the popularity that it later attained in the craft cycles. Among all the incidents of the Christmas season, liturgical dramatists preferred the coming of the Magi (Matthew 2:1-12), which growing by accretions at the beginning and end tended to absorb the shepherds' play and the other chief nativity play, the Slaughter of the Innocents.

The preference for the Magi had several reasons. The Feast of the Epiphany (January 6) which celebrates this episode, called Twelfth Night in English-speaking lands, is an older feast than the nativity proper,* and it seems to have been celebrated with greater elaboration in the Middle Ages. The adoration of the Magi, or Three Kings as they were known, lent itself more to procession, pomp, and ceremony—the strong points of liturgical drama—than the shepherds' play. The democratic implications of the first annunciation of the Saviour to "certain poor shepherds," so often expounded in modern pulpits, had to wait for the vernacular plays for development. There the shepherds became vehicles for all sorts of political and social satire, horseplay, and crude humor.

The Magi plays, which exist in considerable number and variety, carry the liturgical title "Office of the Star," after the chief property used. Many call for a star, pulled along on a cord, which the Magi follow to the manger. In some instances the star seems to have been an elaborate candelabra of several candles called a "corona." The core of the Office of the Star is, however, an imitation of the shepherds' play, itself an imitation of the Easter play: the dialogue between the Magi and the midwives.

This appears in its simplest form in a play belonging to Rouen. The Three Magi come from three different parts of the church, meet at the high altar, kiss each other, then move in procession to the nave. As they approach the manger, the midwives ask "Who are these approaching us, who, led by a star, bear strange things?" The Magi answer that they are

* Which was not instituted until 354.

22

kings of Tarsus, Arabia, and Saba* with gifts to the new born Christ. They fall prostrate in adoration, then each offers his symbolic gift: gold for the king, frankincense for the God, myrrh (used in embalming) for the mortal. The Magi pray, then fall asleep. An angel appears to them telling them to take another way home. The play closes with a cantor summing up the symbolism of the gifts and the choir giving a resume of the action.

The Rouen play is unique in its simplicity. Most include one or two other incidents. The first of these is a pure invention, without scriptural warrant, the meeting of the Magi and the Shepherds, who are returning from the manger.

MAGI.   Shepherds, tell whatever you have seen, and announce the birth of Christ.

SHEPHERDS.   An infant we saw wrapped in swaddling clothes, and a chorus of angels praising the Saviour. [*Exeunt Shepherds*]

MAGI.   Behold the star in the east seen before. Again it goes before us. . . .

This dialogue, found in many of the Magi plays, makes a bridge with the shepherds' play (or perhaps substitutes for it) and prepares for its eventual absorption into an elaborated Magi play, which then becomes the Christmas play, as at Fleury.

The incident which offers most dramatic opportunities, however, is the encounter between the Magi and Herod, which is scriptural. In Matthew's account of Herod's curiosity, duplicity, and rage, liturgical dramatists found a subject to their liking. The appearance of the Magi at Herod's court afforded a chance for spectacle—think of it, four kings on stage at once—and Herod is the first villain in the drama of Western Europe. Haughty, pompous, menacing, blood-thirsty, and insanely angry, he is the progenitor of a long line, of all the Pharoahs, Herods, and Pilates of the craft cycles, of the foiled vice in the moralities, of King Cambyses in the play of Shakespeare's youth. Hamlet naturally turns to Herod as an example of uncontrolled passion, and the vulgar acting thereof: "it out-Herods Herod."

The Herod of the Compiègne play is typical. He is attended by an entourage of courtiers and scribes, whom he orders about impressively. A legate meets the Magi and conducts them to the court, where a messenger announces them in proper style. Herod then wants to know from his scribes who this "king of kings" the Magi are seeking may be.

HEROD.   Attendants, call here to me the scribes skilled in the prophetic books.

ATTENDANTS.   You, experts in the Law called by the king, come quickly with the prophetic books.

* Based on Psalm 72:10.

HEROD. You scribes, I ask you, tell me if you can see anything in the book about this child.

SCRIBES. We see, my Lord, in the lines of the prophets that it is clearly written: "Bethlehem thou art not the least among the princes of Juda; for out of thee shall come a Governor, that shall rule my people Israel; he indeed shall save his people from their sins."

HEROD. [*to Magi*] Go and diligently search for the child, and when he is found bring me word again.

The Magi depart, adore the infant (the incident is considerably abbreviated), and, warned by the angel, take another way home. The inevitable attendant reports that the Magi have eluded Herod. A soldier then counsels a general slaughter of male infants, and Herod gives the command.

Numerous elaborations and refinements appear in later versions. In a twelfth-century manuscript, now at Montpelier but originally connected somehow with Rouen, two Magi speak a mishmash of Latin, Hebrew, and gibberish—no doubt an attempt to characterize them as aliens. A play from Bilsen in Belgium builds up suspense by having a series of messengers report the activities of the Magi with a great deal of running to and fro. When Herod hears their mission he throws swords to the ground and asks whether they believe that this king which they seek really reigns. On hearing their assurance that they do so believe and have brought gifts to the king, he orders them taken to jail. Then, perhaps on second thought, he consults his scribes, hears the prophecy, and releases the Magi, in hope that they will lead him to his rival. Herod's questioning of the Magi is admirably insulting: "You, therefore, where do you come from? You other one, where do you come from? . . . . you third, where do you come from." No desk sergeant could do better.

The Freising play provides a moving choral procession for the entrance of Herod—a distant ancestor for the fanfare of trumpets with which Shakespeare's Kings enter. With unconscious irony Herod refers to the Magi as "tyrants," and borrows a phrase from Sallust: "I will extinguish my fire in destruction."

Full scope for the elaboration of the raging Herod, who verges on the comic* and is frequently thought to owe much to the boisterous festivities of the Christmas season with their parodies of divine service in the Boy Bishop and the Mass of the Subdeacons, is afforded by the incident of the

---

* This is the common opinion of critics, though perhaps one should be sceptical about the contemporary effect of a scene written hundreds of years ago and played to an audience with decidedly different notions of what was comic. The old tear-jerker melodramas, such as *Thorns and Orange Blossoms*, *The Drunkard*, and *Ten Nights in a Barroom*, were not intended as comic when they were written, and their original audiences did not so regard them; yet they are universally played as comic in modern revivals.

Slaughter of the Innocents. Some folklorists see in the raging Herod a remnant of the old pagan ritual play: he is the old king who must be killed before the new king can reign.

One of the Magi plays, that of Laon, has the Slaughter as an epilogue to the Magi play, and it is present in the Freising Office of the Star. Freising, however, as well as the Monastery of St. Martial at Limoges and that of St. Benoit at Fleury, has a separate play of the innocents, called "The Office of Rachel," so named after Matthew 2:18: "Rachel weeping for her children and would not be comforted, because they are not."

In the Fleury version, the most complete and skillfully constructed, the action begins with a procession of the innocents (probably the younger postulants of the monastery) singing a hymn. A lamb leads the procession. An attendant offers Herod a sword, a cliche to identify the king and symbolize his power. An angel then warns Joseph to flee with Mary and the Baby to Egypt. The attendant reports the departure of the Magi. Herod, desperate, tries to kill himself. The innocents apparently parade past Herod just at this moment, and this suggests a course of action to the attendant, who counsels killing all of the male babies of Bethlehem in the hope that the new-born king will be among them. Herod gives the command and the soldiers fall on the innocents. The lamb they have been following is symbolically removed. Despite the plea of the mothers and the cry of the innocents themselves, "Why do you not defend our blood, O God of ours?" the soldiers kill all.

As they die an angel consoles them: "Suffer a little while, until the number of your brethren is fulfilled." The lament of Rachel, standing for the mothers, and the attempts of the consolers to comfort her are developed in well-turned verses. Rachel faints and has to be revived, then falls on the bodies of the innocents in grief. Two consolers carry her off and the angel sings, "Suffer little children to come to me, for of such is the kingdom of heaven." At the angel's voice the innocents arise and enter the choir, probably to symbolize their entry into heaven. Herod dies and his son Archelaus takes his place. The angel then commands Joseph to return from Egypt, and with Joseph's hymn of praise the play closes.

With Herod's death and the return of the Holy Family the liturgical drama of the Christmas season naturally ends. But, in its completed form, it did not begin with the annunciation of the nativity to the shepherds. In the liturgical year Christmastide is prefaced by Advent, the four weeks preceding Christmas, sometimes held to figure the four thousand years from Adam to Christ. Advent is a time of expectation and preparation. The gospels of the sundays of Advent, unlike those of the rest of the year, are from the Old Testament prophecies of the Messiah.

The dramatic offices of the Christmas season parallel in spirit the liturgical year. The Orders of the Shepherds, the Star, and Rachel are naturally completed by a prologue consisting of a procession of prophets, each fore-telling the Messiah. The Order (or Procession) of the Prophets, as this play is called, is unique in liturgical drama in having its source in a sermon. Through the whole of the Middle Ages a piece called *A Sermon About the Creed Against Jews, Pagans and Arians* was ascribed to St. Augustine, though modern scholars assign it to some anonymous author a century or so later.

The sermon is itself rather dramatically constructed, especially the section dealing with the Jews, which is the main source for the Prophet play. The author attempts to convince the Jews that Jesus was the true Messiah by citing their own prophets and showing in each instance that the prophecy was fulfilled in Jesus. "Speak, Isaiah," the preacher demands, "your testimony of Christ." And then he quotes Isaiah: "Behold a virgin shall conceive, and bear a son, and shall call his name Immanuel" (7:14). And so on through Jeremiah, Daniel, Moses, David, Habbakuk, Zachariah and Elizabeth (the parents of John the Baptist), John himself.

Then the surprise. Though the section of the sermon is directed to the Jews, the preacher produces three pagans. Nebuchadnezzar is scriptural; the fourth youth whom he saw in the fiery furnace (Daniel 3:24-25) after he had cast only three into it was commonly construed as a prophecy of the Messiah. The two other pagans give the modern reader a start: Virgil and the Erythraean Sibyl. But Virgil's fourth eclogue, celebrating the birth of Pollio's son, was always regarded as a prophecy of Christ, and we remember how Dante looked on the Roman poet. Verses prophesying Christ circulated widely under the name of the Erythraen Sibyl (also the Cumaean), and the sibyl or sibyls appear commonly in Christian literature and art, most famously in Michaelangelo's Sistine frescoes and the *Dies Irae*:

> The day of wrath, that dreadful day
> Shall the world in ashes lay,
> As David and the Sibyl say.

This sermon, or rather the portion of it addressed to the Jews, was a favorite liturgical reading for the Christmas season, used at different times in various monastic communities, on the fourth sunday of Advent, on the day before Christmas, on Christmas day, even on the Circumcision (January 1). It is from this liturgical form that it passed into drama. Little was needed to make a play of it. Divide the dialogue of the sermon among a lector or interlocutor and several persons representing the prophets. Provide the prophets with suitable dress and properties, and the sermon becomes a play. A version in a thirteenth-century manuscript from the cathedral of Laon (there were probably earlier versions) gives us the form which passes into the vernacular of the cycle plays. The prophets are listed in a sort of dramatis personae at the beginning with a detailed description of each. Isaiah is bearded, dressed in a dalmatic, with a red stole hanging down his front and back. Jeremiah lacks the stole. Moses, bearded, carries the tables of the law. David is dressed as a king. Habbakuk is a hunchback. Elizabeth is pregnant, John the Baptist has long hair and carries a palm. Both Virgil and the Sibyl are crowned with ivy; Virgil carries an inkhorn and pen, the Sibyl acts like one insane. And there is one addition to the prophets of the sermon. Balaam appears riding an ass and spurring it forward to curse the Israelites. According to stage directions "a boy under the ass" does the speaking for the animal: "an angel with a sword whom I see before me prevents me from going. I fear lest I perish."

There are several liturgical prophet plays, with the usual variations, additions, and refinements. The Rouen play goes in for spectacle with a furnace burning oakum for the Nebuchadnezzar episode. The complete Christmas play from the Bavarian abbey of Benedictbeuren, which has in addition to the Shepherds, Magi, and Slaughter, an Annunciation and a Salutation, personifies disbelieving Jewry in the character of Archsynagogue.* He violently objects to the Messianic prophecies, "imitating the action of a Jew in everything," and has to be silenced by Augustine himself, whose argumentative technique seems modeled on that of Abelard.

This play is unusual in introducing the figure of the Boy Bishop, an import from the profane and riotous Christmas festivities. From the Benedictbeuren Christmas play comes that extraordinary stage direction: "Later let Herod be eaten up by worms, and falling from his seat dead, let him be taken by Devils greatly rejoicing." The author or authors were evidently men of good education and high literary attainments. Every internal consideration justifies the guess that one or more wandering scholars are responsible for the Benidictbeuren Christmas play; moreover, the chief anthology of the poetry of these wandering scholars was found at the famous *Carmina Burana* from Benidictbeuren. Familiarity with nascent scholastic dialectic shown in the argumentation of Augustine likely comes from the experience of the author.

The prophet plays furnished the basis for one of the most famous theories of the development of medieval drama, that of the French scholar, Marius Sepet. He saw in the Prophet play the origin of all medieval Old Testament plays. Various incidents of the prophet play expanded and broke off into separate plays, Sepet thought. The chief criticism of the theory is that the Old Testament plays which we have in the medieval drama of England, France, and Germany contain episodes

* Borrowed from another pseudo-Augustinian sermon, *The Dialogue of the Debate between Church and Synagogue.*

(The Fall of Adam and Noah's Ark, for instance) lacking in any of the prophet plays now extant; and the vernacular mysteries do not contain material (Isaiah, Jeremiah) found in all the extant prophet plays. So one has to hypothesize entirely too many "missing links." Nevertheless, Sepet's theory, when it was first enunciated in 1867-68, marked a decided advance in the systematic study of medieval drama. Its refutation was accomplished by Sepet's own methods of collection, analysis, and arrangement of numbers of liturgical texts.

We should expect the liturgical drama to abound in passion plays. Indeed when the modern reader thinks of religious drama, he almost automatically lights on the passion play, perhaps because of the world-wide fame of Oberammergau. Study of medieval drama in the vernacular confirms this impression. The most numerous plays from medieval France are the *passions* or *mystères de la passion* and from Germany the *Passionspiele*. The English cycles treat the passion extensively, and there are records of non-extant English passion plays. But it is otherwise in the liturgical drama. Only two complete samples of a liturgical passion play are extant, both found in the *Carmina Burana*, from Benedictbeuren, plus a few fragments. Nor do records indicate that there was ever any great number.

It is difficult to assign a cause. Some of the episodes of the passion do not lend themselves to representation in the liturgical manner. The crucifixion does not, but liturgical dramatists were most resourceful in the symbolic representation of events beyond realistic portrayal, and some scenes of the passion—the trials before Pilate and Herod and the journey to Calvary—seem made to order.

A more compelling reason is that the liturgy of Passion Week is so moving in itself, as scarcely to require, or even profit by, dramatic treatment. The chanting of the passion account in the Gospel of John on Palm Sunday, even when done by only one voice instead of being divided among three, is a powerful emotional experience. Add the ceremonies of the Adoration of the Cross and the Deposition of the Cross, the covering of all the crosses in the church with purple cloth, the mass of the presanctified, and the singing of the Lamentations of Jeremiah on Good Friday—anyone who has participated in these ceremonies will find it difficult to see how dramatic presentation could enhance the emotional appeal.

Still another reason occurs to one: the Easter season immediately following is most richly endowed with liturgical drama. Perhaps abbots, deans, and choirmasters thought this was enough; perhaps also they were too busy preparing and rehearsing the Easter plays to attempt any for the preceding week.

Nevertheless, one type of liturgical literature contributed powerfully to the vernacular passions, even if it was rarely, if ever, presented dramatically in liturgical surroundings. This is the "Complaint of Mary." The "complaint" is a common medieval lyric form, suitable for the expression of any sort of sorrow or disappointment, whether in love, in fortune, or in religion. The word *complaint* (*Planctus* in Latin) merely means expression of sorrow or disappointment, with or without the hostility and accusation which the word now connotes. And of all sorrows, which was keener or deeper than Mary's? She with her women companions and John, alone of all Jesus' friends and followers, kept their vigil under the cross,

> Stood the mournful mother weeping
> Beneath the cross her vigil keeping,
> Whence hung her son.

The *Stabat mater* is only the most famous of the lyrics on this subject. The ones that contributed most to the drama are earlier, and they are in the first person. Mary tells directly of her sorrow, sometimes accuses the Jews, questions providence, asserts the innocence of her son. One of the most famous, the *Complaint before the Unknown** has Mary sing these words:

> What crime, what offense
> These mad people commit.
> Chains, rods, wounds.
> Spittle, thorns—all
> Without blame he suffers.

Still another runs:

> Weep, faithful souls,
> Weep sisters best
> That there should be so many
> Reasons of sorrow
> Of complaint and tears.

Some complaints are dialogues between Mary and Jesus, Mary and John, or among all three. In at least one late instance, at Regensburg, a complaint was sung "alternately" by singers portraying Mary and John, but there is no evidence that this custom was early enough or common enough to have been a basis for dramatic development. One rather suspects that liturgy is here imitating the already flourishing vernacular

---

* If that is the proper translation of *Planctus ante nescia*.

drama, just as it apparently did in dividing the Palm Sunday Passion among three voices, called Petrus, Pilatus, and Christus.

The two extant liturgical passion plays seem to derive directly from the gospels, principally John and Matthew. The *Shorter Play of the Passion*, as it is titled in the *Carmina Burana*, does not go beyond direct quotation or paraphrase in its dialogue, except that the directions call for Mary's singing the *Complaint before the Unknown*. All the main events of the passion, from the Last Supper to the Burial by Joseph of Arimathaea, are represented, but with a maximum of brevity. It has perhaps the largest proportion of stage business to dialogue of any play in existence.

The longer passion play, untitled in the manuscript, incorporates much material before the passion, thus resembling the later German and French passions, which frequently begin with the Baptism by John, or even earlier. So much attention is devoted to the career of Mary Magdalen that scholars have argued that the Magdalen sections were originally a separate play. Magdalen's licentious life, her conversion, her purchase of ointment and anointing the Lord are included. She is identified, as commonly in medieval times, with Mary the sister of Lazarus, so that we have a scene of the raising of Lazarus. Another interesting feature is that Magdalen sings several songs in German. Apparently the author felt that the vernacular is more suitable to the portrayal of a harlot than Latin—a use of language which we shall find, often for the opposite effect, in the English cycle plays.

The chronicle of liturgical drama is not quite finished with the series of orders and offices developed for the great seasons of Easter and Christmas. There are a score or so of dramas produced for other feasts and connected more or less with the liturgy. Several of these take subjects from the New Testament. Two plays concern the raising of Lazarus, one from Fleury and one written by the scholar Hilarius, of whom more later. The conversion of St. Paul, memorialized as a feast on January 25, is the subject of a Fleury play. An elaborate play of the presentation of the Virgin in the Temple, which if not scriptural is liturgical, was presented at Venice in the 1360's, at Avignon, then the seat of the papacy, in 1372 and again in 1385. It is especially notable for having been sponsored by the famous soldier, crusader, and diplomat, Phillipe de Mézières and for giving a complete account of the costumes, staging, and dramatis personae. Other subjects in the life of the Virgin are an Annunciation contained in a fourteenth-century manuscript from Cividale, in Italy, performed on Lady Day (March 25); a Purification (February 2), likewise fourteenth century, from Padua, and meager records of an Assumption (August 15) in Halle in the sixteenth century.

Several Old Testament plays are also extant. A late twelfth-century manuscript found in Steirmark, Austria, but otherwise unlocated, contains a play dealing with the device by which Jacob got Isaac's primogenital blessing. An incomplete thirteenth-century play from Laon tells the story of Joseph and his brethren, from the selling of Joseph into slavery to Joseph's demand that his brothers bring Benjamin with them to Egypt.

The story of Daniel, which offers numerous chances for the spectacular, appealed to Hilarius and to a group of students at the cathedral school of Beauvais. The plays are somewhat similar, and scholars have argued that the Beauvais play is modelled on that of Hilarius. Both have Belshezzar's feast, the conquest of Babylon by Darius (not Cyrus), King of Persia, and the episode of the lions' den.

A special category is the miracle or saints' plays. Extremely popular in the later Middle Ages, especially in France and in the form of the miracle of our Lady, the saints' play is represented by eight extant plays, all dealing with St. Nicholas. The legend of St. Nicholas, little beholden to any ascertainable facts, characterizes him as a friend of the unfortunate and a reliever of poverty. He seems to be some sort of translated heathen god of generosity, and his feast on December 6 is sufficiently close to Christmas to explain why, as Santa Claus, he has displaced Father Christmas in the United States and Canada.

Two plays, one from Hildesheim in Germany and one from Fleury, dramatize the legend of three indigent virgins whose father was too poor to provide dowries for their marriages. As a last resort, the eldest offers to sell her body in prostitution to recoup the family fortunes. A bag of gold is thrown in the window—by St. Nicholas, of course. A suitor instantly appears, and with the gold as a dowry the eldest is promptly betrothed. The Hildesheim play stops here, but the Fleury one goes on for substantially identical repeats of the scene for the second and third daughters.

Two more plays, likewise from Hildesheim and Fleury (plus a fragment from Einsiedln) present the episode of the three clerks who, murdered by an innkeeper and his wife, are restored to life when St. Nicholas shows up at the inn and by demanding fresh meat forces a confession from the innkeeper. Hilarius wrote a play about the statue of St. Nicholas which watched over the treasure of a pagan so well that the pagan was eventually converted. A version from Fleury substitutes a Jew for the pagan, and still another play from Fleury concerns the saint's protection of the son of the Emperor Getron. This play foreshadows the wilder romantic drama of Elizabethan times, such as Shakespeare's *Pericles* and Heywood's *Four Prentices of London*, in the span of time covered, the number of episodes, and the rapid movement of the action from place to place.

It is always dangerous to fix a terminus for any literary development.

31

Nevertheless, we can say that by 1200 the liturgical drama had matured. To be sure, it is often impossible to know the exact date when a certain play was produced; we can only know the approximate date of the manuscripts in which it comes to us, and many of these dates are after 1200, some after 1300, and few even after 1400. But virtually every elaboration in staging or plotting, every refinement of characterization or versification, every type of use of scriptural, apocryphal or even classical material can be illustrated from plays safely datable before 1200.

Two developments which carry drama to the limits of, if not beyond, the liturgical are illustrated by twelfth-century plays. One is the complex of individual (and ascertainable) authorship and conscious craftmanship exhibited in the plays of Hilarius. Now, Hilarius is known to us in other connections. He was a wandering scholar, possibly an Englishman, almost certainly a subject of the English King, who at that time was also Duke of Normandy and lord of sundry other territories in France. Hilarius was one of those citizens of the Anglo-Norman community who, like Thomas à Becket and John of Salisbury, cultivated the arts. He wrote some verses to his master Abelard on the occasion of the latter's retirement from teaching to enter a monastery about 1125. Hilarius' life and learning partially explain the elaborate versification of the plays, where the metric form is masterfully fitted to character and mood.

Perhaps, too, it explains why the three plays are tenuously connected to the liturgy. The St. Nicholas play is appropriate to the feast; the Lazarus would conceivably be for the Feast of St. Lazarus (December 15), or even for that of St. Mary Magdalen (July 22). Its closing lines suggest performance at matins or vespers, which tells us that it was rather to be introduced into the liturgy than that it grew out of it. The Daniel play has no discernible pertinence to any known liturgy. And none of these plays use liturgical material—hymns, responsories, readings, or the like—in any recognizable form. With Hilarius we are on the verge if not completely into a world in which individual authors write plays in free composition for primarily artistic reasons.

With Hilarius, also, the full force of the literary and cultural "renaissance" of the twelfth century invades the drama. Nor is he a solitary case. The presence of the names *Jordanus*, *Simon*, and *Hugo* on the margin of the Beauvais *Daniel* suggests that these are the names of three individuals who collaborated in writing a piece, which one critic has labelled distinctly "au théatre." The invasion of classical, secular knowledge is also visible in borrowings from such classical authors as Sallust and Virgil in several plays. We should expect Virgil's fourth eclogue in the Prophet play, but there is no external reason why Herod should borrow a line from Sallust in the Strassburg and Freising Magi plays, nor for the echoes of the *Aeneid* in plays from Strassburg, Bilsen, and Fleury.

32

The most elaborate play in the liturgical tradition is the *Antichrist* produced in the Bavarian abbey of Tegernsee, probably about 1160.* Only the form of the Tegernsee *Antichrist* suggests liturgical drama. Otherwise it is quite outside the bounds. It was not written for any feast day. It is not founded, except remotely, on Scripture, nor yet on the life of any saint, but on apocalyptic legend. In fact its specific source is a letter of the monk Adso to Gerberga, Queen of France, written about 950.** It can hardly have been performed in a church, doubtfully even in a cloister. The principal purpose of its author is patently political propaganda, though as so often in the Middle Ages using quasi-theological concepts. Only the dramaturgy is liturgical.

A word about the medieval legend of Antichrist is necessary. Based on various apocolyptical passages in the New Testament, the legend made Antichrist the final adversary of God, a sort of upside-down Christ, whose appearance just before the Last Judgment would mark the last struggle of Satan against God. Son of a harlot, descendant of the tribe of Benjamin, able to duplicate Christ's miracles by Satanic fraud, Antichrist will seduce almost the whole world.

The play itself divides into four parts, almost acts. In the first the Roman Emperor demands fealty of the Kings of the French, the Germans, the Greeks, and Jerusalem. All give it, the King of the Germans only after resistance. Thus the whole Christian world is united. In the second part, the King of Babylon standing for the infidel world, makes war on the King of Jerusalem, who, defeated, is rescued by the Emperor. When the Emperor conquers the King of Babylon and offers up the spoils of conquest in the Temple of the Lord, all the world is united under Christian rule—except the Jews (personified by Synagoga in the play) who still refuse belief.

Now begins the drive of Antichrist. A sort of fifth-column in the form of the Hypocrites soften up all resistance and prepare the way. Antichrist subdues the King of Jerusalem by force, those of the Greeks and the French by bribery. The King of the Germans alone holds out; he has to be convinced by the faked miracles of Antichrist. Once convinced, he leads the forces of Antichrist against Gentilitas (paganism) and conquers him. Even Synagoga submits under the prompting of the hypocrites. Antichrist is supreme.

Enoch and Elijah, the two human beings who have never died and hence have to return to earth to die, appear, preaching Christ and even converting Synagoga. Antichrist unleashes a persecution of all who refuse to worship him as God. Enoch and Elijah and their followers die. Thunder rolls from on high, Antichrist tumbles from his throne, his

* Accepting Young's proposed date. Others date it all the way from 1155 to 1189, depending on their interpretation of the political allegory.
** Commonly called *The Booklet concerning Antichrist* (*Libellus de Antichristo*).

followers flee. The Church then converts all, who praise God and prepare for the coming of Christ to judge the living and the dead.

This is drama in the grandest manner. Its cast of characters is humanity, its scope all history, "till time stand fixt." The author's vision is as bold as Milton's or Dante's, and it is a measure of the technical resources developed by the liturgical drama in the two hundred years since the dramatized quem quaeritis of *Regularis concordia* that the Tegernsee author found a vehicle adequate to his design.

What sort of technique did the liturgical drama develop? Its chief accomplishment was the processional drama, in which the action takes place at or near one or more "stations" and in the "place"* between. This was a natural development from the architectural organization of the churches for which it was designed. The various parts of a church, high altar, side altars or chapels, choir, and so forth, each have a function. Moreover movement from place to place in a church can be symbolic, as when the priest goes from the right (epistle) side of the altar to the left (gospel). This is the principle of staging which governs liturgical drama, and, of course, thereby controls the structure of the plays themselves.

The station starts out as a fixed object, such as the sepulchre used in the Easter services, which in many churches was a permanent stone structure. The angel takes his position beside or behind the sepulchre, the Marys approach him, Peter and John race to the sepulchre. Later, when the scene of the purchase of ointment is added, another station, for the merchant, must be provided. So in the beginning the station is the location of some important character. The manger is the Christ child and the Holy Family. Herod's court is another station. The Magi do not need a station. Their business is to move from parts unknown to Herod's court, thence to the manger, and thence back to parts unknown. When we add the flight to Egypt, we use a station for a geographical location, Egypt. Already, of course, Herod's court is partly that. Besides being Herod, the station is also Jerusalem, just as the manger is also Bethlehem. We can also have a station for Rachel, and here the station is neither geographical nor personal. Rachel is the mourning mothers of the slaughtered innocents, and, in a measure, her station is unconsolable sorrow. The process is complete, when, as in the *Antichrist*, pure abstractions like Gentilitas have stations.

How this scheme works, how action moves from station to station, from one set of characters to another, from one intellectual concept to another is shown in the plat which Young worked out for the presentation of the Fleury Rachel play.

* "Station" translates the Latin *sedes*, "place" *platea*.

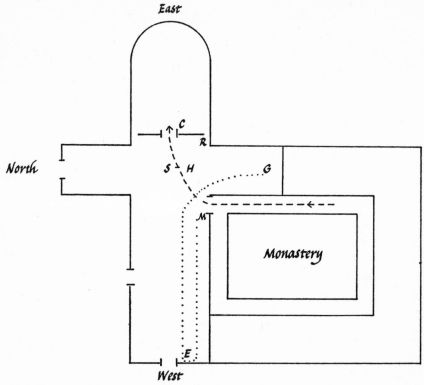

(Adapted from Karl Young, *Ordo Rachelis* [University of Wisconsin Studies in
Language and Literature, No. 4], Madison, Wis., 1919)

M is the manger, *H* the station of Herod, *R* that of Rachel. The broken
line is the route of the Innocents. Starting in the ambulatory of the
monastery they enter the door leading from the monastery to the church,
pass before Herod, are killed at *S*, arise and enter the choir at *C*. Meanwhile the Holy Family flee from *M* to *E*, Egypt, by the route of the
dotted line. They return not to *M*, which is Bethlehem, but to *G*, their
home in Galilee. *G* does not need to be so specific as the other stations,
since no action takes place in Galilee; it is only a terminus for the journey,
and for the play also.

Such an arrangement of playing space presents the dramatist with
enormous opportunities. It provides for movement of all sorts, the effect
so necessary for the emotional intensity requisite to living drama: the
formal procession of the innocents, the flight of the Holy Family, Peter
and John's race to the sepulchre, the attack of the King of Babylon on
Jerusalem. It also makes the handling of symbolic and allegorical figures
easy. The spirit of Jewry acquires not merely a name but a local habita-

tion. The audience knows that Synagoga represents Jewry, because he wears the costume, perhaps the yellow star of David, which Jews were required to wear in the Middle Ages. Furthermore, the audience knows that anything taking place at or near Synagoga's station is action affecting the Jews.

The station-and-place pattern also frees the dramatist from the tyranny of the "unities" of place and time. By making one station represent Jerusalem and another Damascus, he can tell the story of the conversion of St. Paul who receives from the High priests in Jerusalem instructions to seek out the Christians of Damascus, sets out on the journey, receives his vision somewhere between the two stations, goes to the house of Ananias in Damascus for instruction and baptism. If the station for Damascus is some place already built above the church floor (the pulpit, for example), or if a raised platform is constructed for the station, the business of St. Paul's escape from Damascus in a basket lowered from the walls is easily played.

Without any interrupting lowering of curtains, without the use of placards or program announcements, without even prologues or choruses, dramas traversing time and space, like the *Antichrist*, are possible. Audiences absorb such conventions as easily as those of the early cinema learned that a shot of the Eiffel tower meant that the action of the film takes place in Paris. Hence, the excitement of rapid movement from place to place, what the cinema accomplishes by "short cutting," is abundant in the liturgical drama. We shift naturally and easily from Magdalen anointing the feet of the Saviour in Simon's house, to the death of Lazarus in Bethania, to Jesus and his disciples in Galilee. There has never been another stage so flexible as that of the liturgical dramatists.

It combined the graphic quality of naturalistic staging with the complete utilization of symbol and allegory. In the Rouen Prophet play the spectator need not imagine Shadrach, Meshach, and Abednego in the fiery furnace; he can see the youths and smell the burning oakum. On the other hand, the Church, Jewry, Paganism become credibly concrete. An audience accustomed to such methods of representation, will have none of the troubles which Miss Tallulah Bankhead reports that one "Park Avenue birdbrain" had with Mr. Thornton Wilder's *Skin of Our Teeth*, a play conceived in the cosmic dimensions of the *Antichrist*:

". . . I don't understand a word of the play. I haven't any notion of what it's about. Have you?"

Her companion stammered slightly, then said, "Yes, I think so." "What?" she snapped. "Well, in general terms it's about the human race."

"Oh," jeered the belle, "is *that* all?"*

* *Tallulah*, (Dell paper edition), pp. 288-89. Originally published by Harpers. Copyright by Tallulah Bankhead.

The methods of the liturgical dramatists have been amply justified in our own day. After three hundred years of a gradually constricting stage, until it became only a room with one wall knocked out, and an abnormally restricted drama—it must be ordinary conversation merely overheard—playwrights, directors, and audiences finally aroused to what they were missing. They have taken the play beyond the proscenium arch, put the audience around the stage instead of before it, introduced music, set the drama free to charge through time and space.

All this the liturgical playwrights, who did not even know they were writing plays, had achieved before 1200.

Chapter IV. FROM LITURGY TO POPULAR RELIGIOUS DRAMA

BETWEEN THE MATURE liturgical drama of about 1200 and the four English cycles of scriptural drama, which comprehend the whole of history from creation to doomsday, lies a somewhat shadowy period of transition. Though the cycles come to us in roughly their fifteenth-century form, we know from records that some were formed in the fourteenth. The period of transition must therefore cover a time from somewhat before 1200 to past 1300. Many stages in the process rest on logical necessity rather than documentary proof. Transitional texts are rare, records rarer, and the blank space has to be filled in with speculation and hypothesis, which the scholars have provided in abundance.

It is not entirely correct to speak of a transition. There are several. In language, the vernacular, English, German, French, and the others, replaces the Latin of liturgical usage. Perhaps here England is a special case; Latin may first yield to French of the Anglo-Norman variety, which was in the thirteenth century and well into the fourteenth, the speech of the educated classes; then perhaps in the fourteenth century English replaces French. There is a little evidence for this double shift, as we shall see. But language is only one change.

The laity replace the clergy as actors and producers. In some measure, varying from place to place and time to time, the church loses control of the drama to guilds, either trade or religious, and to the city authorities. The theater is no longer the church, but probably first the church precincts, then the town commons, the streets, or any open space suitable for plays.

These replacements, Latin by the vernacular, the clergy by the laity, the church by other places, all produce changes in the nature of the plays themselves, more emphasis on the human than on the divine, greater amounts of comedy, more social and political satire, freer use of a greater variety of sources. Yet none of the changes is complete and absolute. Latin is never completely cast out, the clergy retains some connection with the drama, liturgical motifs and techniques still operate in very late vernacular plays. And there is no reason to suppose—and many reasons to doubt—that when the citizens of York and Chester could witness their respective cycles, the monks and secular canons entirely gave up the presentation of liturgical plays, though it is probable that the impulse to create new liturgical plays or elaborate existing ones gradually ceased.

Of the various transitions, that from Latin to the vernacular is the easiest to trace, because the preserved texts illustrate various stages of this change. For the other changes we need records, and of these there is a great dearth. Late and well developed liturgical plays, as well as some early ones in the vernacular, furnish sufficient material for reconstructing several steps in the process. We are on quite firm ground, so long as we do not oversimplify or oversystematize. We must allow for sudden leaps in one place and great lags in another. England, for instance, is rather meagerly represented—only one document in English of a thoroughly transitional nature. But England in the twelfth and thirteenth centuries speaks two languages, French and English, and of the two most interesting transitional plays in French, one is certainly and the other possibly of English provenance.

Another caution: when the scholar speaks of transition, development of technique, primitive and mature stages, he speaks as a historian, not as a critic. Literary genius is apt to appear at any stage, and to make its presence felt, no matter how crude the technique. It is quite possible to argue that, technically, a contemporary B film is superior to *Hamlet;* it certainly is if naturalistic representation is your criterion for technical excellence. But Shakespeare's technical resources were adequate to his genius, and so it sometimes happened in the twelfth century, witness the Tegernsee *Antichrist.* So we are following a development, which is not in every instance a literary improvement.

The first stage of the introduction of the vernacular into liturgical drama appears when, as at Freising, the congregation sings a vernacular hymn at the end of the liturgical play. Many of the German Easter plays have directions for the "people" to sing *Crist ist erstanden,* "Christ is risen," which is actually the well-known *Victimae paschale,* provided with German words.* Apparently the purpose behind this assignment of a song to the congregation is to include them in the act of worship of which the play is a part. It makes good sense, both devotionally and dramatically.

Another way in which the vernacular invades liturgical drama is illustrated in Klosterneuberg Easter Office. After Pilate sets the guard at the tomb, the soldiers patrol, singing a song with the refrain *Schowa propter insidias,* "a guard against plots," one word of German and two of Latin. Such macaronic verse was quite popular in the Middle Ages. There is a quantity of verse with alternating lines in different languages (usually Latin and the vernacular), with one half of the line in Latin and the other in the vernacular, or with the front of the verse in the

---

* This custom of writing vernacular words to well-known liturgical pieces is widespread, its best known English example being the lovely *Singe cucu.* The manuscript of this song contains words for both the Latin liturgical piece and the English secular one—an example of both vernacularization and secularization. The Middle Ages saw nothing unseemly in borrowing church music for profane songs, even drinking and love songs.

vernacular and the refrain in Latin (or vice versa). They are often, though not exclusively, for comic effect.

In liturgical drama the use of the vernacular in this fashion often serves as a method of characterization. Less dignified characters speak wholly or partly in the vernacular, or it is used in less dignified situations. The effect is not unsimilar to that achieved by Shakespeare when Hamlet speaks in prose to the grave diggers but in blank verse in the immediately following scene of Ophelia's burial. So we find Mary Magdalen, when she is a prostitute, singing a gay song in German in the longer Benedictbeuren Passion Play, and in Hilarius' *Raising of Lazarus*, her lament for her dead brother is partly Latin, partly French.

The later liturgical drama affords several instances of this sort of thing. In early—and sometimes even in quite late—vernacular drama we find a reversal with the major portion of the text in the vernacular, but specially solemn utterances by Christ or God the Father in Latin. Often the Latin is a direct quote from the Latin Vulgate Bible or from the liturgical drama that underlies the vernacular. Sometimes every important speech is given first in the Latin then paraphrased, and usually expanded, in the vernacular. The Trier Easter Play (possibly late fourteenth century) presents the scene at the sepulchre thus:

ANGELS. [*singing*] *Whom seek ye. O fearful women, in this grave, weeping?**
FIRST ANGEL. [*speaking*] Whom do you seek, you three women, with clamor and sorrow so early in this grave on this Easter day?

This is an interesting device. The Latin, which we recognize as a version of the quem quaeritis, is sung by probably three angels, because it is the more solemn part of the text; the German is merely spoken by one of them, as though he were an interpreter. In the Frankfurt Passion Play of 1493, which is of course based on earlier plays, in the raising of Lazarus, Christ starts off in the Latin of the Vulgate, then shifts to a German paraphrase.

SAVIOUR. *I am the resurrection.* I am the eternal life and may make the dead to rise. Whoever can believe in me, even if he were a dead man, he shall live again. Do you believe that, Martha?**

This mixture of Latin and vernacular is not so usual in the later French and English plays as in the German, but by good luck we have one

* In this and the following samples of Latin-vernacular dialogue, I put the Latin in italics, the vernacular in roman.
** Compare John 11:25-26: "Jesus said unto her, I am the resurrection and the life: he that believeth in me, though he were dead, yet shall he live. And whosoever liveth and believeth in me shall never die. Believest thou this?"

English sample of precisely this practice. A manuscript in the library of Shrewsbury School, discovered about 1890 and first printed by the great Middle English scholar Skeat preserves, together with a miscellany of liturgical pieces, three plays in which liturgical Latin is paraphrased in English. The plays are all familiar ones, a Shepherds, a Sepulchre, and a Pilgrims. The text, however, is not complete; actually it is only one part with cues in each play, but there is enough to make clear the nature of the play. It is obviously an actor's copy. Its occurrence in a liturgical manuscript is significant. The plays were apparently thought of as liturgical, for one, the sepulchre, is titled, "Here begins the office of the resurrection."

The manuscript is of the fourteenth century, and the language used in the English portions appears to be of about this time, but of course the Latin play is much earlier, being similar to many twelfth-century pieces from the continent. Earlier scholars were of the opinion that the Shrewsbury Fragments, as they are called, came originally from Yorkshire, probably the city of York itself. Young, however, preferred Lichfield. The language is more like that of the Northwest Midlands; the manuscript containing the Fragments has a processional concerning the translation of St. Chad, a seventh-century bishop of Lichfield whose cult centered there in the later Middle Ages; and records show that in the thirteenth or fourteenth century precisely these liturgical pieces were presented at Lichfield. The ascription cannot, however, be certain.

Wherever they originated, the Shrewsbury Fragments show many similarities to parallel scenes in the York plays, including one passage of twelve lines which is almost identical. One further interesting feature is that many of the Latin passages are provided with scores for singing, exactly the practice we observe in the Trier and other Germany plays and a sure evidence of liturgical origin.

In the Sepulchre, which gives an adequate notion of all the Fragments, the individual, presumably a cleric, for whom the parts were written, played the Third Mary.

3 MARY.   *Alas! the redemption of Israel, that he should suffer such a death!*
1 MARY.   . . . . . .
2 MARY.   . . . . . pain.
3 MARY.   Alas! he that men weened should buy
          All Israel, both knight and knave,
          Why suffered He so for to die,
          Since
          Sithen He may all sickness save?
1 MARY.   . . . .
2 MARY.   . . . . . .

3 MARY. *Alas! Why was so mild a teacher fixed to wood with nails?*
Alas why was the one born that pierced His side?

1 MARY. . . . .

2 MARY. . . . . is aught

3 MARY. Alas that we such bale should bide
That sudden sight for to see.
The best teacher in world wide
fixed
With nails tatched to a tree!
Alas! that ever so should betide
Or that so bold man born should be
For to assay our Saviour's side
And open it without pity!

ALL. *Now, now, behold we now approach the tomb, anointers of the*
most holy body of the beloved one. [Approaching the sepulchre,
they sing] *O God, who will roll back for us the rock at the entrance*
of the tomb?

1 MARY. . . . .

2 MARY. . . . . him laid.
naturally   made known
3 MARY. He that thus kindly us has kenned
Unto the hole where He was hid,
Some succor soon He will us send
At help to lift away this lid.

Here must have followed the dialogue with the angels, some version of
the quem quaeritis, in which Third Mary apparently had no lines. Her
next speech, after the announcement of the resurrection reminds us that
the visit to the sepulchre originated in a trope of the alleluia:

3 MARY.   Alleluia shall be our song,
Since   voice
Sithen Christ, our Lord, by angels' steven
Shews him as man here us among,
And is God's Son, highest in heaven.

1 MARY. . . . . .

2 MARY. . . . . was gone.

3 MARY. [presumably to Peter and John] *Christ has risen, our hope.*
He goes before you into Galilee.
Christ is risen, witness we
By tokens that we have seen this morn!
health
Our hope, our help, our heal is he
And has been best, sith we were born.
If we will seek him for to see,
Let not this lesson be forlorn:
But go even unto Galilee;
There shall ye find him you beforn.

42

That is all, but it is enough to furnish a completely satisfactory transitional piece reaching back to familiar forms of the liturgical drama and forward to perhaps the most developed of the English cycles, that of York. The fragment of the pilgrims is similar in general make-up, that of the shepherds is rather less liturgical, including only two passages in Latin and many in vernacular that are not translated from or corresponding to anything in any extant liturgical shepherds play.

The most interesting of transitional plays is in French. Contained in a manuscript at Tours, the handwriting of which most scholars place in the latter half of the twelfth century, the *Play of Adam* is chronologically much earlier than the Shrewsbury Fragments, but represents a later stage in development. The language is Norman French, but the extant text was copied by a scribe whose dialect was of the south of France and who altered many of the linguistic forms. One editor, Studer, dates the composition of *Adam* as about 1150. Opinion is divided concerning its original home, whether in England or in France. Certainly it comes from the Anglo-French community, which in the later twelfth century included not only Normandy, but also Anjou, and after the marriage of Henry II and Eleanor in 1152, Aquitaine.

Adam contains both liturgical and non-liturgical elements, rather more of the latter than the Shrewsbury Fragments. Strictly speaking, it is not a play about Adam at all, but a prophet play to which have been added two episodes, one about the creation and fall of Adam and Eve, the other about the murder of Abel by Cain. These two episodes now occupy over three-quarters of the play, but this is partly because the manuscript is incomplete. Of the prophets we have Abraham, Moses and Aaron, David, Solomon, Baalam, Daniel, Habbakuk, Jeremiah, and Isaiah. Almost certainly the play included Nebuchadnezzar, Virgil, the Sibyl, Simeon, and perhaps several others, so that as much as half the play may have been given over to the prophets.

An even closer connection with liturgy is the fact that at the beginning and at several other places within the play the choir sings verses from the first four chapters of Genesis, which were used as readings on Septuagesima (the third Sunday before the beginning of Lent) and the following week. Whether the play was intended for performance then we do not know. The more normal time for a prophet play is before or during the Christmas season, not after.

The prophet section of *Adam* resembles the Shrewsbury Fragments in using both Latin and the vernacular, first the scriptual prophecy in Latin, then a French paraphrase. But the more dramatic episodes dealing with Adam and Cain have no Latin except the stage directions and the occasional verse-and-response sung by the choir. *Adam* clearly goes beyond anything in the liturgical drama, even the Tegernsee *Antichrist,* in its attention to details of production, the freedom with which it uses scriptural narrative, and, above all, the high quality of its characterization and motivation.

A rather long rubric at the beginning sketches one of the important stations, that of Paradise, which is to be in a "somewhat elevated place," is to be surrounded by curtains to the height of the players' shoulders, and is to contain "sweet smelling flowers and foliage" with "several trees," and "fruits hanging from them"—a rather naturalistic setting. Of more interest than the setting and the specifications for the dress of the Figure, as God is called, Adam, and Eve, are the instructions how the roles are to be played. These read like Hamlet's advice to the players.

"Let this Adam," the rubric reads, "be well trained when he ought to answer, lest in speaking he be either too fast or too slow." Any director knows how important tempo is, and how deadly it is when players pick up their cues tardily. "Let not only Adam, but all the players," the directions go on, "be so trained as to speak composedly"—is this a warning against stage fright?—"and make gestures proper to the subject of which they are speaking, and, in [speaking] verses, neither add nor drop a syllable, but pronounce all clearly"—no sloppy enunciation, please!—"and let what is to be said, be said in proper order." Finally, one specific instruction: "Let anyone who names paradise look towards it and point to it with his hand."

Some other details support the conclusion that the author was concerned over how his effort was presented. According to Genesis, after eating the fruit Adam and Eve knew they were naked and made garments of fig leaves to cover their nakedness. The author of *Adam* manages this important business by assigning it to Adam alone and by providing for a "quick change," possibly the first in theatrical history. Adam is to "stoop down [behind the curtains around "paradise"] so that he cannot be seen by the people, and put off his elegant clothes and put on poor clothes of fig leaves sewed together."

In the murder scene Cain has to hit Abel apparently on the head. The weapon is unspecified,* but the author evidently wanted the blow to look lethal; so he calls for Abel's having a "pot hidden beneath his garments," probably over his head as a sort of helmet, but covered by his headdress. Thus Cain could strike a convincing blow and not hurt the actor playing Abel! After the blow Abel is to "fall down, as if dead." Quite apparently the author of *Adam* has a bit of experience in directing amateur theatricals, and it was definitely the theatrical, not the liturgical, effect at which he aimed.

But he was more than a slick playwright. The feature of *Adam* which lifts it out of the category of the historically significant and endows it

* In the usual medieval legend it is the jawbone of an ass.

with permanent literary value is its sensitivity to character. No literary treatment of the temptation of Eve before Milton so succeeds in rendering it convincing in human terms.

To do this the author went far beyond scripture. The Devil makes his first attempt on Adam, who is suspicious and, when the Devil praises the fruit of knowledge, flatly refuses to eat it. Satan goes away, calms down by walking about the square, then returns to tempting Adam. Finding him still stubborn, he finally gives up, goes off to consult with other demons. When he returns, his target is Eve, not her husband. The Devil has apparently studied not only the secrets of Paradise, as he assures Eve, but also feminine psychology—perhaps that is also a secret of Paradise. He promises to tell her something profitable, if she will keep it from Adam:

DEVIL.	Thou'lt keep it hidden?
EVE.	Yea, in truth.
DEVIL.	Nor publish it?
EVE.	Not I! forsooth.

On her agreement, Satan launches on his temptation, a wily combination of flattering Eve and running down Adam. He is a churl, whereas she is delicate and tender, "fresher than the rose in the spring," whiter than crystal, and, moreover, much wiser than Adam. After another warning not to share her knowledge with anyone, especially Adam, Satan is ready for the revelation:

DEVIL.	I'll shew thee, then what crafy plot
	Was 'gainst you in this garden wrought:
	The fruit God gave you to possess
	Hath in it little goodliness,
	But in the fruit to you forbidden
	Exceeding virtue lieth hidden;
	Therein is found of life the dower,
	Dominion, mastery, and power,
	Knowledge of evil and of good.
EVE.	What savour hath 't?
DEVIL.	'Tis heavenly food!
	To thy fair body, to thy face,
	Most meet it were to add this grace:
	That thou be queen of the world—of this,
	Of the firmament, and of the abyss—
	To know all things that shall befall,
	And be the mistress of them all.
EVE.	Is such the fruit?
DEVIL.	Truly, it is.

45

Eve is definitely interested. The flattery, the not-unpleasant hint that Adam is unworthy of her beauty and wisdom, the sense of power in knowing something that he does not, the promise of greater things to come—these are working on Eve. But she is wary. The fruit looks good. She will think about tasting it. Not right now, but after Adam has had his nap. The Devil has brought her to the brink, then Adam walks up interrupting the whole proceedings.

ADAM.	Say, wife, what thing of thee inquired
	That evil Satan?—what desired?
EVE.	'Twas of our honour he conversed.
ADAM.	Believe him not—the traitor curs'd!
	That he's a traitor, I've no doubt.

But Adam overdoes it. He turns down Eve's request to listen to Satan and ends by forbidding her to see him:

> A knave that's done such wickedness
> To thee shall never have access.

For the Devil this is the opportune moment. He had Eve nearly sold on eating the apple, when Adam interrupted. Now Adam, by forbidding Eve to talk with the Devil, has aroused her determination to show who is boss. At this moment a serpent "cunningly contrived"* crawls up the trunk of the tree. It whispers to Eve, who takes the apple and offers it to Adam. He is afraid. Eve uses the argument of Lady Macbeth, "If you don't, I will."

EVE.	Eat! Adam, thou know'st not what is offered!
	Let's take the gift thus freely proferred.
ADAM.	I fear!
EVE.	Then, leave it!
ADAM.	Nay, I'll taste.
EVE.	Faint heart! so long thy time to waste!
ADAM.	I'll take the fruit.
EVE.	Here, eat it! So
	Thou shalt both good and evil know.
	But, first, myself I'll taste it now.
ADAM.	And I next?
EVE.	Marry, next shalt thou. [*Eats part of the apple*]
	I've tasted! Pardi! What a savour!
	I've never known so sweet a flavour!
	With such a savour 'tis endued—
ADAM.	What savour?

* Perhaps "made by craftsmanship" would be a better translation. It is obvious the author has some device in mind, but just what or how it works is beyond us.

46

EVE. —as no mortal food.
Now do mine eyes so clearly see
I seem Almighty God to be.
All that has been or shall befall
I know—am mistress of it all!
Eat! Adam, eat! No more abstain;
Thou'lt do it to thy lasting gain.

What man could resist such urging? And so Adam eats. At once, he knows what he has done, and, as in *Paradise Lost*, begins blaming his wife:

And whom shall I beseech for aid,
When mine own wife hath me betrayed,
Whom God gave me my fere to be?
An evil counsel gave she me.
Alas! O Eve! Insensate wife!
In an ill hour I gave thee life!
O had that rib been burned, alas,
That brought me to this evil pass.

God seeks out the guilty pair, hears their stories, curses serpent, man, and woman, and ejects them from paradise. Adam resumes his laments and his accusation of Eve.

O evil woman, full of perfidy!
How quickly to perdition brought'st thou me.

It is Eve, again as in Milton, who is contrite and admits her fault—Adam is sorry only for what he has lost.

Adam, dear lord, much hast thou chidden me,
And much reviled, and blamed my villany . . .
Toward God and thee much evil have I wrought . . .
No ground have wherewith to make my plea,
That God's just doom be not pronounced on me;
Forgive me! no atonement can I see,
Else would my sacrifice be offered free.

It is certainly not in characterization or general dramatic quality that *Adam* is transitional. The rapid-fire dialogue is without peer until well into the fifteenth century. These things we undoubtedly owe to a writer of genius who worked in the drama at a stage between the liturgical and the vernacular. The prophet play, the presence of liturgical chant, these are liturgical elements.

In one respect, the staging is also liturgical. *Adam* seems to use the church in its staging, which is a liturgical characteristic, but also an area outside the church. The choir may be within the church, or just outside it, on the porch. The Figure comes out of the church and returns to it several times, and the church may well symbolize heaven, just as the choir does in the Fleury Rachel play.

On the other hand, the chief stations, paradise and hell-mouth, are clearly outside the church apparently in a square or open place before the church. Hell-mouth is something new—we do not find it in liturgical drama, in which devils play little or no part.* In *Adam* they are extremely important concluding each scene by carrying the participants off to hell. There is no sign of the horse-play and low comedy of the devils so frequent in later French and German plays,** but the opportunity has been created.

Was *Adam* played by clerics or by the laity? We do not know, and there is no evidence within the play to furnish the basis for even a guess. The presence of Eve in the cast of characters is, of course, no evidence, for women characters appear in the first liturgical drama, and we know that throughout the medieval drama, throughout the professional drama of Shakespeare's time, until 1660, women's parts were played by men or boys.*** It is hard to imagine Eve played by a boy; but no more difficult than to imagine a boy as Juliet or Lady Macbeth.

Two fragments discovered in the last thirty years suggest that sometimes there was an extra transitional stage in England, from Latin to French. In a text printed by Professor Robbins in 1950, twenty two lines of French are paraphrased by the same number of lines in English, precisely in the manner that the Latin speeches of the Shrewsbury Fragments are paraphrased in English. Dating from before 1300, the age when we should expect such a development if at all, the text cannot certainly be established as dramatic, but the contents, a plea to "set still and harkeneth all" is exactly the sort of speech which we find in the cycles to quiet the crowd and build up the entrance of such figures as Herod and Pilate. Unfortunately, all we have is a fragment of a single sheet, which got bound in another manuscript probably by chance.

We have rather little evidence about the time or the manner in which the laity took over the drama. Transitional plays which might furnish such evidence are lacking, partly because when the transitional plays had been supplanted by something more developed, there was no reason for preserving them, and partly because there was a considerable destruction of ecclesiastical, particularly liturgical, manuscripts in England following the dissolution in 1536.

* Perhaps because liturgical plays were performed inside the church. Devils were expelled at the dedication of the church. Their presence, even in a play, would violate convention and probability.

** The regular German name for the harrowing of hell, the scene in which Christ, after his death on the cross, liberates the souls of the just is *Teufelspiel*, "devil play."

*** See below, p. 95, for a possible exception.

Most scholars believe that the Shrewsbury Fragments were played by a cleric. The extensive use of Latin, the closeness to the liturgy, the fact that the Fragments are found in a liturgical manuscript all point in that direction, but there is no positive proof. *Adam* has no indication either way. It is possible to argue that a large proportion of Latin points to clerical performance, but you cannot reverse the argument—a considerable amount of French does not point to lay performance, for the clergy could speak French as well as the laity.

One must also, in considering the transition from clergy to laity, draw a distinction between plays *for* the laity and those *by* the laity. Liturgical drama is not primarily *for* the laity in the sense that it exists for their instruction, though of course it is for them in the sense of being worship, whose merits are shared by all.

Another Norman French play, perhaps half a century later than *Adam,* and usually called the *Anglo-Norman Resurrection,* hints that the chief purpose of the vernacular drama was instruction. The C text of the play, found at Canterbury and certainly written in England, begins, "If you have a great desire to represent the holy resurrection for the honor of God and to recite it before the people," and then continues with precise instructions about staging. This seems to point to clerics performing a play for the laity. The liturgical purpose, "for the honor of God," and the instructional, "before the people," are balanced.

Another document, written about 1275, seems to draw a distinction between strictly liturgical plays and something else. It is forbidden the priest, says William of Waddington in his *Manuel des Pèchès* "handbook of sins," to play "miracles." This word in English usage is rather broad, certainly embracing plays based on scripture as well as saints' legends. But other dramatic performances are allowed. In the words of Robert Manning of Brunne, who translated William's *Manuel* as *Handlyng Synne* in 1303.

> For, miracles if thou begin,
> It is a gathering, a sight of sin.
> He may in church, through this reason
> Play the resurrection—
> That is to say, how God rose
> God and man in might and lose . . .
> And he may play, withouten plight
> How God was born in yule night
> To make men to believe steadfastly
> That he lit in the Virgin Mary.
> If thou do it in ways or graves,*
> A sight of sin truly it seems.

* I.e., in the streets or in the churchyard, a favorite place for sports and pastimes.

William apparently has two sorts of dramatic works in mind, both played by priests. One is obviously the familiar liturgical Easter and Christmas offices. The other must be something like *Adam*.

An interesting record from Cividale in Italy tells of the production of an extended play comprehending both the passion and the resurrection and ending with doomsday. It was performed in the city courtyard and by the clergy of the city in 1298. In 1303 the same play, plus the creation of Adam and Eve, was performed, but this time, the chronicler says, "by the clergy, or by the lay chapter." What is the "lay chapter"? The Latin is ambiguous, but perhaps the best construction is that it means the laity, perhaps members of some sort of guild or sodality. If so, we have the change from clergy to laity pinpointed in one city in one country.

We can then hazard the guess that transitional plays like *Adam* were played at least in the beginning by clerics. Just when the laity replaced the clergy, or by what stages, we cannot know. The Cividale record would suggest the year 1300, and that date strikes one as not too far afield for England also. At any rate, when the cycles come into existence (perhaps by 1350), the laity have taken over. Play production is a function of the municipality; individual guilds are charged with particular plays, and the regulation is in the hands of the corporation.

But one must not suppose that the clergy was excluded from any participation. The original authors must have been clerics, since hardly anyone else would have been able to handle the materials. Certainly clerics must have been called on for the kind of help they could best give, just as they are today in certain civic enterprises. Doubtless, too, a bishop or a dean could find methods of regulating the plays, if they became offensive or heretical. At Chester an indulgence was granted to spectators, an action which makes the drama a quasi-religious function. Secularization of the drama does not mean entire withdrawal of the church and its clergy. The medieval drama was, after all, a religious drama.

Aside from the use of the vernacular instead of Latin, there is more continuity than change in the manner in which the vernacular plays were written. Even the most developed English cycle plays use the framework of a liturgical play, where one is available, as in the Christmas and Easter offices. How persistent this liturgical element is appears in the fact that all four cycles preserve, practically unchanged, the visit to the sepulchre as we find it in the later liturgical drama. Three of them have the quem quaeritis. The York-Towneley version (York and Towneley have an identical resurrection play) runs

FIRST ANGEL.   Ye mourning women in your thought
                            Here in this place whom have ye sought?

MARY MAGDALEN.   Jhesu that unto dead was brought
                     Our lord so free.
SECOND ANGEL.   He is not here, the sooth to say,
                     The place is void therein he lay,
                     The sudary here see ye may
                         Was on him laid;
                     He is risen and gone his way,
                         As he you said.

And so on, just as in the liturgical drama. Chester is very similar. The Ludus Coventriae omits the quem quaeritis, but otherwise the visit to the sepulchre is pretty much as in liturgical drama. If we had more liturgical material from England, we should probably see in the finished cycle plays even greater dependence on the liturgical drama. As it is, numerous passages similar in wording in all the cycles suggest a common liturgical origin.

Other scenes apparently have no liturgical forerunner: the passion play (except for the Complaint of Mary), the public life of Jesus, most of the Old Testament material (except for the prophet play, found in all four cycles), and various individual plays found in only one of the cycles. Here the process of composition is about the same as that found in the later liturgical drama. The bible, the apocrypha, and legend are used when liturgical material is lacking.

In staging, one has to discriminate between two types of drama. In the one the station-and-place pattern developed by liturgical drama was taken over, moved outdoors, amplified and refined, but essentially unchanged. This is what we find in *Adam*, the *Anglo-Norman Resurrection*, the great French and German passion plays, the Cornish plays covering the creation, the passion and the resurrection; and several English plays, such as *Mary Magdalen*, the *Conversion of St. Paul*, and the morality, *The Castle of Perseverance*. It also seems to have been the method of numerous passion plays and other "miracles" not now extant, which were performed in the south of England. So it was without doubt the most popular method of staging.

But it is not the method of the English scriptural drama that has come down to us, except for one cycle. The scriptural drama which we have is a form peculiar to England and known as the craft cycle, the guild play, or the Corpus Christi play, pageant, or cycle.* Two differences dis-

* The term *mystery* is also sometimes used, but rather unfortunately. It is the appropriate term for the long French plays on scriptural subjects. Probably derived from Latin *ministerium*, it means "trade" or "craft": "He will discredit our mystery" says Abhorson in *Measure for Measure*. As a term for a dramatic presentation it was not used in England until the eighteenth century. The two terms used in medieval times for the sort of play we are describing were *miracle* (which was not limited to a saint's play) and *Corpus Christi Play*.

tinguish this sort of play from those found on the continent. It consists of a considerable number of pieces, separate plays, as it were. They were usually performed on pageant wagons, one after the other; and the separate plays together compose a cycle running from the creation of the angels to the last judgment.

This is a rather different scheme from what we find in the later and more developed French and German plays. These usually center around the passion. Most have episodes from the public life of Christ, and go through the harrowing of hell to the resurrection. In a few instances, a prophet play precedes the passion, and sometimes the play goes on to the ascension, or even to the destruction of Jerusalem. There were also independent plays, on both Old and New Testament subjects, the most notable being the French *Mystery of the Old Testament*. It has been generally thought that the continental drama had nothing like the creation-to-doomsday cycle.

Recently, however, Professor Craig has shown that in several parts of Europe, perhaps even in France, there were early developments towards the cycle play. Eger, in modern Czechoslovakia, had such a play, and one from Künzelau (1479) not only runs from the fall of Lucifer to Judgment day, but is actually called a "Corpus Christi play." Fragments in Low German and records from Barcelona indicate the existence of something similar. We have already noticed the account from Cividale. The Ste. Geneviève manuscript has a series of French plays which, if performed consecutively, would make up a cycle comparable to those in England. The conclusion seems to be that, though there were European developments which point towards, and sometimes achieve, a true cycle, only in Northern England did this become the dominant form. Here, old liturgical plays, most probably in transitional forms like the Shrewsbury Fragments, were gathered together, edited, provided with new material, and produced by the guilds of a city, generally on Corpus Christi day.

The last fact, the connection of the plays with the feast of Corpus Christi has given rise to much speculation. In the fourteenth century, when the cycles came into existence, Corpus Christi was a new feast. Celebrated on the Thursday after Trinity Sunday (eleven days after Whitsunday), it was first proclaimed by Urban IV (d. 1264) as a feast to honor the real presence of Christ in the Eucharist. Urban died before his proclamation was implemented, but it was confirmed by Clement V and the observance ordered by the Council of Vienne (1311). A little later John XXII established the chief feature of the feast, a procession of the clergy and laity behind the Eucharist. John's action probably institutionalized and regularized what was already the practice in many places.

Falling between mid June and mid July, Corpus Christi is an ideal time for outdoor spectacle—including the production of plays.

Records show that Corpus Christi was celebrated at Canterbury in 1318, Ipswich in 1325, London in 1347, Coventry in 1348. These are not necessarily the first celebrations, only the first of which there is record. These and other records also show that the guilds, religious or trade (if one can draw such a distinction), played a part in the procession. The earliest record of a Corpus Christi play is apparently one from Cambridge about 1350, when one William de Lenne joined the Corpus Christi guild and contributed one mark (thirteen shillings, fourpence) to the expenses of producing a play, probably the Slaughter of the Innocents. Other records of Corpus Christi plays come from Beverley (Yorks), 1377; York, 1378; and Coventry, 1392. There are many in the fifteenth century.

It is a great temptation to put these records together and to speculate, not that the feast of Corpus Christi or the procession was somehow connected with the cycle plays, but that the procession was the origin of these plays. Even the great Chambers saw the procession as giving birth to the plays. The procession, according to this hypothesis, included pageants of various scriptural episodes, which then developed through dumbshow into real plays of the kind we have in the cycles.

The theory was never of great utility. It did not explain the peculiar direction which the drama took in Northern England. There is nothing in the feast of Corpus Christi to impel the creation of the cycle play, as distinct from the other variety, so popular on the continent. Indeed, there is nothing in the feast of Corpus Christi to produce drama of any kind, as for instance there was in the Easter services. Nor do the Corpus Christi plays show any special connection with the liturgy which St. Thomas Aquinas composed for the feast. The plays make no attempt to demonstrate the truth of the real presence. Moreover, most of the steps which have to be postulated between a simple procession and a cycle of plays are quite unsupported by documentary evidence.

For all these reasons, Professor Craig has recently entered a strong dissent. Why, he asks, look for an alternative origin when we have a thoroughly satisfactory one in the long development of liturgical drama? England already had plenty of plays, liturgical and transitional, before the establishment of Corpus Christi as a feast. "What happened," says Professor Craig, "was that the plays were gathered together from the traditional periods of Christmas and Easter and, no doubt, from other parts of the year, arranged in chronological sequence, and played all together at a new and better time of year."

The feast provided a convenient time. It was a new holiday, and so not already preempted by other traditional festivities. It was in early summer, when the weather is reasonably dependable. This is the main connection of the feast with the cycle. Other minor connections are that the guilds marched in the procession and also produced the plays. Hence, in getting up their part of the procession, they might well use their costumes and properties, might even pull their pageant wagons along in it. This is the extent of the connection of the plays with the feast.

The peculiar cyclical form of the plays has to look elsewhere for its impetus, to the incremental and agglutinative tendencies of the liturgical drama itself; to the liturgical year, which is roughly organized in a historical sequence from creation to doomsday, or at least to the foundation of the church; to literary works like Peter Comestor's *Scholastic History*, which is so organized, or the English *Cursor Mundi*, which relies heavily on Comestor.

To account for the craft cycles one has only to observe that several things came together in the fourteenth century in England: the establishment of a new feast; the existence of a mass of dramatic works in a fairly well-developed state; the triumph of English as a national language; the achievement of power, prestige, and wealth by the manufacturing and trading classes; a vigorous civic life in the cities; a movement, partly initiated by the friars, towards a more popular religion, with wider participation by the laity; an increasing literacy and interest in things cultural; a tendency, best seen in scholastic philosophy, towards systematic and complete treatments of a subject. Add to these the presence of several genuine, though anonymous, dramatic geniuses, and you have the causes producing the four great cycles of scriptural drama in English.

Chapter V. SCRIPTURAL DRAMA IN ENGLAND

WHAT REMAINS of the scriptural drama of medieval England is only a small fraction of what once existed. We have four complete cycles, two definitely localized in York and Chester. Another, the Towneley Plays, is generally thought to be the Wakefield cycle. The fourth, called variously the *Ludus Coventriae*, Hegge, or N-town Plays, is certainly not from Coventry, but may be a form of the Lincoln cycle. Of the once flourishing Coventry plays two remain, and Norwich and Newcastle-on-Tyne are each represented by one play. A piece found in one of the Digby manuscripts is all that remains of a small group, of perhaps four plays, whose location is unknown. Two plays on Abraham's sacrifice may have formed parts of cycles at one time, though they may also have been independent.

This is the complete inventory of scriptural drama, unless one wants to include a play on the conversion of St. Paul and one on Mary Magdalen, both in the Digby manuscript and a Burial and Resurrection found in a Bodleian manuscript. The former two are, however, probably best regarded as saints' plays and the last as scarcely more than a translation of the liturgical Easter play, perhaps not even intended for dramatic representation. Also one ought to mention three Cornish plays on the story of the cross, the passion, and the resurrection. These are in the ancient Cornish language, and their organization and method of presentation are totally different from that of the extant English plays on similar subjects.

That this is but a small remnant of the drama that flourished in the fourteenth and fifteenth centuries appears from the mass of records compiled by Sir E. K. Chambers. Beverly, in East Riding, had a complete cycle of scriptural plays, first mentioned in 1377 and described in 1390 as of "ancient custom." Records throughout the fifteenth century testify to its vigor, and from 1520 comes a complete list of the thirty-six plays of the cycle. Doncaster, Chelmsford (Essex), Dublin, Hereford, and Kendal certainly had cycles, and London, the largest and wealthiest city in the realm, was a center of dramatic activity. The chronicler Malvern in 1384 speaks of a play produced by the "clerks" of London which lasted five days and included subjects from both Old and New Testaments, in 1411 there was a still longer play, running seven days. These must have been gigantic spectacles of a scope beyond any of the extant cycles. Scholars guess that they resembled the long French passions, like that of Jean Michel, but not a scrap of text remains to confirm their speculations.

Records abound from almost every part of England, which attest productions of plays of one sort or another, many of which are labelled "Corpus Christi plays," and must have been extended and cyclical. The towns and villages from which these records come run all the way from New Romney in Kent to Kendal in Westmorland, or if one wants to cross the border, to Aberdeen, which had a "haliblude" play given apparently on Corpus Christi and a nativity play at Candlemas. Other places supported a shorter play, as Hull, which had, appropriately for a maritime town, a play of Noah's ark. There are even records of something like touring companies. The New Romney players seem to have played at Lydd several times, and New Romney was host, at various times, to players from Hythe, Lydd, Wittersham, Herne, and other places.

The import of all this information is clearly that a vast deal of dramatic writing has perished. To the literary historian this means not only the loss of valuable material, which could fill in many gaps in our knowledge of the extant cycles, but also the entire absence of examples of other types of scriptural drama which certainly existed, the passion play on the German and French model, for instance. More serious, there is no reason to suppose, as there is with Greek and Roman drama, that the best was preserved. In fact preservation seems largely to be accidental, and where not accidental dependent on religious or civic, rather than literary, considerations.

It is worth noting, when one considers the problems of preservation, that dramatic manuscripts were not multiplied, as were the poems of Chaucer and Langland. The attitude towards them was rather like that which we take towards cinema or radio scripts: their sole utility was to the actors and producers of the plays. There was at any one time apparently only one complete copy of a cycle, that in the official register kept by the town authorities. There might be one additional copy of an individual play in the possession of the guild responsible for its production. One such guild copy is extant. On these two copies and possibly on the memory of the actors depended the life of the play.

Hence the bulk of our knowledge of Medieval English drama rests on unique manuscripts. Except for the Scrivener's Play of the "Incredulity of Thomas" in the York cycle, and the Norwich creation play, which exists in two versions, the only medieval drama for which we have more than one text is the Chester cycle.* This has five texts, all copied in the late sixteenth or early seventeenth century, when the plays had ceased being produced and had become a subject of antiquarian interest. The five manuscripts preserve substantially the same text, but give us two sets of banns, or announcements, one late (about 1575 and inaccurate), the other earlier, perhaps as early as 1467, and reasonably accurate.

Scholars have generally regarded Chester as the earliest of the extant

* One of the moralities, *Wisdom*, is extant in one full text and a fragment.

56

cycles. Numerous documents of the sixteenth century and the early seventeenth-century account of Archdeacon Rogers of the customs of Chester are responsible for the belief that the plays were first made in about 1327 by Ranulf Higden, a monk of Chester otherwise famed for his historical writing. The chief authority on the Chester plays, Professor F. M. Salter, has recently questioned both date and authorship. The documents on which it rests are confused and conflicting and require a good bit of interpretation to make them square with known facts. Professor Salter argues that they were falsified in the reign of Elizabeth, when civic authorities, desiring to produce the plays against the opposition of the Protestant church authorities, tried to conceal their real origin, which they feared smacked too much of popishness. Professor Salter would date them from the 1370's and would accept Henry Francis, also a Chester monk, as their author.

The circumstance which induced scholars to accept the earlier date— and some still do despite Professor Salter's cogent arguments—is the primitive structure and tone of the Chester plays. Despite revisions—of which both Salter and Greg postulate several, the last in the 1570's—they retain a rather simple narrative form, with markedly less interest in character and motivation than the York or Towneley plays and less realization of spectacular theatrical effects than the Ludus Coventriae. The cycle contains fewer plays, twenty-four in its present state, than any other, but this is largely because each play contains more material.

Critics, too, have found a more religious and devotional tone in them, but a recent rereading makes me less than sure of this. I fear that many critics have unwittingly opposed devotional to theatrical—devotion is naturally a dull business, and if a set of plays is somewhat dull by accepted theatrical standards, then it must be devotional. They are certainly no nearer liturgical drama than either York or Towneley, and I do not find that they conduce more to devotion than, say, Ludus Coventriae. It all depends on what one regards as a proper devotional state of mind. Is it calm? or intensely emotional? The qualities of Chester about which they can be little doubt are a calmness, an evenness, a narrative and lyrical rather than a theatrical technique. Some unexplained conservativism has kept out of Chester the spectacle, the fervor, and naturalism which fifteenth-century revisers introduced into the other cycles.

Two of the extant cycles, York and Towneley, come from Yorkshire and are somehow connected. York is undoubtedly the older of the two. It was in existence though doubtless not in its present form, in 1378, and some scholars would put its origin as early as the 1350's. In 1415 the town clerk Roger Burton prepared a list of the plays, fifty-two in all, together with the craft or crafts responsible for their productions and the chief actors and principal actions, in this fashion:

TILERS. 14. Mary, Joseph, the midwife, the newborn child resting in a crib between an ox and an ass and the angel speaking to the shepherds, and they praising in the following pageant.

Many of the plays here described are recognizable in the cycle as we now have it. Others have been dropped or changed, and the number of plays is somewhat fewer, forty-eight, in the extant text than in Burton's list, which has fifty-two. A second list, made a few years later by the same Burton, agrees, curiously, somewhat less with the contents of the extant cycle.

The manuscript in which the York plays come to us is an official register of the plays prepared towards the middle of the fifteenth century. Some plays omitted from this register are supplied in a sixteenth-century hand. The manuscript abounds in changes and corrections, some made apparently as late as the last quarter of the sixteenth century. This is evidence of what we know from other sources, that the cycle was not static but ever changing. Plays were added, dropped, coalesced, altered, broken up not only in accordance with changes in taste and dramatic technique, but also in guild structure.

This flux naturally produces its effects on the cycle. The wonder is not that there are many styles of dramaturgy and versification and much unevenness in dramatic execution but that the fundamental purpose and the basic structure were never completely lost sight of. The phenomenon is not unlike York's other glory, the York Minster, which took two and a half centuries to build, and for which there was probably never any over-all plan.

The mixture of styles and dramatic techniques in the cycle has posed severe problems to the textual critics. Certainly one can detect several layers of composition. There is a rather primitive layer, reflected in the scene where the three Marys visit the sepulchre, already quoted, which is very close to liturgical drama. Also primitive is some of the Shepherds' play, which, as we have noted, incorporates some of the Shrewsbury Christmas fragment.

On the other hand, some of the most advanced dramaturgy and the best verse in the whole corpus of medieval drama is found in a series of plays on the passion. One of the features of this mature writing is the extensive use of alliteration, sometimes as a structural feature, sometimes as an ornament in rimed verse. Some scholars have seen two hands here, whom they have labelled the "dramatist" and the "metrist." But the basis of this division has recently been called in question and probably the whole matter needs restudy. Suffice it for our purposes that the York plays were built, like York Minster, by diverse authors working over a long span of time, possibly on different plans, but yet have a remarkable unity.

The last stage of the York plays, apparently only projected never realized, is probably responsible for their preservation. The burgers of York wanted, like those of Chester, to keep their plays going in Elizabethan times. They met opposition from Edward Grindal, the Archbishop of York and a stiff Protestant, whose opposition to the popish superstition of the plays had to be overcome. Either he or his successor Sandys got hold of the plays, doubtless for the purpose of censorship. There are indications that some such censorship was undertaken. The Archepiscopal authorities seem to have solved the whole problem of the plays by just holding on to the manuscript, which then eventually found its way into the Fairfax family, thence into the libraries of various gentlemen, ending up in that of Lord Ashburnam, whence it came to the British Museum. There are probably few other examples in history where intent to destroy insured preservation.

The second of the extant Yorkshire cycles is the Towneley plays, preserved in a manuscript of the mid-fifteenth century, once in the possession of John Towneley (d. 1813) of Towneley Hall, Lancashire. For the better part of this century most students of the plays have been convinced that they are the Wakefield cycle. The evidence is the occurrence of the name "Wakefield" in the hand of the chief scribe of the manuscript on two of the plays, and the presence of at least two allusions to places in or about Wakefield. The two mentions of a civic cycle in the records of Wakefield are late, 1554 and 1556, but all records from Wakefield in the fifteenth century when the plays in the present form must have been given are sparse; so that one can draw no conclusions. One corroboration of Wakefield as the correct provenance is the fact that the language of much of the cycle agrees with what is known about the dialect of Wakefield and the West Riding area. Many of the linguistic forms would rule out Beverley, Lincoln, and other towns where there were cycles. So one can be reasonably sure that the Towneley plays are the Wakefield cycle.

That is not to say that Wakefield was necessarily the original home of all the plays. Towneley is even more a patchwork cycle than York. Six of the plays are, in fact, virtually identical with York plays. Passages in several other plays have more than accidental resemblances to York and many plays or scenes possess structural similarities. Certainly Towneley is closer to York than to the other two cycles which we possess. One theory, originally advanced by Marie Lyle and recently championed by Professor Craig, would see in the two cycles divergent developments of a single parent cycle, presumably an early form of York.

In the form in which it has been presented, this theory runs into the difficulty, pointed out by Chambers, that Wakefield was hardly large enough a city to have a cycle of plays before 1425, and the York cycle of that time was, as Burton's list shows, far different from anything we can accept as the original form of Towneley. Nor is it likely, or even possible, that Wakefield could have got hold of an obsolete form of the York cycle—medieval clerks did not carefully file away superseded papers as we do. The difficulty could, of course, be solved if we supposed that starting at York the cycle spent some time in another city, say Beverley, before moving on to Wakefield. But this is to buttress one hypothesis with another.

I have always preferred to believe that the Towneley cycle was put together at Wakefield, perhaps mostly from materials borrowed from York—I do not even guess whether procured openly or by subterranean methods—but also some materials from elsewhere and with a good deal of editing and local work. One of the marked features of the Towneley plays is the work, readily identifiable, of a dramatic genius who wrote his contributions in a unique nine line stanza. The rather tumbling rhythm, the sharpness of social criticism, the broad humor, as well as the peculiar verse form are the trademark of an unknown author, called for want of a better name the "Wakefield Master." He wrote several whole plays, parts of others, and a stanza or two in still others. The best known of the Wakefield plays, indeed the best known piece of medieval drama with the possible exception of *Everyman*, the *Second Shepherds' Play* is his. He has been rather accurately dated, from several kinds of evidence, as writing in the 1430's. His work thus may have been at the very first stage of the compilation of the cycle, or it may have been a dozen or so years after the compilation, but certainly at a formative period, and I cannot help feeling that his interests and predilections, his world view, so to speak, spread through much of the cycle that does not come directly from his pen.

This is, of course, pure hypothesis. What can be proved is that there are several textual layers in Towneley, perhaps as many as five or six, that there are sufficient differences in language to suggest diverse origins, either in time or place, for some of these layers, and that the literary merits, even those usually credited to the Master, are not confined to any one layer. The Towneley cycle is thus a patchwork, but an inspired one. I can only attribute these features to careful editing and purposeful selection of material. One other characteristic of the Towneley cycle deserves mention: of all the cycles it takes most liberty with scripture, and at the same time uses least legendary material.

The most legend and apocrypha is found in the cycle variously known as the Ludus Coventriae, Hegge, or N-town plays. The last name comes from the cycle itself, whose banns after enumerating and describing the plays promise that:

> A Sunday next if that we may
> At vi of the bell we gin¹ our play
> In N. town.

¹ begin

Before 1629 the manuscript of these plays was owned by the Durham antiquary Robert Hegge (to rime with wedge), who left two signatures in it. It then passed into the possession of the great manuscript collector, Sir Robert Cotton. His librarian, Richard James, wrote on the manuscript a note containing three bits of misinformation that confused scholars for over two centuries. The note states that the manuscript contains the "contents of the New Testament expressed in scenes and formerly acted by monks or mendicant friars. This book is commonly called the Coventry play or the play of Corpus Christi. It is written in English verses."

The last two assertions are true; the rest quite mistaken. The plays include subjects from the Old as well as the New Testament (and several in neither); they were not acted by monks or friars; and they do not come from Coventry, for we have two long authentic Coventry plays with which to compare them. It may be that, as some have argued, James regarded "Coventry play" as a generic rather than a peculiar designation, and that a "Coventry play" could come from Lincoln just as easily as china can be made in Staffordshire. More likely he was simply mistaken. At any rate, some scholars have tried to undo his work by calling the cycle Hegge or N-town, though most, I believe, stick to his designation.

Even without James's false leads, the cycle holds enough problems. The manuscript itself is puzzling. It is written on several kinds of paper and in several hands, though the bulk of it is in the same hand. There are numerous cancels, corrections, and marginal notes. More seriously, the itemization of the plays in the banns does not agree with the actual contents of the manuscript, one important piece having been omitted and others misdescribed. The cycle is apparently made up of forty-two separate plays, in the manner of the other cycles, but the numbers that indicate the plays are in red in the margin and often do not correspond with any real break in the text. The splitting up into separate plays would indicate production on pageant wagons, as at York, yet the stage directions of the two plays on the passion definitely call for a station-and-place stage, such as was used in the continental plays. The prologue of the second of the two passion plays says that the first passion play was produced "last year"—an impossibility in a true Corpus Christi cycle.

In large outline it is clear what has happened. The Ludus Coventriae is an assembly of at least three different pieces: a Corpus Christi cycle, a St. Anne's day play on the life of the Virgin, and a two-part passion play, the parts given in alternate years and on a multiple stage. The latter two pieces, and probably one on the Assumption of the Virgin have been interpolated into a Corpus Christi play, and the editing and fitting together is rather mechanical, as though done by a scribe rather than a real editor.

Ludus has other peculiarities as well. It is easily the most atypical piece of scriptural drama we have. The attention given to the Virgin, especially her early life in the temple, is without parallel elsewhere in vernacular drama, although Young found a French semi-liturgical drama on the Presentation of the Virgin which it somewhat resembles. Several other subjects treated in Ludus are also unique. Instead of a prophet play, the cycle has one in which the ancestory of Jesus, as enumerated in St. Matthew's genealogy, bear witness to Him—the famous root or tree of Jesse theme, familiar in stained glass and mural but otherwise unknown in drama.

The chief literary feature of Ludus—and an unexpected one in so learned a piece—is its theatrical maturity. No other cycle devotes such attention to working out exciting bits of stage business, no other is so deft in what the cinema calls "short cutting," the rapid alternation of scenes to advance a plot along several lines almost simultaneously.

Once scholars had eliminated Coventry as the original home, the search for the right locale began, just as with the Towneley plays. Some sought to interpret "N-town" as an actual place, perhaps Norwich or Northampton. But we have a play from Norwich, and it is quite different from the parallel one in Ludus. Northampton does not seem to have had plays. There is now general agreement that N stands for *name*, in other words, the name of the town is to be inserted by the crier. This would seem to point to a touring play performed at different towns, and the preparation of such may be the reason behind the form of the cycle as we have it. There are objections to this view, however. For one thing, plays are usually cut, not expanded, before going on tour.

Professor Craig has made a strong case for Lincoln as the original home of the cycle. Its language is remarkably appropriate for Lincoln. Records make it clear that Lincoln had much dramatic activity, including a cycle of plays, a St. Anne's day play, and others. The cycle was probably produced on St. Anne's day (July 26) and by the Guild of St. Anne. Lincoln likewise had a long tradition of learning and close ties with Oxford, which lay in the diocese of Lincoln. One interesting detail is that the play of the Assumption, one of the interpolated sections, calls for an organ and has pronounced liturgical elements. Lincoln records indicate that from the middle of the fifteenth century an Assumption play was acted in the Cathedral itself, which would account for both the organ and the liturgical elements. All in all, the case for Lincoln as the original home of Ludus is almost as strong as that for Wakefield as the home of Towneley.

In addition to these four complete cycles, we have four plays from cycles otherwise lost. The rather important Coventry cycle, performances of which were frequently attended by kings and the last performance of which may have included in the audience a Warwickshire lad named William Shakespeare, is represented by two extant plays. Coventry seems to have had fewer plays than other cycles known to us, possibly as few as ten, but to judge from the two extant ones, each play included more material than common. Records indicate that there were no Old Testament plays.

The Shearmen's and Taylors' pageant, which was copied from a now perished original by the Coventry antiquary, Thomas Sharp, before 1817, compasses the whole of the nativity group from the annunciation through the slaughter of the innocents. The Weavers' play is somewhat shorter containing the presentation in the temple and the disputation with the doctors. Both plays have a sort of interpretative chorus of prophets, who explain the significance of the events dramatized. It looks as though an old prophet play has been reoriented, cut up, and distributed through two (and possibly more) plays. Both plays come to us in a version prepared in 1534 by Robert Crow (sometimes spelled Croo), who was not merely a scribe but also rewrote or added some scenes in a turgid, Latinate style reminiscent of Shakespeare's pedant, Holofernes. The structure of the plays, however, is probably what it was in the fifteenth century; the language and metrics have been gravely damaged in Crow's recension.

The Norwich cycle was, like the Coventry, shorter than the four extant ones. Its twelve plays included Old Testament subjects, but, to judge from the records, no passion, ascension, or last judgment. The cycle was apparently in existence in 1478, when Sir John Paston refers to one of the plays. All the records, however, come after 1527. Only one play remains, that of the Grocers, which deals with the creation of the world, man's fall, and the expulsion from paradise. The original manuscript has long since been lost. We have to depend on a seventeenth-century transcript, which gives two versions, an earlier one dated 1533 and a later one of 1565. The earlier breaks off as God comes to judge Adam and Eve after the fall. The later version has been completely recast, probably to bring it into line with Protestant sensibilities.

The sole remaining play of the Newcastle-on-Tyne cycle, also extant only in a transcript of the eighteenth century, is a Noah play—or perhaps one should say half a Noah play, since it breaks off with the completion of the ark. Perhaps there was another play of the flood proper; perhaps we have only a fragment. The original text was doubtless in the Northumbrian dialect, which was quite beyond Bourne, the transcriber, who made many mistakes. Though unable to restore the original, modern editors have produced a satisfactory reading text, by which we can follow the action of the play. The play itself has some interesting features.

It is hard to know whether to call the Digby *Slaughter of the Innocents* part of a cycle. It was part of a small group of plays given in successive years, but these did not compose a cycle in the usual meaning of the term. The Digby manuscript 113 in the Bodleian Library at Oxford contains several plays, and is written in two different hands, possibly about 1512. The plays themselves are probably much older, and the manuscript seems actually to be a sort of anthology, the first in the history of English drama. A prologue spoken by Poeta tells us that the play is in honor of St. Anne, and it is thus our only pure representative of a form we know existed also at Lincoln. Poeta tells us, too, that last year a play of the shepherds and the magi was presented, and as epilogue promises us that next year a doctor's play will be shown.

A hand identified as that of the Elizabethan chronicler, John Stowe, has written on the manuscript "the vii book." This might mean that there were eight plays in all, but this seems too many. Four sounds more likely: one on the childhood of Mary, the nativity play, the slaughter, and the doctors. The original locale of the Digby *Slaughter* is unknown, except that the language, though mutilated by being transcribed by a scribe whose speech was southern, seems to be of the East Midland area—somewhere in Essex, Suffolk, Cambridge, or Ely would be a reasonable guess.

Two plays on Abraham's sacrifice of Isaac, a subject both dramatically pregnant and theologically important, may or may not have once formed parts of cycles. There is no evidence either way. One is found in a commonplace book written at Brome Manor, Norfolk, between 1470 and 1480. The Brome Abraham and Isaac is distinctly based on the Chester play on the same subject, one passage of more than a hundred lines being virtually parallel in the two plays. Critics have generally found in the Brome play the most skillful use of pathos in medieval drama. Almost as excellent is another Abraham play, preserved in a mid-fifteenth century manuscript in Trinity College, Dublin. Since the manuscript has a list of mayors of Northampton up to 1458, the piece has naturally been ascribed to that city. That is not impossible, but neither can it be proved. The Dublin Abraham is similar in tone to Brome and Chester, but exact lines of influence cannot be established.

Of course, the first-time reader is apt to find most cycle plays on the same subject remarkably similar, just as one Gothic cathedral looks like another when the tourist is seeing his first half dozen. The cycle play as a form was founded on scripture. It tried to trace the whole history of humanity; the major part of its attention was focused on such events as the fall, the flood, the birth of Jesus, His passion, resurrection and ascension, and that terrible day when He will come to judge the quick and the dead. Scripture, canonized legend, received theology, the amount of universal truth one can safely and effectively dramatize—these are common elements in all cycles.

Greater familiarity with the form and closer inspection of individual samples, whether of plays or cathedrals, produces astonishment at the inexhaustible variety. It has always seemed to me that modern authors try to hide an essential sameness behind the mask of discrete originality; the medieval author did just the opposite. He ardently pursued the universal; he assured his readers at every turn that he was only repeating the "old story"; he fled all deviation from tradition and authority—and he succeeded in being most original, most individual, most various.

This is the reason that any cycle will have at least one play found in no other, that it will develop scenes just hinted at in the others, will find motivations not discoverable elsewhere, will have its own unmistakable dramatic construction and tone. A resume of the contents of the four cycles, the fragments of non-extant cycles, and independent plays on scriptural themes makes this abundantly evident.

Chapter VI. FROM EDEN TO DOOMSDAY

OF THE CREATION PLAYS all but one, the Norwich later version, begin with the same formula. God the Father announces, "I am the alpha and omega, the beginning and end," and then creates the heaven and the angels. None of the plays has a very convincing interpretation of Lucifer, or Satan; and it is perhaps significant that all the extant plays are of a primitive sort. The subject seems not to have appealed to any of the several geniuses, the Wakefield Master for instance, who recast plays in the fifteenth century. After creating the angels, God leaves his throne, Lucifer begins to boast that he will be equal to God. Some of the angels follow him, some remain faithful to God, who returns, catches Lucifer sitting in his throne, and casts him into Hell. This action, of course, must be taken symbolically, but even so it disappoints us.

Then follows the creation of man and woman. Norwich had among its properties a "rib colored red," and Chester has a scene in which God puts Adam to sleep and creates Eve of his rib, but York, Towneley, and Ludus follow the account of Genesis 1, "Male and female created he them," rather than the detailed one of Genesis 2, with only a passing allusion to the rib. All emphasize the prohibition of the fruit of the tree of knowledge, mistakenly called the tree of life in Towneley.

The temptation of Eve, which gave so much opportunity to the author of *Adam,* is hastily dealt with in all the plays. The only appeal the tempter uses is that God is jealous and fearful of man, and Eve makes but token resistance, as does also Adam. Chester provides Satan with an "adder's coat"; elsewhere the manner of presentation is not specified. A lacuna of twelve leaves in Towneley deprives us of the temptation; the length of the gap might indicate a greater development here than in the other cycles. York has two bits that, had they been followed up, might have improved the play: Satan tells us that he is envious because God will take the form of man—a forecast of the incarnation. The quarrel between Adam and Eve after the fall faintly suggests Milton, especially Eve's reply to her husband's reproaches: if woman is so weak, as he says, men should exercise greater mastery.

It is only with the Cain and Abel play that the cycles begin to take advantage of their opportunities. All follow the standard explanation that Cain cheated on his sacrifice, giving God his worst corn. Abel chooses his best sheep, and the fire from his sacrifice ascends heavenwards; whereas the smoke from Cain's sacrifice blows back in his own eyes, a sign that it is unacceptable. Towneley and York both build up Cain's character. He

66

is a rough farmer, driven to exasperation by wet weather, bad crops, and grinding toil. The York Cain grumbles at the uselessness of sacrifice:

> Ya, devil, me thinketh that work were waste
> That he gave us [to] give Him again.

Both Towneley and York provide their Cains with a comic servant. After his condemnation by God, the Towneley Cain in a spirit of defiant bravado makes a proclamation for himself, which Pikeharness, the servant, burlesques:

CAIN.	I command you in the king's name
PIKE.	And in my master's, false Caim
CAIN.	That no man at them find fault nor blame.
PIKE.	Yea, cold roast is at my master's hame. home

(above "hame" is written the gloss: home)

Except for Ludus, which has an out-of-place scene of the blind archer, Lamech, shooting Cain by mistake for a beast, the cycles pass on to Noah and the flood. All four cycles follow the scriptural account that God repented Him of man, the command to Noah to build an ark, the building of the ark, the animals and the voyage, the releasing of the raven and the dove, and the final thanksgiving. The rather dull Ludus play sticks close to these topics; the other three and the Newcastle play, which goes only to the completion of the ark, have several elaborations.

The most prominent of these are the themes of old age and the shrewishness of women. Noah in all five plays is characterized as an old man.

> Sick, sorry, and cold
> Like muck upon mold,
> I wither away,

says the Towneley Noah. Sometimes he grumbles at the prospect of so much work. But the major trial is his wife. She protests against the whole project; she is willful and refuses to enter the ark. In Chester she will not go on unless her "gossips" accompany her. Either Noah takes them along or he can "row forth" and get himself a new wife. In York she protests that he has not taken her into his confidence and told her about the ark. Early and late he has been away from home working on the ark. She is a sort of medieval "office widow." She adds the demand that her gossips come along.

The Towneley Mrs. Noah is the most cantankerous of the lot. Although the waters are rising, she stubbornly insists on finishing her spinning, presumably to assert her ego and keep everybody waiting. A daughter-in-law tactfully suggests that she can spin just as well on the ark, but she will have none of that. After exchanging insults, Noah and wife come to blows. Only the intervention of the sons and daughters-in-law shames her into getting aboard. The Newcastle play adds one detail to her motivation. The devil appears and urges her not to enter the ark, giving her a drink for Noah. The parallelism with Eve's temptation of Adam is obvious, and this is the original form of the legend, which has been lost in the other plays.

The next Old Testament incident is Abraham's sacrifice. Of the six plays on the subject, Dublin and Brome plus the four cycles, only Chester devotes attention to other incidents in the life of Abraham. It dramatizes the rescue of Lot, the offering of Melchizedek, and Abraham's prayer for a son. The other five plays begin with God's command to Abraham to go to the "land of vision"* and there sacrifice his son Isaac. Abraham reluctantly accepts his duty, but conceals the real purpose of the journey from Isaac. Though Sarah is mentioned in all plays, only in Dublin does she actually appear. There she objects that Isaac is too young for such a long journey. Abraham replies that he must learn the rite of sacrifice. Sarah sees Abraham and Isaac off with several warnings: don't give the boy a wild horse to ride, mind that he doesn't get muddy, stay away from pools. In several plays Isaac wonders what they will sacrifice, is told that God will provide a beast.

All the plays develop the situation pathetically. Towneley and York lose force because they apparently do not conceive Isaac as a child.** In Towneley, Isaac is afraid and loath to die, implores to be spared for his mother's sake. In York he asks forgiveness for his faults and begs a kerchief over his eyes.

Each play has its own selection and arrangement of pathetic details. In Ludus Isaac suggests that his father may be able to perform the deed if he turns his eyes away. This concern of Isaac for his father's feelings is commonly emphasized. In Chester and Dublin he offers to take his clothes off lest they be bloodied. In Brome, Chester, and Dublin it is Isaac who has to urge Abraham to perform his duty to God. You have other children, says the Brome Isaac,

> nature
> The which ye should love well, by kind.
> I pray you, father, make ye no woe,
> gone
> For, be I once dead and from you go
> I shall be soon out of your mind.

* Following the Vulgate reading for the Authorized Version's "Land of Moriah."
** The preponderance of commentary opinion favors Towneley and York. The notion that Isaac was a child is an artistic, not a theological, interpretation.

In all plays the intervention of the angel brings a shout of joy from both Abraham and Isaac, and the latter skips off to find the ram which will substitute for him as a blood sacrifice.

In Chester Abraham's sacrifice directly precedes the prophet play. Only Towneley gives any attention to Jacob and Esau. Two leaves torn out of the manuscript apparently dealt with Rebecca's scheme to secure the blessing for Jacob; only the actual blessing is extant. This is followed by another play of Jacob, which though quite short, presents Jacob's vision of God and God's promise and his return to Aran to meet with Esau.

Ludus has a play in which God appears to Moses in a burning bush and gives him the commandments, a curious telescoping of Exodus. York and Towneley have an identical Moses play, in which Pharoah is the central character, beginning the play with a conventional tyrant's boast. Soldiers report that the Jews are overrunning the land. Enslave them, Pharoah orders, and have the midwives kill all Hebrew infants. Moses sees God in the burning bush and receives a command to liberate His people. Appearing before Pharoah, Moses shows him the wand that changes to a serpent and, when Pharoah is stubborn, calls up the ten plagues, which are reported one by one by messengers. After the tenth plague, Moses leads Israel out of Egypt and through the sea, the stage direction saying simply, "Here they cross through the sea." Pharoah's army is drowned, as Pharoah himself calls on Mahound, and the play closes with Moses' thanksgiving.

In Chester a Moses episode is part of the Prophets, which is also the next play in York. The order of the Towneley cycle seems to have suffered from a scribal error which places the Moses play after the Prophets. Chester and Towneley most nearly preserve the liturgical form of the Prophets. The play has two episodes, one in which God gives Moses the Law (not the commandments), typified by such details as the offering of first fruits; and the Baalam story, complete with a talking ass named Burnell. The rest of the play consists of the prophecies of Isaiah, Ezechiel, Jeremiah, Jonah, David, Joel, and Micah. The Expositor appears after each of the episodes and each of the prophets with his interpretive comments. The end of the play is somewhat confused. It has obviously been cut, either from an earlier version or from the liturgical original, for Expositor assures us that they could play many more prophets but it would "tarry the day."

The Towneley Prophets is similarly constructed and was probably even nearer its liturgical original. Moses, as prologue, recites with comment the ten commandments. Then follow the prophecies of David, the Sibyl, and part of Daniel. Here the manuscript breaks off. Doubtless more was to come. The prophecies are in Latin with English paraphrase. The York Prophets is only a vestigial remnant in which an unnamed prologue recites several of the prophecies as a prologue to the Annunciation play. This, however, probably does not represent fifteenth-century practice, but is later.

It is at this point that Ludus deviates most markedly from the other cycles. The prophets are combined with several kings of Israel and Judah in an arrangement in which each king is followed by a prophet, David by Jeremiah, Solomon by Ezechiel, and so on. The manuscript itself calls the play "Jesse," and it is obviously the author's intention to put in dramatic form the well-known iconographical theme in which the ancestors of Jesus form a tree, the root of which is Jesse.

Ludus follows with four plays* without parallel, so far as I know, elsewhere in medieval drama. These deal with the life of Mary and her parents, Joachim and Anna. They are based on well-known legends, immortalized by Giotto. In form the plays have many liturgical elements, suggesting a closer connection with church services than usual in the vernacular drama.

After a prologue by Contemplatio, we meet Joachim and Anna, an old childless couple. Joachim fears that his sacrifice in the temple will not be acceptable because of his childlessness. Anna takes the fault on herself and weeps as Joachim leaves. When the priest refuses Joachim's sacrifice, he goes off to live with his shepherds. Anna prays for a child. An angel then appears to Joachim and promises that Anna will bear a child, who shall be offered in the temple and who will bear the Saviour. He commands Joachim to return to Jerusalem and meet his wife at the Golden Gate.

In the next episode Joachim and Anna keep the angel's command by presenting the three-year-old Mary in the temple. When the Bishop receives her, Mary recites the fifteen gradual psalms,** a miracle in so young a child, as the Bishop points out. The Bishop then instructs her in the commandments and turns her over to the virgins of the temple, whom she edifies by reciting seven petitions to the Lord. An angel brings manna to her in a cup of gold.

The betrothal of Mary, which follows, is built around the miracle of Joseph's blossoming rod. The Bishop reminds Joachim that, according to the law, every damsel of fourteen must choose a spouse. When the Bishop urges this duty on Mary, she protests that she has vowed virginity. The Bishop approves this, but has to maintain the law. Puzzled what to do, he prays. An angel appears with the message that God wishes all the youth of the house of David to be assembled, each with a white rod in his hand. The one whose rod blossoms is to wed Mary.

* According to the artificial numbering of the manuscript however it seems certain they constituted but one play. One of the marginal numbers indicating a new play comes in the middle of a speech.
** Psalms 120-34.

When he hears the command, Joseph, whose lineage is of David, is reluctant, since he is old and has always remained a virgin. Nevertheless, he obeys the command, and, of course, it is Joseph's rod which blooms. The Bishop performs the marriage ceremony. Mary and Joseph promise each other ever to keep their chastity. The Bishop warns Joseph that old men with young wives are often targets of slander. He provides three damsels to dwell with Mary and to bear witness to her virtue, an obvious preparation for the situation which follows. Mary and Joseph leave for their home in Nazareth.

As a sort of prologue to the annunciation, Ludus dramatizes another topic prominent in medieval art and didactic literature but without parallel in the drama: the Parliament of Heaven. This is a sort of allegory of the scheme of salvation based on Psalm 85:10, "Mercy and truth are met together, righteousness and peace have kissed each other." Truth, Mercy, Righteousness (Justice in the play), and Peace are the "four daughters of God," and they debate what should be done about mankind. Truth and Righteousness demand his punishment; Mercy and Peace plead for him. After hearing the debate, the Father decrees that Mercy and Peace shall have their wish, but Truth and Righteousness shall also be satisfied, for the Son will take on him mankind's debt and discharge it fully.

With the annunciation, for which the Parliament of Heaven prepares, Ludus joins company with the other cycles. The group of plays concerning the nativity is variously organized in the four cycles and in Coventry, whose two extant plays belong to that part of the cycle. Coventry has one long play comprising everything in the whole Christmas group except the flight to Egypt and the slaughter of the innocents. Chester has one play for everything up to the adoration of the shepherds; Ludus, York and Towneley, have several plays for the same material. All five cycles have plays or scenes in which Gabriel announces the incarnation to Mary, and Joseph is suspicious of his wife's pregnancy.

All but Coventry also present Mary's visit to her cousin, Elizabeth, though the order differs, Ludus and Towneley putting the suspicion of Joseph before the visitation, Chester and York after. The handling of the three episodes is rather close to scripture, except that all four cycles use Joseph's suspicion as an occasion to introduce the January-and-May theme, the old husband beguiled by a young wife, a favorite in medieval fabliau and romance. The Chester Joseph complains that he is too old to beget a child,

> This thirty winter, though I would
> I might not play no play.

71

There follows a scene in which Mary pleads her innocence, seconded by her maidens in Ludus, but Joseph cannot believe that God or an angel is the father of Mary's child. An angel appears to Joseph, in York and Chester while he sleeps, and he is persuaded of Mary's innocence. Ludus adds a play, lacking elsewhere, in which Mary and Joseph are formally hailed into court by a comic summoner, to answer before a bishop and two doctors the charges of two detractors. Both Joseph and Mary undergo an ordeal; they drink of the "bottle of vengeance," and then go seven times about the altar without falling. The first detractor drinks and falls, exclaiming that his head feels on fire. He asks Mary's pardon for his slander.

Chester at this point has an episode in which the Emperor, called Octavian, proclaims a universal census, and a messenger takes the news to Joseph. Included in the episode is an interesting scene in which the Sibyl, presumably moved here from the prophets, foretells the birth of Christ. Octavian unhistorically refuses to be deified. The portrait of the Emperor is rather kindly, exactly the opposite to that in Towneley, where Caesar Augustus is a boasting tyrant of the Pharoah and Herod stamp. He sends for Sirinius (Cyrenius of the Gospel of Luke) and tells him that the birth of a rival king has been foretold. What shall Caesar do? Sirinius suggests that the boy be sought out and killed, the Herod motif. As proof of Caesar's power, let him proclaim a head tax. Caesar rewards Sirinius for this good advice and sends forth the messenger with the blessing of Mahound.

York and Coventry omit all reference to the edict of Caesar. Joseph merely tells Mary they must go to Bethlehem. In Ludus there is a slight reference to the edict, and the journey to Bethlehem is dramatized. As usual Ludus relies on legend, here the famous cherry-tree story. As they journey on, Mary asks Joseph what tree stands on yon hill. A cherry tree. In season she might eat of its fruit. Turn again, says Mary, it is in bloom, is loaded with fruit. Joseph grumbles at his inability to pluck the cherries, the tree is so high. At Mary's word it bows down. Chester supplies a detail of a different sort—from everyday life instead of romantic legend. As they leave Joseph ties an ox to the ass on which Mary will ride. The ox is to sell for their head tax.

The nativity is staged in all the cycles except Towneley. The simplest play, and perhaps the most effective, is the York. Joseph tells Mary that there is no room for them except in the stable. Then, says Mary, the child will be born here. It grows dark and cold, so Joseph steps out of the stable for light and fuel. Once outside, he sees a sudden light within and rushes back. Mary joyfully announces that the child has been born. Joseph adores the infant, repeating several of the prophecies of His coming. But there is no bed and no fire. Mary has to put the Infant in the crib between the ox and the ass, who recognize their Lord and warm him with their breath.

Other plays elaborate this action. In Chester, Coventry, and Ludus Joseph leaves his wife in the stable to seek help for her accouchement. In Coventry the action is a little difficult to follow, because of an intervening scene with the shepherds—it would probably have been clear when staged. Apparently Joseph hears the angelic message and rushes back to find the Baby born. In Ludus and Chester he returns with midwives. The Babe has already been born when the Ludus Joseph returns, but the Chester midwives arrive before the birth. Their assistance, however, is not needed. God will work all of His power, Mary assures them. In both plays the function of the midwives is not obstetrical but theological. In Chester Tebella bears witness that Mary had no pain in childbirth; in both Chester and Ludus the other midwife, Salome, doubts that Mary is a virgin. When she touches Mary her hand is withered. An angel appears and tells her to touch the Child, and the hand is healed.

Chester closes its nativity play with another scene from legend. Expositor tells the marvels at the birth of Jesus. There were three suns in the sky (obviously a sign of the Trinity), and a temple in Rome fell down. Then Sibyl bids Octavian the Emperor to look on high. He sees the birth star and in it the new born Babe and His mother. Expressing an ardent desire to honor Him, he hears the angels' song.

In all other cycles the shepherds are the first to hear the angels and to worship Jesus, and, of course, Chester has a shepherds' play also. Towneley makes up for the lack of a nativity by having two shepherds' plays, both by the Master. Apparently the producer may take his choice. The most devotional of the shepherds' plays is that of Ludus, in which the shepherds repeat several prophesies of the Messiah, hear the angels' song, and worship the Babe with songs of praise.

These are the bare essentials; all other plays have more or less elaboration, much of it comic. The discussion of the angelic announcement, found also in Ludus, becomes the occasion of rustic humor in Chester, and the two Towneley plays. The Third Shepherd of Chester claims as the eldest of the group the right to expound the song:

> It was glarum, glarum, with a glee;
> It was neither more nor less.

Others however have diverse interpretations, and the issue is almost decided by blows. Another comic addition is the gifts of the shepherds to the Babe, found in all plays except Ludus. Most of the gifts are ridiculous, a horn spoon holding a hundred peas, a pipe, a hat, a "pair of my wife's old hose."

73

Chester and the two Towneley plays go far beyond this in expansion of the comic elements. Chester introduces a clown, Trowle, servant to the shepherds, who exchanges insults with them and throws all three in wrestling. In the same three plays the shepherds eat a meal of curiously assorted foods. Two of the shepherds of the First Towneley play get into an argument over where to pasture some sheep which one of them intends to buy. Only the appearance of the third and his ridicule prevents a fight over the non-existent sheep. Political and social satire appear in these three plays, attaining its greatest development in the Second Towneley play. Here the one shepherd vents his bitterness against "these gentlery men" who, with their proud manners, make the husbandman miscarry; another's trouble is domestic, a wife sharp as a thistle and rough as a briar; and the third complains of the weather, floods, rains, and storms worse than any since Noah's time.

This attitude of protest is developed in the famous Mak episode. As the three shepherds prepare to settle down for the night, Mak, a suspected stealer of sheep, joins them. Undeceived by Mak's effort to pass himself off as a stranger by using the Southern dialect of English, the shepherds make him lie down in their midst. When they are all asleep, Mak arises and takes one of their sheep to his hovel, where Gill, his slatternly wife, tells him he will be hanged for his thievery. She is glad enough, however, for the food, and she helps him when the shepherds, discovering their loss, come to Mak's house. The sheep is concealed in a cradle, Gill groans in pain, and Mak tells the suspicious shepherds that she has just given birth to a bairn.

The shepherds are almost taken in—but just as they are going, one turns around and makes for the cradle. He must give the baby a present before he leaves. When he pulls off the covers, he sees the long snout of a sheep. Gill's protest that it is really a baby, but has been bewitched is of no avail. Mak must be punished, but the shepherds are poor men themselves and have noted that the home has not a crumb of food in it. So instead of turning him over to the law, they merely toss him in a blanket.

The angelic announcement and the adoration of the babe seems to come almost as an afterthought. There is a connection, however, in the grotesque parallel between the sheep in the cradle and the infant Jesus in the manger.

Following the adoration of the shepherds comes that of the Magi, found in the four cycles and in the Coventry nativity play. Though the different cycles organize the material somewhat differently, in the main they all follow the lines of the developed liturgical plays. Three kings, following the star, come to Herod's court, where the doctors read the prophecies of the Messiah to Herod, who shows his rage in various ways. He allows the kings to depart, intending to have them lead him to the new-born king. In the adoration of the Infant, all treatments emphasize the symbolism of the gifts. After the adoration, an angel warns the Magi not to return to Herod and commands Joseph to flee with Mary and the Babe to Egypt.

Of the flight into Egypt we have six extant treatments. It occupies separate plays in York and Towneley, but is compressed into short scenes in Chester, Ludus, the Coventry Shearman's and Taylor's Play, and the Digby *Slaughter of the Innocents*. York and Towneley achieve their fuller development by characterizing Joseph. He is a chronic grumbler, but for different reasons in the two plays. The York Joseph is impatient because Mary, instead of preparing for the journey, mourns Herod's command to kill all male children. The Towneley Joseph, though also urging expedition, is sorry for himself and warns young men against marriage. Nevertheless, he comforts Mary and helps her by bearing the pack. The grumbling Joseph appears also in Coventry Weaver's Play, where he protests at having to find two doves for the purification of Mary in the Temple.

Herod is the dominant figure in the slaughter of the innocents. When the news of the escape of the Magi reaches him, the Coventry Herod rages "not only in the pageant, but in the street also," and the Chester Herod denounces the Magi as "traitors." In all treatments he consults with his counsellors and determines on a general slaughter of male infants. In Chester and Coventry the soldiers object. One of the Chester soldiers says that he is ready to fight any knight or champion, even "though / stiffer than ever Samson was," but killing babies "me shames sore by St. Mahound." The objection of the Coventry soldier is more political: so great a slaughter is likely to provoke insurrection. Elsewhere the soldiers are quite willing, sometimes even advising the action.

In the actual scene of the slaughter, the mourning Rachel of the liturgical drama often becomes a cursing Rachel, who defies the soldiers and calls down vengeance on Herod and his soldiers. In Digby a comic servant named Watkin, desirous of proving his valor, is beaten with distaffs by the women and flees. In Towneley the episode closes with Herod apparently victorious, rewarding his followers, and boasting of the slaughter. In Coventry and York Herod learns that Jesus has escaped, and Chester, Ludus, and Digby show Herod's death.

In Ludus Herod is celebrating the elimination of his rival at a banquet, when the figure of Death appears. Death strikes down Herod and two of his soldiers, and the Devil receives their souls. Death then moralizes that Herod now lies under earth, where worms will eat him. In Digby Herod goes mad, and apparently dies repentant. Chester has a unique account, which I have not seen elsewhere. Herod's own son is slain by mistake along with the other infants, and the news apparently causes his death. He complains that his legs and arms are rotten. The Devil receives his soul and predicts his eternal punishment. The Chester play is the only one that closes with the return of the Holy Family from Egypt.

In all but Ludus the Purification of Mary in the Temple, also sometimes called "the Presentation of Jesus," follows. Ludus achieves perhaps a better chronological arrangement by making the purification a scene in the slaughter play, placing it before the flight to Egypt. The York play is out of place in the manuscript, following the Easter play, but doubtless it was originally played after the slaughter, which position it occupies in Towneley, Chester, Coventry, and Digby.

The principal actions covered in all these plays or scenes are the presentation of Jesus, the prophecies of Simeon and Anna, and the offering of two turtle doves by Mary. Several marvels appear in one or other of the plays. The Chester Simeon reads in Isaiah that a virgin will conceive and bear a child. Believing this a mistake of the scribe, Simeon erases the word "virgin" and substitutes "good woman." An angel restores the original reading. Simeon is amazed, and to make sure that he has witnessed a miracle again erases "virgin," and again it is restored. In Coventry an angel furnishes the two doves when Joseph fails to catch any. In York an angel tells Simeon he will see the Messiah. The incomplete Towneley Purification has the bells of the temple ring by themselves.

In Chester and Coventry the disputation between Jesus and the doctors of the law, an incident which Luke describes as taking place when Jesus was twelve, forms the second part of the purification play. Chester violates chronology and perhaps secures dramatic compactness by making the two episodes continuous, but Coventry indicates a lapse of time. York and Towneley have a common, and separate, play of the doctors, and the Ludus play also bears a separate number. In all the plays the doctors are scornful of Jesus when he enters—they are learned in the law, and a mere child should not meddle in such matters. The Ludus Jesus proceeds to show his knowledge of the law by inspiration. In all but Ludus He recites with comment the Ten Commandments. In Ludus Jesus' teaching is more esoteric: He propounds the mystery of the Trinity, by analogy with the sun, which has three qualities, splendor, heat, and light, just as the Godhead has three persons.

When Mary and Joseph discover that Jesus is not in their company, they return to Jerusalem. The Joseph of Chester and the common York-Towneley play hesitates to enter the Temple to seek Jesus. He is just a poor, ignorant man and cannot go among the learned doctors; so Mary has to lead the way. In all the plays Jesus leaves in his parents' company, saying that he will be obedient to them.

Scripture gives no account of the life of Jesus between his twelfth year and His baptism by John, traditionally placed in his thirtieth year. The cycles are similarly silent. In fact, the public ministry, which is extensively treated in the gospels, is rather sketchily dramatized in the cycles, at least in comparison with the wealth of development in the Christmas, Passion, and Easter groups.

York, Towneley, and Ludus have plays on the baptism of Jesus; Chester, York, and Ludus present the temptation in the desert. The raising of Lazarus appears in all, though out of place in Towneley. All but Towneley contain plays or scenes of the woman taken in adultery, the healing of a blind man, Mary Magdalen's anointing the feet of Jesus, and the triumphal entry into Jerusalem. Only York has the transfiguration, only Chester the driving of the money-changers out of the temple. One misses entirely such episodes as the Sermon on the Mount, the miracle of the loaves and fishes, the marriage at Cana, though York once had such a play, now lost.

On the whole the plays concerned with the public ministry are rather sketchy, and, do not exhibit the ablest dramatic writing in any of the cycles. One reason is obviously the lack of precedent in the liturgical drama, but there is also lack of precedent for the vastly elaborated passion scenes. Perhaps a more powerful reason is that the dramatists apparently did not find in the public ministry those qualities of conflict, contrast, suspense, irony, spectacle, and character which called forth their best efforts. Except for a few scenes, the healing of the blind man in Chester and the woman taken in adultery in Ludus, all the plays on the ministry are excessively prosy and narrative—and rather dull.

The three plays of the baptism begin with John identifying himself. In Towneley and York an angel tells John that Jesus will come to him for baptism. In all three plays John objects his unworthiness, but Jesus persuades him. John or Jesus or both develop the doctrinal significance of baptism, and the plays close with John's praise of Jesus.

The main theme of the three plays on the temptation in the desert is the confusion of Satan, who cannot find who was Jesus' father and is uncertain whether or not he is the promised Messiah. He must tempt Jesus to find out. He uses three temptations, gluttony (changing the stones to bread), vainglory (standing on the pinnacle of the temple), and covetousness (the kingdoms of the world). The Chester Expositor parallels these with the temptations of Adam, and makes the oft-repeated point that Jesus is the second, and perfect, Adam.

York and Chester have slight treatments of the woman taken in adultery, each occupying only a portion of a play. In both the actual taking is only reported and the emphasis is on Jesus' writing the sins of her accusers in the sand. Ludus builds up the episode into a whole play by making the appeal to Jesus a plot of the Pharisees and by staging the detection of the woman and her lover. Somewhat the opposite happens with the healing of the blind man. In Ludus and York it is a short episode, part of the entry into Jerusalem, but Chester develops it into a considerable scene.

Chelidonius, as Chester names the blind man, enters led by a boy. Peter and John ask Jesus the cause of his blindness, whether because of his own sin or that of his parents. For neither, but to show God's glory. Jesus sends Chelidonius to the pool of Siloam to wash his eyes. Chalidonius is healed and praises God. Two neighbors take him to the Pharisees. Denying that Jesus, who violates the sabbath, could do any good, they send for his father and mother, who come reluctantly, fearing the Pharisees. The parents of Chelidonius witness that he was born blind, and Chelidonius himself, despite the efforts of the Pharisees to convince him that Jesus is a sinner, honors Jesus as the Son of God. The Pharisees in their anger propose to stone Jesus, who vanishes.

The raising of Lazarus follows the episode of the blind man in Chester, that of the woman taken in adultery in York and Ludus. It is the only scene of the public ministry in Towneley. All the cycles follow the gospel account fairly closely, except that, as usual in the Middle Ages, Mary the sister of Lazarus is identified with Mary Magdalen. Ludus gives the fullest representation of Lazarus' death. Lazarus, ill, wishes that Jesus were there. A "consolator" goes to fetch Him. Lazarus dies and is buried before the consolator can return with Jesus. Mary and Martha are mourning; Jesus is taken to the sepulchre, raises his eyes to heaven, and summons Lazarus to come forth; all confess Jesus their saviour. The Towneley Lazarus preaches a sermon of some length on the favorite medieval topic of death, how it levels all men and brings them to dust and worms.

The cycles exhibit extreme variation in handling the events just before Jesus' capture and the passion. Chester has one play which deals with Jesus' visit to the house of Simon the leper, Magdalen's anointing His feet, and the conspiracy of the Jews with Judas to take Jesus. York has a play on the preparation of the Passover, the triumphal entry into Jerusalem, and the healing of a blind man and a cripple, with another play given over to the conspiracy. In Ludus these matters occupy the beginning section of the first passion play. Towneley begins the passion group with the conspiracy.

The episode of Magdalen's anointing the feet of Jesus, dramatized in Chester and Ludus and reported in York and Towneley, is important in establishing Judas' motivation for the betrayal. As treasurer of the band, Judas is wont to take ten percent of all their goods. The ointment with which Magdalen anoints Jesus is worth three hundred pence. In so wasting it instead of selling it, Judas reasons, she has, with the commendation of Jesus, cheated him of thirty pence, and this is his price for betrayal.

The action of the passion begins with the conspiracy of the Jews. In Ludus the conspiracy is interlarded with scenes of the entry into Jerusalem and the Last Supper. In the other three cycles the events are presented separately, the conspiracy, then the Last Supper, then the capture of Jesus. In Ludus Annas consults two doctors of the law about measures to be taken against Jesus. As the conference proceeds, Caiaphas, who describes himself as a judge, Rewfyn, Leyon, and Gamaliel all give their opinions. Chester has fewer consultants and simpler action, but the same charges are made: Jesus heals on the sabbath, He says He is the son of God, above all He will destroy "our laws." This is the theme of all the dramatizations of the conspiracy. To persuade Pilate, the accusers emphasize another charge: Jesus is a threat to Caesar's sovereignty.

York and Towneley include Pilate among the council. The York Pilate prepares for his role in the passion by saying that Jesus is innocent and the actions of the high priests and Pharisees are motivated by envy and spite. Only when they allege Jesus' treason against Caesar, does Pilate consent to their proposals. The Towneley Pilate is, however, from the beginning the arch-enemy of Jesus. He identifies himself with the Jews, often speaks of "our laws," words used elsewhere only by Annas, Caiaphas, and the other Jews.

During the deliberations of the council Judas comes in. In Towneley and York he has difficulty getting a hearing. A beadle refuses admission to him in York and the Towneley Pilate orders him thrown out. Nevertheless he manages to get a hearing for his proposal, and instantly the attitude of Pilate, Annas, and Caiaphas changes. For thirty pence—what he would have gained had Magdalen's ointment been sold—he will betray Jesus. The Jews (with Pilate in York and Towneley) call out soldiers to capture Jesus.

Of the four treatments of the Last Supper only Ludus dramatizes the institution of the Eucharist. The eating of the paschal lamb, Jesus washing the feet of Peter and the other apostles, the prophecy "one of you shall betray me"—these incidents appear in all. Following the Last Supper, Jesus and the apostles go to the Mount of Olives and Jesus prays, while the apostles sleep. The band of soldiers advances to capture Jesus, whom Judas identifies with a kiss. Peter cuts off the ear of Malchus, and Jesus heals it. In Towneley Pilate commands the soldiers, and lurks in the background supervising everything. In York Annas is in charge, in Ludus and Chester Jews of lesser rank.

Ludus follows the capture by a unique scene, in which Mary Magdalen tells the Virgin the sorrowful news. The trial before Caiaphas, the high priest, is depicted in all the cycles as brutal and rigged. Accusers, called "torturers" in Towneley, elsewhere simply Jews or soldiers, bring the expected charges. Caiaphas attempts to examine Jesus. The Towneley play, one of the Master's pieces, presents the starkest picture of hate and cruelty. Caiaphas is so violent that even Annas had to remind him that he

79

is a "man of holy kirk" and should control his passion. The torturers blind-fold and beat Jesus unmercifully, asking Him to prophesy who struck Him. Annas finally advises Caiaphas that Jesus must be tried by secular authority, and suggests sending him to Pilate. All but Towneley stage Peter's denial and repentance either during or after the trial before Caiaphas.

The first trial before Pilate is short in Ludus and Chester, absent from Towneley. Annas and Caiaphas are the accusers. When they mention that Jesus has preached sedition from here (i.e. Jerusalem) to Galilee, Pilate asks if He is a Galilean. Then he must go to Herod for trial. York ampli-fies this episode by prefacing it with a scene of domestic banter between Pilate and Percula, his wife. They are going to bed when Pilate is aroused by Caiaphas and his company. Pilate rises and goes to the judgment hall, and his wife sleeps. During her sleep the Devil, who fears that the death of Jesus will bring to an end his power over mankind, appears to Percula. She must tell Pilate to free Jesus. Ludus also has the dream of Percula, but later on in the passion.

Towneley entirely omits the trial before Herod, though there is a covering allusion to it later. Herod in the other three cycles is at first friendly to Jesus. He has heard of Jesus' miracles and would like to see a sample. When Jesus remains silent despite coaxing and promises of help, Herod grows angry and turns Jesus over to the soldiers. They dress him in white and scourge him. Herod then commands the soldiers to take Jesus back to Pilate.

At this point York inserts the remorse of Judas, found, in abbreviated form, elsewhere in Ludus, but not in Chester or Towneley.* In the York version Pilate is listening to the charges of Annas and Caiaphas (for the third time!) when Judas enters, repenting that he has sold guiltless blood. He begs Pilate to take back the money and free Jesus. When all jeer at him, Judas throws down the money and leaves to hang himself. Annas, Caiaphas, and Pilate debate what to do with the money. As the price of blood, it cannot go into the treasury. Pilate suggests that they buy a "spot of earth" in which to bury pilgrims. A squire wishes to mortgage a piece of land, "Calvary locus," for thirty pence. Pilate asks to see the title. Once it is in Pilate's possession, the property is his. The squire, cheated out of his property, curses all of the company.

The second trial before Pilate is the climax of the Passion, dramatically speaking. If one can speak of suspense concerning an action, the outcome of which is already known to the audience, the suspense of the passion is

---

* At the end of the Towneley manuscript, is a fragment called *Suspencio Judae*, "the hanging of Judas." It is in a later hand than that of the rest of the manuscript, and it is a monologue with no indication of action. I do not believe it is a play, or ever formed a part of the Towneley cycle.

altogether confined to the trial before Pilate, for his is the power to condemn or release Jesus. All the enmity of the Jews, the capture and the inquisition before Caiaphas and Annas, the trial before Herod can avail nothing, if Pilate determines to find Jesus innocent. Hence Pilate is the key figure, and his court the focal point of the tragedy, just as the Forum is in *Julius Caesar* and "The Mousetrap" in Hamlet. Here the issues are settled, and all that follows is, barring a miracle, inevitable.

The trial before Pilate is therefore a significant test of dramatic construction in all four cycles. There are two possible methods of development, both dependent on the interpretation of Pilate's character. One is to portray Pilate as vacillating, desirous of releasing Jesus but also afraid of what the Jewish leaders may tell Caesar if he thwarts them. This is the dominant impression one gets from the gospels, particularly John, and it is the line that Chester, Ludus, and especially York, pursue.

York greatly augments the gospel account. It introduces the apocryphal story of the bowing of the banners. When Jesus enters Pilate's court, all the banners held by the soldiers bow to Him. When Pilate asks why, the soldiers reply that it was beyond their ability to keep the banners upright. Pilate sends for the two strongest soldiers in the country. They cannot hold their lances straight; even Pilate is forced to kneel. Dramatically, this is waste motion—it makes no point, and the outcome of the trial is unaffected by the incident.

But another type of development is purposive. York greatly lengthens the trial. Pilate keeps insisting that he can find no guilt in Jesus. Annas and Caiaphas reiterate their charges, coming back several times to the threat against Caesar's power, which always produces its effect. Pilate tries one maneuver after another. Try him after your own law. Shall I release Barrabas or Jesus? Let Jesus be scourged, perhaps that will content you. Let his blood be upon your head. No doubt much of this added length is due to the necessity of providing plays for guilds grown numerous and prosperous, but the dramatic point is no less valid. Pilate squirms and wriggles; does everything in fact except face the issue. The high priests, aided by the mob, wear him down, and in the end he capitulates, just to be rid of them, one feels. He washes his hands. His refusal to change the legend over the cross, "Jesus of Nazareth King of the Jews," to something like "He said he is King of the Jews," is a last petty defiance.

Chester and Ludus follow substantially this line, but with less elaboration and repetition, hence with diminished force. Towneley follows a daring alternative quite without parallel or precedent, so far as I have observed, in medieval treatments of the Passion. It boldly makes Pilate the main villain, proud, cruel, crafty, but not weak or changeable. By omitting such scriptural episodes as the trial before Herod, the dream of Pilate's wife, the denial of Peter, the despair of Judas, it centers on Pilate and Jesus, the two real adversaries. Pilate preludes the Passion group by saying that he means to destroy Jesus, identifies himself with the Jews, conducts the negotiations with Judas, briefs the guard as they go out to capture Jesus, and prefaces the trial by a soliloquy in which he clearly states that, though he will appear to be Jesus' friend, Jesus will before nightfall be slain on the cross.

The trial is completely rigged. Pilate goes through the motions of hearing Jesus' defense, pretends he finds no fault in the man, orders the scourging, washes his hands—all so rapidly that it has the appearance of a well rehearsed play, as, indeed, it is. Jesus speaks exactly two lines, his enemies a hundred or more. As Jesus is pushed off to Calvary, one supposes that Pilate congratulates himself on a masterful performance.

This profound difference in interpretation is not continued into the following crucifixion. Here all the cycles are in substantial agreement in choice of incidents and in attitude toward them. In all Simon of Cyrene is forced to carry the cross for Jesus. The Chester Simon sympathizes with Jesus; others merely grumble. Ludus alone has the incident of the wiping of Jesus' face by Veronica—the imprint of his face is left on the towel. All four have more or less extensive complaints of Mary, standing with John and Magdalen at the foot of the cross. The Ludus presentation is especially pathetic. Mary swoons, embraces the cross, has to be pulled away from it. In Towneley Mary, John, and Magdalen meet Jesus on the way to Calvary. Mary laments, Jesus says he must die and rise again to save mankind. The soldiers push John and the women away.

The physical process of the crucifixion is brutal in all the plays. The soldiers, Jews, or torturers, as they are variously called, strip Jesus, stretch him out on the cross. The carpenter has erred in the dimensions of the cross; the feet and arms do not reach to the holes where the nails must be driven. The soldiers get ropes and stretch arms and legs, pulling them out of their sockets until they reach. Then they must elevate the cross. It is heavy, and they tug on the ropes. Finally, it lurches into the hole prepared for it, tearing sinew and flesh. Through the whole scene the soldiers fiendishly enjoy their grim work.

On the cross Jesus speaks to John and Mary, prays for his persecutors, talks with the two thieves, called in Ludus Dismas and Jesmas. He asks for drink, cries, "Eli, eli, lama sabachthani," which his persecutors misunderstand as a prayer to Elijah. Finally he murmurs, "It is finished," and dies. All four cycles dramatize the refusal of Pilate to change the legend over the cross and all show the incident of Longeus, the blind knight who is commanded to pierce the side of Jesus with a lance. The blood runs down the shaft and when Longeus puts his bloody hand to his eyes, lo, he sees again.

In Chester and Ludus a centurion is converted by the miracles attending the crucifixion. Towneley and York use this scene also, but later on in their common resurrection play. All the passion groups close with Nicodemus and Joseph of Arimathea begging from Pilate the body of Jesus and preparing to bury it.

The division of Jesus' garments among the soldiers, which occupies a scene of eighty lines in Chester and a much shorter one in York, is developed into a whole play in Towneley. As in Chester the Towneley *Procession of the Talents** has the soldiers throw dice to see who gets Jesus' seamless coat. But in Towneley Pilate gets into the game. The three torturers run in, one after another, each one fearful lest the others cheat him out of the garment. They ask Pilate to settle the dispute over its possession. Pilate himself wants it, for it has magical properties. One of the torturers takes out three dice and suggests settling the matter that way. Pilate assents, but insists on the first throw. He throws thirteen. One torturer makes eight, another seven, but the third shows fifteen. Pilate then bluffs him out of the coat. The play closes with a homily by the three torturers on the evils of gambling.

The whole play is a study in grim humor, resembling in its effect such Shakespearean scenes as the gravediggers in Hamlet or the knocking on the gate in Macbeth. Its mood is an effective transition from the defeat of the crucifixion to the victory of the following episode, the harrowing of hell, found in all four cycles, and a separate play in all except Ludus, where it is divided into several scenes which alternate with incidents of the burial and the resurrection.

The theological basis of the harrowing of hell is an early, though not scriptural, tradition that Jesus' first act after his death was to rescue from hell the souls of the just, who could not enter heaven, closed by Adam's sin—"suffered under Pontius Pilate, was crucified, died, and was buried; *descended into hell*, and rose again the third day," in the words of the Apostles' Creed. Liturgically, the drama of the harrowing seems to derive from the ceremony for the dedication of a new church. The heart of this ceremony and of the dramatic versions of the harrowing is Psalm 24:

JESUS. Lift up your heads, O ye gates; and be ye lift up, ye everlasting doors; and the King of glory shall come in.
SATAN. Who is this King of glory?
JESUS. The Lord of hosts, he is the King of glory.

In the four cycles this entry of Jesus into hell is preceded by speeches of several patriarchs and prophets, Adam and Eve, Seth, Moses, David, Isaiah, Simeon, John the Baptist, the number and order varying in different

* The scribe obviously miswrote *talentorum*, "talents," for *talorum*, "bones," i.e. dice, but the name has stuck.

plays, who mourn their imprisonment in hell and express longing for release. When Jesus demands entrance in a paraphrase of the psalm, the devils try to bar hell's gates against him. He breaks them down, the liberated souls express their joy and gratitude, and the devils mourn their loss of power. The Chester harrowing has features borrowed from the prophet play, which also affects in a lesser degree the common York-Towneley play.

With the resurrection we are, for the first time since the nativity plays, on material which had been well developed in the liturgical drama, and the cycles exhibit fewer differences with one another here than in the passion or the public life. The common York-Towneley and the Chester plays of the resurrection begin with speeches by Pilate. In York-Towneley the centurion then reports the marvels at the crucifixion, which have made him believe in the divinity of Jesus. Annas, Caiaphas, and Pilate try to dissuade him and, failing, realize that to prevent the spread of this heresy they must guard the tomb of Jesus, lest his disciples steal the body and say he has risen. The Chester Pilate fears he has done wrong, or at least offended Caesar. Annas and Caiaphas use this opening to persuade him to cover up his fault by having the tomb guarded well. Ludus has already briefly handled, in the episode of the harrowing of hell, the placing of the guard.

All four cycles dramatize the resurrection. In Chester, Towneley, and Ludus, Jesus delivers a speech, sometimes called "The Charter of Christ," in which he demonstrates to "earthly man, that I have wrought," how He has saved man from sin, pleads with him not to corrupt himself again, and promises that in the form of the Eucharist, He will always remain with man. The Chester and Towneley charters are quite similar, even in language, Ludus is briefer, and York omits it entirely. Ludus here deviates from the other cycles in following the old tradition that the first appearance of Jesus was to His mother.

From this point the order of incidents varies somewhat. York-Towneley follows the resurrection by the visit of the Marys to the tomb, followed by the report of the soldiers to Pilate. Ludus and Chester reverse this order. All follow the pattern of liturgical drama: the mourning woman going to anoint the Lord's body, the question, "Who will roll back the stone for us?" the dialogue of the women with the angel(s). The awakening of the soldiers also follows the familiar outline. When they report the resurrection, Pilate berates them as cowards and traitors. Annas and Caiaphas prevail on him to bribe the soldiers to tell a fabricated story how they were overpowered and the body stolen. Ludus motivates the bribing better than the others. In resentment against Pilate's tongue-lashing the soldiers threaten to tell the truth, that Jesus is really risen by his own power. Frightened, Pilate asks them to wait a while until he can consult

Annas and Caiaphas. After a secret conference, Pilate offers to placate them with a bribe, if they will disseminate the story of the theft of the body. Chester has only a stage direction to indicate the bribing. Probably a passage has dropped out.

Chester and Ludus follow the visit of the Marys with the race of Peter and John to the tomb, lacking in York-Towneley. All, however, close the resurrection sequence with the appearance of Jesus in the guise of a gardener to Magdalen, built around the "Touch me not, for I have not yet ascended to the Father" motif from liturgical drama.

Appearances of Jesus to his followers make up the rest of the Easter group of plays. The first appearance is to two disciples on the way to Emmaus. A stranger joins Cleophas and Luke, as the disciples are called in all plays but York, while sorrowfully they review the events of the last few days. They have heard a report that some women found the tomb empty, but they are not sure that Jesus is actually risen. The stranger then blames them for their lack of faith and summarizes the prophecies that prove the Son of Man must rise on the third day. They do not, however, recognize the stranger until, at their invitation, He eats with them at Emmaus. When Jesus breaks the bread as though it were cut by a knife, they recognize Him and ask mercy for their unbelief.

In Chester and Ludus, Cleophas and Luke then report their experience to the other apostles and disciples, who have assembled together. The Towneley Magdalen tells the news to Peter and Paul, who is unhistorically written into the scene. In York Jesus merely appears to the group, without previous announcement of his resurrection. In all but Ludus Thomas is absent at this second appearance, when Jesus eats with the group. Jesus disappears, Thomas returns and doubts what the others tell him, and Jesus reappears to convince Thomas. Ludus telescopes this action. When Luke and Cleophas report having seen Jesus, Peter believes them, but Thomas doubts. The two argue, Thomas vehemently affirming that he will not believe until he has seen and touched. Jesus then appears and Thomas believes. All cycles close with Jesus' reproof of the apostles and disciples for their lack of faith and His blessing of those who will believe without seeing.

The ascension, the next episode dramatized in the cycles, lacks the liturgical precedents of the Easter plays, and hence is susceptible to more variation in representation. Nevertheless, the pattern is about the same in all four cycles: Jesus delivers several exhortations, all based more or less on scripture, to his followers and prophesies their hardships and their success; bids them farewell; and then ascends out of sight. Ludus ends its play here. All the others add a scene in which angels explain what has happened. Within this framework, there is considerable difference in details. York and Towneley, for instance, include Mary in the company which witnesses the ascension. The apostles John, James, and Peter promise to care for her and she asks them always to follow her Son's teaching.

An unfortunate gap of twelve leaves in the Towneley manuscript deprives us of any treatment of Pentecost, which immediately follows in the other cycles, and probably also of one or more plays on the death and assumption of the Virgin, found in York and Ludus. The three plays on Pentecost are quite different from one another. All begin with the selection of Matthias to replace Judas as an apostle, though York only mentions this without dramatization. In Chester the apostles then kneel and sing "Veni Creator Spiritus," which they paraphrase in English. God the Father reviews the redemption, promises to send the Holy Spirit, and gives power to the kneeling apostles. The Spirit then descends as tongues of flame. Two angels say that the apostles will preach to all men, each understanding in his own tongue. The apostles testify to their new power and each in turn paraphrases one of the twelve sections of the Apostle's Creed.

The York play includes Mary in the company, and Peter announces that they are met to replace Judas, but drops the matter there. Four apostles recall Jesus' promise to send the Holy Spirit. Two Jewish doctors outside the chamber think the apostles are afraid. Angels sing "Veni Creator" and the Holy Spirit descends. When the apostles excitedly testify to the new spirit which fills them, the doctors outside think they are drunk. Peter preaches, apparently to these doctors, and Mary closes the play by predicting Peter's success in his mission. John and James will remain with her.

The Ludus dramatization is short and much simpler than the other two. It presents in rapid succession the selection of Matthias, a prayer for guidance and strength by the apostles, each saying one line; the descent of the Holy Spirit, the belief of the Jewish crowd that they are drunk, and a short sermon by Peter.

As usual, Ludus has compressed the scriptural narrative to make way for an elaborate presentation of apocrypha and legend, here the death and assumption of Mary. It begins with a prologue in which Doctor assures us that a book called "Apocriphum" by St. John the Evangelist gives an account of the life of Mary after the ascension. She visited all the places where her Son had ministered and spent much time in prayer in the temple. The play opens with a council of a "Bishop of the law," that is, a high priest, and three "princes." Killing Jesus has not ended the menace to Jewish law. His followers preach everywhere and His mother still lives. The Bishop thinks it would be best to burn her and scatter her ashes and to kill and dismember all His followers—apparently to prevent their resurrection.

86

Mary prays at the temple. Sapientia* receives her prayer and sends down an angel to tell her to prepare for death. First John, then the rest of the apostles, including Paul, appear. They were miraculously snatched up by clouds and set down at Mary's home. Jesus with the "court of heaven" descends and the play becomes for a time definitely a liturgical ceremony with responsive chanting in Latin by Jesus, Mary, and the Apostles. As Mary dies, Jesus receives her soul to His breast and welcomes her to heaven. A chorus of martyrs, virgins, and angels sings her welcome.

The apostles kiss her body and carry it in procession to burial. The Jewish Bishop and his princes attack the procession. One of the princes lays hands on the bier and cannot pull them loose until, at Peter's suggestion, he confesses belief in Jesus and His mother. John leads the apostles in blessing the body, while the first prince, released from the bier, converts the others. Devils flee from them. Jesus descends again and, at John's prayer, rejoins Mary's soul to her body and takes her to heaven with him as the Archangel Michael blesses Him for "this holy assumption" at which all heaven makes melody.

York devotes three plays to a less liturgical and somewhat less fantastic presentation of similar themes. Gabriel announces to Mary that she will die in three days. John arrives and, hearing the angelic message, hopes the other apostles will come. They all appear miraculously. As Mary dies, she prays for all men in trouble and all women in childbirth. Jesus appears to grant her prayer and promise that angels will protect her from the assaults of the fiend as she dies.

In the next play, Thomas, apparently somewhere in India, laments the tortures and death of Jesus and recalls how sinfully he doubted the resurrection until he touched the wounds. Suddenly by a miracle he is in Judaea. He hears angels singing praises to Mary and sees her borne aloft by angels in a blaze of light. Mary commands him to tell the other apostles what he has seen. When he doubts they will believe him, she gives him her girdle as a token and promises to intercede for all in trouble and pain. Indeed, the apostles do disbelieve his story, until at Andrew's suggestion they go to the grave and find it empty. All praise Mary and separate to their missionary work, Thomas back to India, Peter to Rome, James to Samaria, Andrew to Achaia, and John to Asia.

The final play of the series looks as though it should be second—or perhaps it was an alternative to the second. In it Jesus sends four angels to bring Mary to heaven, where she is to be queen. The angels salute Mary, who blesses God and says she is ready. In the next scene Mary in heaven is welcomed by Jesus and the angels recite her five joys. Jesus then crowns her. York had also, in the early fifteenth century, a play on

---

* Miss Block, the editor of Ludus, thinks Sapientia should be Jesus.

the burial of Mary, containing the scene in which the Jew, apparently called Fergus, lays hands on Mary's bier. This play was apparently suppressed in 1485, possibly because the antics of Fergus had developed into irreverent low comedy. At any rate, the play has completely vanished.

Chester, which has no treatment of the death and assumption of Mary, makes up for the loss by being the only cycle to offer a play—actually two plays—on Antichrist. In the first play four apocalyptic prophets foretell doomsday: Ezechiel 37 in the vision of the valley of dry bones; Zachariah 6 in that of the four chariots; Daniel 7 in the four beasts, the last of whom will reign three and a half years; and St. John the Evangelist in the two witnesses of Revelation 11. All these prophecies Expositor interprets of the end of the world and the reign of Antichrist. In structure and intent this play parallels the prophet play preceding the nativity. The prophets of doom prepare for the third and final great event in human history as the prophets of Christ had for the second.

To the prophets Chester adds an account, spoken by Expositor, of the fifteen signs of judgment. Ultimately suggested by Matthew 24, this medieval theme had a long and colorful development in eschatological literature. Though credited to Jerome, the version followed by Chester seems to be that of Jacobus a Voragine's *Golden Legend*. It is simply an enumeration of the marvelous catastrophes that will precede doomsday:

> The fifth day, as read we
> All manner herbs, and also tree
> Of bloody dew all full shall be
> And man and beast all dazed.

The second play opens with Antichrist's boast that he is the Messiah. He converts four kings by calling the dead to life and by himself dying and rising again. To the converted kings he gives lands and power. Enoch and Elijah then denounce Antichrist as a fiend. As they preach he rages against them. They demonstrate the diabolic origin of his power by offering food to the dead he has restored to life. When these refuse to eat bread blessed in the name of the Trinity, the four kings see that Antichrist is the Fiend. He then kills Enoch and Elijah and the kings. The Archangel Michael appears. Antichrist's three and a half years are up, and Michael slays him.

All four cycles end with a doomsday play. York and Towneley are partly identical. The essential action consists of the summons to resurrection by the angels, the separation of the saved from the damned, and the sentencing of the one group to heaven, the other to hell. Before He orders the angels to blow the trump which will summon all to judgment, the

York God reviews the whole of human history, emphasizing the redemption. Chester begins with God ordering the summons, Ludus with the summons itself, and Towneley (which may have lost its beginning) with speeches by the damned souls after the summons.

Before proceeding to judgment God (or Jesus)* in all but Ludus alleges his rights to man's love, another "charter of Christ" enumerating all the sufferings on the cross. Chester even illustrates these:

> Behold now on me
> And see my blood fresh out flee
> That I bled on rood tree
> For your salvation

And the stage directions call for blood to flow from Jesus' side.

Then the saved and the damned stand forth. In all but Chester the saved are represented by two or more "good souls" and the damned by an equal number of "bad souls." Chester represents the saved by a pope, an emperor, a king, and a queen, each of whom confesses his sins, but adds that he died in contrition and has suffered in purgatory. The damned are also represented by a pope, an emperor, a king, and a queen, plus a judge (or lawyer) and a merchant—apparently the author did not expect any who pursue law or commerce to be saved. In all the plays Jesus then turns to the saved and says they have fed Him when he was hungry, clothed Him when he was naked, have performed all the seven corporal works of mercy. But when have we done these things to you? ask the saved. When you did them for the poor and needy, replies Jesus.

The demons now ask judgment on the wicked, pleading their rights to the possession of these souls. Jesus again enumerates the corporal works in all plays but Ludus, where the seven deadly sins are substituted. When Jesus pronounces sentence on the damned, devils carry them off to eternal torment, doubtless to the accompaniment to weeping and clamor, though this is only hinted at. Ludus is incomplete. Towneley ends with the rejoicing of the saved, York with the "melody of angels going from place to place," Chester with speeches by Matthew, Mark, Luke, and John to the effect that in their gospels they warned the wicked, who therefore are justly damned.

A characteristic Towneley expansion by the Master just before Jesus comes to judge introduces us to the irrepressible devil, Tutivillus. He has charge of the account books in which the sins of men are entered and must also gather up, with the help of several devils, the sinners them-

---

* All the cycles but Towneley name the judge simply *Deus*, but Jesus is obviously meant in York, and probably in Ludus and Chester. So henceforth I call the judge Jesus.

selves. If the world had not ended when it did, hell must have been enlarged.* He proceeds to enumerate the varieties of sinners in his bags. In addition to the usual adulterers, gluttons, and the like, he has a list reminding us of that of the Lord High Executioner in the *Mikado*. He bears down especially hard on "raisers of false tax" and "gatherers of green wax," i.e., those who used the royal commission, sealed in green wax, to extort money from the people. The "female gender" also makes up a good part of his freight, especially those who disguise themselves with cosmetics and wear headdresses "horned like a cow." We never learn what punishments suited these crimes.

* Tutivillus was originally the devil appointed to gather up the words mumbled, mispronounced, or skipped by monks in singing their office. He is usually complaining about his terrible burden and demanding more assistants. We shall meet him again in the morality, *Mankind*.

Chapter VII. THE CYCLE PLAYS: PRODUCTION, STAGING, AND DRAMATIC TECHNIQUE

THE CYCLE PLAYS were a product of the municipal enterprise of fourteenth, fifteenth, and sixteenth century England. A group of plays such as that of York is as unthinkable in the eleventh century as it would be in the twentieth, for in the eleventh century the town life which supported them scarcely existed. The manner of their creation, the fashion of their production, their financial support, even many of the literary features they exhibit are understandable only against the background of the society which gave rise to them, the medieval town.

One of the fundamental facts of the medieval town is the guilds, those combinations of trades unions, manufacturers associations, and religious fraternities that were both the body and the soul of the medieval town. They were the political parties, the pressure groups, the organs of public opinion of the medieval community. From the guilds came the aldermen and the mayor who governed the town. These and their deputies exercised general supervision over the whole cycle, the individual plays of which were financed, produced, and acted by the various guilds.

The corporation, as its share of the municipal enterprise, determined which crafts were to produce which plays, set standards of performance that must be met, and saw to it that each guild carried its proportional share of the financial burden. It is from the town and guild records of York, Chester, Coventry, Beverley, Norwich, and other places that we learn virtually everything we know—outside the texts of the plays themselves—about the conditions under which the cycle drama was produced. The first act of the yearly presentation of the Chester plays, for instance, was the proclamation of the banns on St. George's day by the city crier, accompanied by a steward from each craft. Then followed a proclamation by the mayor warning potential disturbers of the peace, which was read on the Roodee.

York had a definite mechanism for insuring competent production and acting. During Lent a sort of committee, presumably appointed by the mayor or by the aldermen, and consisting of the "four ablest players" in the town came before the mayor to "search, hear, and examine all players, plays, and pageants," a casting session. Doubtless, too, York fined incompetent actors, as did Beverley, where in 1452 Henry Cowper was fined for not knowing his part. Coventry in 1441 ordained that "Robert Greene and all others who play at the feast of Corpus Christi shall play well and sufficiently," under pain of a fine of twenty shillings.

Another of the chief duties of the corporation was the assignment of plays to the individual guilds. Only in a few instances can one discover any reason why a particular guild should have a particular play. The play of Noah's flood, in every town from which we have records, is given to some craft occupied with boats or water, the watermen in Beverley, the waterleaders in Chester, the shipwrights at Newcastle, and of the two York plays on the subject the shipwrights played one, the fishers and mariners the other. At Hull, a maritime town, a guild of mariners and pilots apparently had a Noah play. The Magi play was presented by the goldsmiths at Beverley and by the "orfeverers" (goldsmiths), goldbeaters, and moneymakers at York, probably because these crafts could provide suitable properties, but at Chester the goldsmiths had another play, the slaughter of the innocents, and the two Magi plays belonged to the vintners and mercers, respectively.

Doubtless, a more complete knowledge of the patron saints of crafts and occupations and of the patron saints of individual guilds at various towns would show that often a craft had a play involving its patron saint. But generally, though one could add other examples of appropriate assignments, no reason or principle of assignment is discoverable.

Rather, what we have is the result of inter- and intra-guild politics and the exigencies of time and place. The principal task of the corporation was to see that each guild pulled its weight. There were always the smaller guilds, consisting of two, three, or half a dozen members, who could not be asked to undertake the expense of a whole play by themselves. Unless someone kept close check they might escape all responsibility. Other guilds, once numerous and prosperous, fall on evil days (think what happened to the harness makers in the last fifty years) and can no longer carry a play all by themselves. At the same time a small craft may grow into a large one and be capable of supporting a whole play. Such a craft may even, in an understandable desire to show off its new strength, insist on having a play all by itself.

The records are full of accommodations to such circumstances. The chandlers and cooks are commanded to contribute to the smith's play, the butchers to pay sixteen shillings and eightpence yearly to the whittawers' play, and the like. In Beverley the guild members felt aggrieved that many citizens of the town were well able to contribute to the cycle but escaped because they belonged to no guild. So in 1411 it was ordained that the "more worthy," i.e. the wealthier, men of the town should appoint four representatives and support a play. Probably this action is the reason why, in the Beverley play list of about 1520, we find, along with tilers, scriveners, bakers, weavers and such, one play assigned to the "gentlemen" and another to the "priests."

This background of financial support is important to the historian and

critic of the cycle drama, for the reason why a subject is quite un-
treated in one cycle but treated in all the others, and apparently necessary
to the representation of the scriptural story, may well be that the guild
to which that subject was originally assigned has decayed and so the play
has dropped out of the cycle. Contrariwise, the explanation for the
presence of two plays on a subject, where one would suffice, is possibly
the growth of some guild. The Beverley drapers originally were in the
same guild with the mercers. The two trades separated, and their play,
which comprehended the trials of Jesus before Herod and Pilate, was
divided in two, one called "Sleeping Pilate" and the other "Black Herod."

In addition to setting standards of production and providing for the
support of the plays, the municipal authorities had custody of the text
of the cycle, called the "original" (spelled with bewildering variety), and
they regularly spent sums of money for copying parts, making additions,
and the like. Presumably they commissioned the writing of the whole
cycle in the first place, but we have no records from any town or guild
early enough to give us details of authorship. The nearest we get is an account that Beverley hired one Thomas Bynham, a Dominican friar, to write
banns, and records of several Coventry guilds that Robert Crow copied,
apparently with some revision, their plays. This is not very helpful, since
the Beverley plays, including Brother Thomas' banns, are lost, and Crow's
aureate verbosity labels him a botcher rather than an author.* In addition
to the corporation copy of the whole cycle, individual guilds also sometimes had copies of their particular play, of which one "The Incredulity
of Thomas," played by the scriveners of York, is still extant.

The individual guilds, or sometimes an association of several guilds, were
the immediate producers of the plays. However much the corporation
might try to oversee the production, outfitting, acting, and financing was
the province of the guild. Theatrical enterprises were expensive then as
now, and perhaps proportionally as expensive. Without any prospect of a
box-office, the guilds could pay for their productions only out of their
income and by an assessment on their membership. In York this seems to
have run from one penny to eightpence a member. The Coventry records
are more explicit and the assessments apparently higher. In 1443-4, for
instance, each member of the cardmakers, saddlers, masons, and painters,
four crafts which had a common play, paid a shilling a year to the pageant
master responsible for their play.

How the money so collected was spent may be seen from the accounts
of the smiths' company of Coventry, which had a play dealing with the
trials of Jesus before the high priests, Herod, and Pilate. In one year, 1490,
they spent, mainly for food and drink, two shillings twopence for the

* Crow was apparently a theatrical factotum, for he also received money for
providing costumes and props and for acting.

first rehearsal and twelve shillings, and a penny halfpenny for the second. For costumes and props they laid out a total of fifteen shillings. Included are such items as four jackets of black buckram for the "torturers" and— apparently to provide a change of costume—another four with damask flowers, a cloak and a hat for Pilate, a gown and a hat for his son; a gown, a faulchion and a sceptre of Herod, two mitres for the "bishops" (i.e. the high priests, Annas and Caiaphas), four scourges and a pillar, and a head for the Devil.

The largest outlay, totalling twenty nine shillings and twopence was in wages for the players, of whom the best paid were Pilate at four shillings followed by Herod at three shillings and fourpence, Caiaphas at three shillings and threepence, Annas at two shillings and sixpence, Jesus and Procula, the wife of Pilate, at two shillings each, and so on through the bits and walk-ons. There are other expenses for storage of the pageant wagon and for repairs to it. The expenses for producing the Smiths' play total two pounds, eighteen shillings, and fivepence halfpenny, a sizable sum in an age when a fat lamb fetched around sixpence and a nutritious meal cost a penny.

Other records tell similar stories of expenditures on plays. Pageant wagons, properties, and costumes are the most frequently mentioned in account books. The pageant was always needing repairs or ornamentation, pensils of cloth, iron vanes, guilding. In the book of the Norfolk Grocers' company we encounter sums spent for "a rib colored red" (for the creation of Eve), two coats and two pairs of hose for Eve, a coat and hose for Adam,* a face and hair (wig) for God the Father, and a precious tree which apparently bore fruit. Pages could be taken up with such lists.

The total impression which they create is that productions of the cycle plays must have approached the lavish. The extravagant taste of the fifteenth century to which the decorated architecture of the period and the work of illuminators and painters, especially in the Low Countries, testify is supported by the records of the playing guilds. In the nature of things, we cannot know what we would most like to know, how competent the acting and direction was, but perhaps we can infer something from the care taken to provide costume, properties and scenic effects. The inference must be that the municipal authorities and the pageant masters of the guilds did the best they could, sparing no pains to get everything a liberal budget and conscientious supervision could get.

The inference is perhaps weakest with authorship. The records tell us nothing about what was paid the original authors and little about the succession of adapters and revisers. The texts show that there were plenty of these, some of them of great theatrical talent, but we don't know how

---

* Early critics who had the fantastic notion that Adam and Eve were played in the nude apparently hadn't seen these accounts. The coats and hose, however, may have been of white (or even flesh colored) leather and fit tightly like a leotard.

a corporation or a guild went about getting good dramatists. How, for instance, did the Wakefield Master come to write his magnificent work? Did the mayor and the aldermen of Wakefield, feeling that the town ought to have a cycle like York and Beverley, appoint a committee to make a diligent search for dramatic talent? Did this committee interview school-masters, the abbots of monasteries, the priors of friaries, university men, professional scribes, and all who might know about literary ability in the vicinity, in hopes of finding the best man to edit and rewrite their plays?

I once suggested that something like this must have happened. Some scholars objected that this was too unmedieval a procedure: the authorities would just borrow or steal a set of plays from anywhere they could get them. Perhaps so, but in 1475 York set up just such a committee for examining and selecting actors. If actors why not playwrights? Or were the managers of the cycle plays so unintelligent as to believe that the play doesn't matter, so long as you have big name actors, slick direction, and lavish decor? That kind of stupidity is reserved for Hollywood and the professional theaters of Broadway and the West End.

Until evidence to the contrary appears I will prefer to believe that the care and expense which the records show was spent on material furnishings and on acting was also spent on writing. I am willing to go a step further, even, and to suppose that some of the writers were also actors, pageant masters, costumers—that they were professional men of the theater, like Will Shakespeare, who was certainly an actor, and probably a director, as well as an author.

One detail suggested by the Coventry records is that women's parts were played by men, or perhaps, as on the Elizabethan stage, by boys. In 1495 the Smiths' accounts contain a payment to "Ryngold's man Thomas that played Pilate's wife," and in 1498 two shillings went to "Pilate's wife for his wages." That this custom may not have been universal, however, appears from the early banns of Chester, which include among the plays one on the Assumption of the Virgin (lacking in the extant manuscripts) supported and possibly played by "the worshipful wives of this town." Two late Coventry payments testify to child actors, one in 1551 "to the woman for her child" and another in 1553 "to the little child."

For in the fifteenth century, when the Corpus Christi cycles had become an established fixture, when the cycle was the outward and visible sign of the town's inward vitality, when it attracted visits from nobility and royalty,* a considerable measure of professionalism is evident. The Smiths' company of Coventry, whose records for the year 1490 we have reviewed, spent half its budget for acting, one pound, nine shillings, and twopence out of two pounds, eighteen shillings, and fivepence halfpenny.

* Queen Margaret saw the Coventry Plays in 1457, Richard III in 1485, Henry VII in 1486 and again in 1493. Perhaps Richard II inaugurated the custom when he visited York to attend the plays in 1397.

It is hardly likely that these Pilates and Herods were all amateurs. By 1446-47 York was importing and paying players from Donnington, Wakefield, and even London, and these can hardly have been "rude mechanicals" playing only for the glory of their town, their guild, and their God. The professional producer-director makes his appearance at Coventry when in 1452-3 the smiths make a twelve year contract with one Thomas Colclow to produce their play for a yearly salary of forty-eight shillings and eight-pence.

By the middle of the fifteenth century, then, the plays of York and Coventry are becoming professionalized, and doubtless the same thing happened in other places as well. The process of professionalization is, of course, not known, but one is tempted to conjecture that it was the same by which amateur sports get professionalized. It is the old inevitable story of the desire for excellence producing specialization. One result is to destroy what we now call amateur status. Apparently the authorities of both York and Coventry felt that the process of bringing in actors from the outside was getting out of bounds, for both cities established pro-hibitions against players appearing in more than one or—a compromise—two plays. One supposes that about this time the spirit of reverence and worship vanished, as the amateur spirit has vanished from American col-legiate sports, but there was likely also an improvement in the quality of the plays.

The least that we can say is that the cycle plays must not, at their height in the middle and later fifteenth century, be regarded as com-pletely amateur performances by untutored craftsmen. What the crafts-men of Coventry showed Richard III in no way resembled the "Pyramus and Thisby" which Bottom and company unfolded before Duke Theseus.

The most significant fact about the staging of the cycle plays is also the most puzzling: the use of the pageant wagons. The oft-quoted account of David Roberts, whose *Breviary, or Some Few Collections of the City of Chester* is found in a British Museum manuscript written in 1609, is the only quasi-contemporary description we have of the use of the pageants. The *Breviary* is based on the notes of David's father Robert, who was Archdean of Chester and who presumably saw the plays, which were last performed in 1575. According to the *Breviary*, the pageant, or carriage, was a "high place made like a house with two rooms, being open on the top; in the lower room they appareled and dressed themselves; and in the higher room they played." These pageants had six wheels and they were drawn by men from place to place, "first from the Abbey gate to the Pentise, then to the Watergate Street, then to the Bridge Street, through the lanes, and so to the Eastgate Street." At each of these five places a performance was given, and each performance was followed by one of the following plays.

Some such procedure—that is presentation on pageants and seriatim performance of successive plays in the same station—was followed in York, Coventry, and Norwich, and presumably also at Beverley and Wakefield. Ludus is an exception, to which we shall refer later. And of course the passion plays of the South of England, the Cornish plays, and probably the Digby plays were done in a quite different manner.

For York and Coventry also we have some notion of how many stops the pageants made. This, of course, varied from time to time, especially in York, where the privilege of having the pageant stop in front of one's house was apparently purchased from the municipal authorities. In 1417 the number of stops was limited to twelve, but possibly it grew, especially since it was a source of revenue to the town and possibly of support for the plays. Craig conjectures that the Coventry plays were given at ten stations, but there is some reason to suppose that in the 1550's the stations had been cut to three.

Roger's account has many details to which exception has been made by scholars. The lower story tiring-room seems quite unnecessary and awkward, and it is difficult to suppose that there was not considerable variation in the pageants, depending on the exigencies of the play and the tastes of the guild supporting it. And of course we would not expect those of York or Norwich to be just like those of Chester. The pageant of the Norwich Grocers, on which they gave their Adam and Eve play, appears in the records as a "house of wainscot painted and builded on a cart with four wheels." It had a "square top" and was ornamented with a "griffon guilt with a vane to set on the said top" and "a bigger iron vane to set on the end of the pageant." In the same inventory is an item of "6 horse cloths, stained, with knopps [knobs or studs] and tassels," which suggests that the pageant was horse drawn.

The chief difficulty, however, is in understanding the staging of the plays on the pageants. If we only had a contemporary picture of the pageant wagon! The nearest thing I have been able to find is some canvases by Denis van Alsloot of a "triumph" of Isabella, Spanish Governor of Belgium in 1615. Two of the paintings depicting the event are in the Victoria and Albert Museum in London, two in the Prado in Madrid. A number of pageant wagons are depicted. Though the scenes are of living tableaux, not plays, two of the scenes coincide with those represented in the cycles, the nativity and the annunciation. From them we can perhaps form some notion of the appearance and use of pageant wagons in Chester, York, and the other cycles that used them towards the end of the period of their production in the third quarter of the sixteenth century.

Judging from the size of the figures alongside the nativity pageant, the wagon cannot have been over eight feet in width by twenty or less in length. The annunciation pageant is smaller. There seems to be an abundance of space for the pageants to move in, a condition not duplicated in York or Chester, where the wagons had to be maneuvered through narrow streets. Too long a wagon would not take the corners, one too wide could not clear the buildings on either side. We should, then, probably not be too far wrong if we computed the extreme possible length as eighteen feet, the width as eight. And this may be too high.

On this diminutive stage must be represented such scenes as the York Tilemakers' play of the second trial before Pilate. This requires a cast of twelve, all apparently on stage at the same time. Pilate must surely be seated in some sort of throne. Annas and Caiaphas presumably stand near him. When Jesus enters he has to pass through or by a line of soldiers, four of whom have speaking parts. Two others are brought on later. At least four of the soldiers have lances with banners on them, and they must dip these lances as Jesus enters. Clearance room is necessary if the lances are not to hit someone. Besides there are a beadle and Barrabas. It is virtually impossible to imagine all this in an eight by fourteen playing area.

Yet York is the most suited of all cycles to playing on pageant wagons, for it has more plays and consequently less material and fewer changes of locale in each play. Chester has the trials before the High Priests, Herod, and Pilate all in one play, together with the carrying of the cross, the crucifixion, the death, the descent from the cross, and perhaps the burial. Symbolic action, a few steps standing for the whole journey from Pilate's judgment hall to Golgotha, would accomplish much, but we still have entirely too much action and too many personages for the area available. And how would you toss Mak in a blanket on a pageant wagon?

Several stage directions in Chester, Towneley, and Coventry suggest the solution. It is simply that the action was not confined to, but only centered in, the pageant stage. In the Chester Abraham and Isaac the Expositor enters "riding," and a stage direction in the Townley Magi play explicitly directs that the three kings alight from their horses and pray. The Coventry Herod rages "in the pageant and in the street also." In the Chester Nativity play Joseph has to bind an ox to the tail of the ass on which Mary rides to Bethlehem; later he lifts her off the ass in his arms. The Towneley Pilate twice asks the spectators to make room for the players:

> Stint, I say! Give men place.

and

> ^{Stand}
> Standis on side or else go sit,
>   ^{walk}   ^{yet}
> For here are men that go not yit.

What all this means is that the action was not confined to the pageant. Expositor rides up to the pageant to deliver his commentary on the action. Quite properly he stays out of the action itself. The Three Kings ride up the street on horseback, looking towards the star which is on the pageant itself. They dismount, pray, and remount. Finally they come to the pageant wagon, where the Virgin and the Child are, dismount, ascend to the pageant stage from the street, and there adore the Babe. Likewise Pilate needs room because the players do not all appear on the pageant stage; some of them stand in the street or open space about the wagon. The business with the ox and the ass can be managed easily if the space about the pageant is used.

If we use this space we can also easily stage the Tilemakers' play. We simply move the soldiers down to the street level and have Jesus enter, probably between two lines of soldiers (we aren't confined to the four speaking soldiers but can have a dozen, if we like), ascend to the pageant stage, where Pilate sits on his throne listening to the accusations of Annas and Caiaphas, who are also on the stage. Later Barabbas and Beadle can enter in the same fashion. Perhaps a set of steps is needed, but that presents no difficulty.

This would be the natural solution for the producers of the cycle plays, who probably saw no problem anyway. The liturgical and transitional drama used the station-and-place method of staging. The pageant is merely a station with wheels under it. So we have movement towards and away from the pageant stage. It is even possible that, on some occasions, more than one pageant wagon was used, perhaps, as Professor Wickham suggests, one pageant as a set and another, entirely bare, placed in front of it as a sort of apron. Or several set pageants could be used side by side or with a few feet intervening. In the Chester passion play, for instance, we can give the high priests, Herod, and Pilate each a pageant for his station and perhaps have another for Calvary. This is of course, pure conjecture. It is entirely possible to stage the play in another manner with only one pageant, which successively represents each of these stations. The players leave the pageant wagon and perhaps walk around it, returning to it (this time as Pilate's hall), and so forth. Processional drama of this sort is typically medieval. The essential thing is that we do not insist on confining the action to the stage of a single pageant.

To much of the foregoing Ludus is an exception. It was not apparently presented as separate plays on pageants, but in the manner of the continental passion plays. The directions of the second Ludus passion play are quite specific about the manner of staging: "What time that procession is entered into the place and the Herod taken his scaffold, and Pilate and Annas and Caiaphas their scaffolds, also then come[s] there an expositor in doctor's weed." So we have clearly three scaffolds, or stations, and an unlocalized "place." A little later the messenger enters and runs about the place shouting "Tidings, tidings, Jesus of Nazareth is take."

The first passion play adds a suggestion that the scaffold was sometimes enclosed and provided with a curtain: "The council house beforesaid shall suddenly unclose, showing the bishops, priests, and judges sitting in their estate, like as it were a convocation." This is doubtless the same as the scaffold of Annas and Caiaphas in the second passion play.

The other parts of the cycle are not so explicit, though, despite the artificial division into plays in the manuscript, large sections seem from their structure to be playable only in this processional manner, with action sometimes centering in one of several stations and at other times flowing processionally from one to another. One direction of the Digby *Slaughter of the Innocents* suggests the same method of production. The knights setting forth to kill the children "walk about the place" until Joseph and Mary have safely taken the Babe to Egypt.

If Lincoln indeed is the home of Ludus, one can find good reasons for the station-and-place method of staging. Lincoln is built on a rather steep hill; the layout of the streets would not lend itself to plays on pageant wagons. The natural place for dramatic presentation is at the top of the hill before the Cathedral.

The Lincoln records show marked differences from those of York, Coventry, Chester, Beverley, and Norwich. Although there are records of one craft, the cordwainers, and although these even mention a pageant, there are none of the usual expenses for the support of a play, nothing about a play book, or hire of actors, or paying for props and costumes. On the other hand, municipal records show the existence of a Corpus Christi Guild and of a St. Anne's Guild. In 1511 every man and woman who was able had to contribute fourpence a year to the St. Anne's Guild. One or both of these guilds must have been responsible for the cycle, perhaps the Corpus Christi in earlier times and the St. Anne's in later. It is also apparent that the clergy of the cathedral were considerably concerned in the plays, a fact not attested to by the extant records of any other town. The dramatic situation at Lincoln was decidedly unusual; and the staging and structure of Ludus exhibit a parallel unusualness. This is one of the most compelling reasons which Professor Craig, who has studied the Lincoln records exhaustively, offers for the hypothesis that Ludus is the Lincoln cycle.

Ludus is the best of the cycles for the study of staging. It has the most complete and explicit stage directions. Critics have often characterized its effects as spectacular. Whether this is entirely just must admit of some doubt. Spectacle it undoubtedly has, like most artistic products of the fifteenth century, but comparatively little of the adventitious sort that the word usually connotes. Mainly, the effects are just good theater. Perhaps it relies more on theatrical effects than on characterization and motivation, but they come mostly from the realization and exploitation of the excitement inherent in the subject matter. It looks as though a talented director had left the mark of his efforts in the numerous explicit stage directions.

We ought not, however, to infer from the presence of such effects in Ludus their entire absence in the other cycles, as they were actually staged. The absence of directions in York, for instance, does not mean that the cycle was presented with almost no stage business, no attention to costume, decor and the other elements that make seeing a play such a different experience from reading it or even hearing it read. Absence of directions from York may mean only that the director's contribution to the performance was never reduced to writing. Whoever is responsible for the York manuscript as we have it did not think it necessary to incorporate long stage directions.

The whole attempt to reconstruct the staging of the cycle plays is attended with much difficulty. Chester has fairly extensive directions, Towneley and the two Coventry plays a few, York almost none. We can infer a good bit from the dialogue. Much more comes from a study of the costumes and properties recorded in the guild accounts. The plastic and graphic arts can contribute much, for there is in all ages a considerable kinship between the drama and all the arts, auditory as well as visual. Dr. Hildburgh has successfully argued that many English alabaster carvings of the fourteenth and fifteenth centuries reproduced scenes which the artists actually saw in cycle plays. Illuminations, wall paintings, and sculpture could be used in similar fashion, and doubtless the influence flows in both directions: artists reproduce what they have seen in plays, but pageant masters also reproduce what they have seen in stained glass windows, bosses, screen carvings, and all the other forms of medieval ecclesiastical art.

Recently, Professor Wickham has produced a mass of information about tournaments, royal entries, court entertainments, disguisings, and mummings—a whole range of quasi-dramatic representations which doubtless made valuable contributions to the staging of scriptural drama. For one thing, his material proves that the skill to produce elaborate spectacles existed in the late fourteenth and all through the fifteenth century.

One of the first conclusions that follows even a cursory examination of the stagecraft of the cycles is that such terms as naturalistic, realistic, abstract, symbolic, stylized, and the others currently used to categorize staging have little meaning when applied to the earlier drama, whether Elizabethan or medieval. For instance, you can say that the Elizabethan stage was not naturalistic, because it lacked scenery, lighting, or a curtain. When Shakespeare wishes to indicate that it is dawn, all he can do is write some such description as

> The grey-ey'd morn smiles on the frowning night,
> Chequ'ring the eastern clouds with streaks of light.

In the modern theater, even more in the cinema, lighting would convey this information. We would see the red glow of the rising sun. That is naturalistic staging.

But what of the handling of scenes of violence? Even in the most grue-some gangster film, I have never seen blood visibly spout from a wound. Yet we know that an Elizabethan actor playing a scene in which he is thrust through with a rapier provided himself with a bag of blood, got fresh from the shambles. It is likely that medieval actors did likewise. When in the Chester Resurrection Jesus recounts his sufferings to redeem mankind, the direction specifically says "Here blood flows from his side." The fact that the guild of butchers played the Scourging in Beverley and the Death on the Cross in York may be meaningful.

The fact is that audiences demand naturalistic effects in some contexts and will not tolerate them in others. Tastes change in such matters. If we could witness the crucifixion as performed in York about 1450 we should probably be made deathly ill by its explicitness. The medieval audience might be equally revolted at the handling of sex in our cinema.

With these cautions in mind, we can note some characteristics and some details of the staging of the cycle plays, as it can be inferred from the texts, the records, and contemporary arts, but sometimes only by conjecture. One feature is certainly the use of symbolic action, props, and cosumes. This principle is implicit in the station-and-place method of staging of liturgical drama, in which one station is Herod's palace, another the manger, and so on. So we find that one part of the pageant represents one place, another part another place—or perhaps, as we have conjectured earlier, two pageant wagons were used. The principle remains the same: motion from one part to another, or from one pageant to another, or from the street to the pageant indicates a journey, some-times of great length.

Another form which symbolism can take is the use of miniatures, dolls, or physical representations of invisible objects (the soul, for instance) or abstract ideas. In the Chester Deluge the animals that entered the ark are represented by pictures painted on the pageant, which was probably in the shape of a boat. Noah's sons and their wives recite the names of the animals, sometimes with a bit of description, meanwhile pointing to the pictures.

According to their accounts the Coventry Drapers, who presented a

Doomsday play, had a "barrel for the earthquake," and paid the ubiquitous Crow for making "three worlds" which some unspecified person was hired to set on fire. Apparently the play was given at three stations, at each of which a "world," probably a globe painted so as to represent the world, was burned. Obviously this is the destruction of the world by fire before the Last Judgment.

Dr. Hildburgh believes that considerable use was made of miniatures and dolls. The evidence of the alabaster carvings seems to indicate that in the adoration of the shepherds and of the Magi the infant Jesus was a doll laid on a platter-like object, painted so as to suggest a halo. This seems altogether probable, since the use of a real infant would present great difficulties. Less convincing, but still quite possible, is his argument that a doll, pulled up by ropes, was used to represent the ascension. The sudden replacement of a living actor—for Jesus speaks to his followers until the moment of ascension—would seem awkward. But we must never underestimate the power of convention and the ability of theatergoers to take the symbol for the reality.

Of one thing we can be sure, the dramatists of the cycle plays were courageous. They did not hesitate to give some sort of representation of the greatest miracles and most sublime mysteries. Whatever their technical limitations, they were not scared by them into using messengers or reports from off-stage, probably because they knew that the audience would accept their contrivances in the proper spirit of belief. Consider, for example, the attempt of Ludus to visualize—at the same time—the mysteries of the incarnation and of the Trinity. This is the stage direction:

Here the Holy Ghost descends with three beams to Our Lady. The Son of the Godhead next with three beams to the Holy Ghost, the Father Godly with three beams to the Son, and so enter all three into her bosom.

It is futile to attempt to understand every detail of this business. The "beams" are doubtless rods of some kind, probably gilded. They must be held and manipulated in some fashion by the actors. Possibly we should interpret the passage to mean that the "beams" are, by legerdemain, made to appear to enter the Virgin's body. These directions are written by the same hand as a number of others whose excellence we can grasp, and we must suppose that the action was meaningful and memorable to the spectators.

Costume and props were used to their fullest in a manner that defies categorization as either symbolic or naturalistic, because it was both. From the texts and the lists of props we know that Annas and Caiaphas were outfitted in the mitres, robes, and croziers of bishops, not those of Jewish high priests, be it noted, for that would be meaningless to the

THE DRAMA OF MEDIEVAL ENGLAND

audience, but those of Christian prelates, the kind of ecclesiastical power which the audience knew. Similarly, the Chester Herod has a staff and a sword, the accessories of majesty in England, if perhaps not in Judaea; and the Coventry Herod had a faulchion, a scepter, and a crest, these apparently made or decorated with "silver paper," "gold paper," "green foil," and "gold foil." He also had a robe of blue buckram.

Knowing medieval principles of clothing design, we should suspect that there is reason for the color, if perhaps not for the material. Chaucer promises to tell us concerning his pilgrims, "what array they were in." And so he does; the Merchant's Flemish beaver hat, the Wife of Bath's scarlet hose, the Friar's cape of double worsted. These details convey as definite information about character, occupation, and degree as most novelists can accomplish in a page. A large part of the splendor of Roman ritual is the symbolic colors of the vestments, black for the dead, red for martyrs, gold for joyous feasts, and all the rest. We keep a faded remnant of this color symbolism in our academic regalia, and a still less frequently used one in the late medieval language of heraldry. But when the cycle plays were at their height in the fifteenth century color and design of garment were tools that could be used for more than merely mood and atmosphere.

Note how carefully the directions of Ludus specify the colors and materials of the chief actors in the Passion. Annas has a "scarlet gown and over that a blue tabard furred with white and a mitre on his head." The two doctors standing by him wear "furred hoods, and one before them with a staff of estate, and each of them on their heads a furred cap with a great knop in the crown." Caiaphas is arrayed like Annas, except that his tabard is red furred. The directions state that these costumes are "after the old law," but of course they aren't; they are after the current English practice for bishops or archbishops, doctors of theology, and judges.

Another of the elements that the cycles use liberally is music. The medieval drama was born of music and music is still a large element in the cycles. Some is purely liturgical, as when the Chester and the Towneley Harrowing of Hell, and probably the York as well, ends in *Te Deum*. The extant manuscript of the York plays contains five pieces of music, all more or less liturgical, sung by the Waferers during the plays on the death and assumption of the Virgin. All cycles abound in such directions as, "Here let the roofers and tilers of houses sing." One of the most frequent expenses is for minstrels.

There are some indications of secular, or at least vernacular, song. The Chester shepherds sing, though the nature of the piece is not indicated, and the Coventry Shearmen's and Taylors' play is followed by three songs and that of the Weavers' by two, all apparently Elizabethan, though we are probably justified in supposing that they replace older songs, or at least continue an older tradition. Apart from the five pieces in York and the Coventry carol all of the music has perished, except as we can restore it from known liturgical music. The Digby *Slaughter of the Innocents* contains not only the "Nunc dimittis," sung by the virgins of the Temple but also a dance led by the prophetess Anna.

One of the most interesting and difficult to analyze of all the effects of staging is that involving two levels of stage. The action of the cycles which is rarely confined to Ibsen's three-walled room, frequently calls for two or more levels. There are frequent scenes in which an event in heaven is followed by one on earth, or even in hell: the creation, the fall of Satan, the deluge, the annunciation, the nativity, the harrowing of hell, the ascension, the assumption of Mary, doomsday. A stage with only one level would be psychologically unacceptable to us, and it must have been to the medieval audience, too, for it was used to seeing its ritual performed on several levels, at the foot of the altar and at the altar itself, on the porch and steps of the church, and even through the streets.

The directions for many scenes seem predicated on the assumption, sometimes only the hope, that a multi-level stage will be available. With Ludus, which was performed on a multiple platform stage, there is no problem. Perhaps the use of the street as well as the pageant provides all that is needed in levels for the other cycles, but something more than that seems intended. For instance, Chester, as well as Ludus, provides for Satan to lead Jesus up to some sort of raised platform in the play of the Temptation. "Satan sets him on the pinnacle of the Temple" says Chester. Was there a raised portion of the stage, perhaps a miniature of the Temple for this scene? The Chester Deluge has another suggestive direction: "And in the first [part of the play?] let God speak in some high place as if in clouds, if that can be done, to Noah standing outside the ark with his whole family."

We could of course take this as merely something the author desired, but could not get. But I suspect that he got his high place and very likely his clouds as well. The Carmelite, Richard Maidstone, gives a detailed description of a pageant presented by the city of London in 1392 on the occasion of a reconciliation with Richard II of some financial disagreements. In one of the tableaux the King and Queen saw a youth, representing an angel, and a girl wearing a crown (perhaps representing Concord or maybe the Queen), surrounded by clouds, descend from a tower without the aid of visible steps or ladder. Maidstone says he doesn't know by what machine this effect was contrived—proof that it was contrived, not just suggested. Obviously, the machinery was available.

Professor Wickham, who calls our attention to this description, refers to several accounts of quasi-dramatic representations which call for mountains and clouds, among other effects. In fact, the medieval mechanic could provide a variety of winches, hoists, lifts, trap doors, ships on wheels, and miscellaneous other engines. The medieval love of pageantry and spectacle created a demand for such contrivances. The only question in the Chester playwright's mind, then, was not whether the effect could be produced, but whether the budget could stand the expense.

Multiple levels of a different sort are required for the resurrection and perhaps for the harrowing of hell. Historically the tomb from which Jesus rose was a cave, but artistic representations of the resurrection from Graeco-Roman times most often use a sarcophagus, and it is likely that the cycle plays conformed to this convention. The alabaster carvings do. An actor playing Jesus might, like Anima in the *Castle of Persever-ance*, lie within the sarcophagus until his cue came, or he might use a trap door and enter from beneath the pageant. A trap door could also provide an exit for Satan when he falls from heaven into hell and for the damned souls as they go to their eternal punishment.

These are minutiae, and considerable speculation is involved in visualizing the staging of such scenes. In any analysis of staging of the cycle plays, the actual directions must be projected a considerable distance, simply because they are so sparse and cryptic. We have to presume that principles ascertainable in other artistic media obtain in staging as well. The result, in all cases, is a combination of symbolic and naturalistic methods of staging, which must strike one as fairly true of all medieval artistry.

In examining dramatic construction we are on firmer ground, for that can be adequately studied from the texts themselves. Dramatic construction, of course, has a good deal to do with staging, for the dramatist always has to fit his method of telling the story to the material means at his disposal. In the cycles, for instance, we can see two polar techniques of construction, one most often (though not exclusively) exemplified by York, the other by Ludus. York has the largest number of separate plays; its story is told by a large number of often self-contained scenes. Its plays deal with one or only a few episodes. Ludus, on the contrary, is continuous action. It has actually fewer separate scenes, but it cuts back and forth with greater liberty.

Partially this is accounted for by the use of pageants in York and a multiple fixed stage in Ludus, but this is not the only reason. The Coventry Shearmen's and Taylors' play is closer in construction to Ludus, and the Chester plays are almost equidistant from York and Ludus. Towneley, as we should suspect, is closer to York, but the smaller number of plays means more episodes in each play and hence more dove-tailing and alternating of scenes.

The extremes in dramatic construction can well be illustrated by the York handling of the nativity as against the Coventry. York has six plays. The first combines the journey to Bethlehem with the birth of Jesus. The second is the shepherds' play, consisting again of two episodes, the appearance of the angels to the shepherds and their adoration of the infant. The third and fourth plays overlap; the last part of the third being verbally identical with the first part of the fourth—apparently an illustration of the common York practice of splitting plays according to the exigencies of guild organization. The two plays together contain the announcement to Herod of the approach of the Magi (third play), the meeting of the Magi and their appearance at Herod's court (both plays), and the adoration of the Magi (fourth play). The appearance of the warning angel to Joseph and the flight into Egypt take up the fifth play, followed in the sixth by Herod's learning that the Magi have gone home, his orders for the slaughter of the innocents, the actual slaughter, and the soldiers' report to Herod.

Coventry dovetails many of these episodes and achieves a development much like that of Shakespeare, in which several lines of action are pushed forward, a bit at a time, in alternating scenes. For instance, in Coventry Joseph goes for midwives to help Mary. In the next scene we see the shepherds. Joseph then returns to find the child already born. We then pick up the shepherds, who hear the angelic announcement. Then the two lines of action join in the adoration of the shepherds.

The superiority of this technique appears most prominently in the handling of the flight into Egypt. York violates not only the Scriptural story but also the natural chronology by showing the flight into Egypt as a completed action before Herod announces his intention of slaying the newborn King. The Ludus handling of this matter is more apropos. A "seneschall" reports the flight of the Magi, and Herod gives his orders for the slaughter. Then we "cut"—as the cinema critic would say—to the Holy Family, where an angel warns Joseph and he prepares for flight. Then cut again to the Herod's soldiers and the slaughter. Ludus even incorporates the Presentation in the Temple into this series of episodes by placing it between the departure of the Magi and the seneschal's report to Herod.

But lest we think that the dramatic laurels rest entirely with Ludus and Coventry, both York and Towneley, and to a lesser extent Chester, offer other excellences, notably the characterization of Joseph. In both he is a grumbler. In York he grumbles about Mary's slowness in getting ready for the journey. While he is bustling about getting packed, she launches into a long lament for Herod's cruelty. "Leave off thy din," he says curtly, "let's get on our way." The Towneley Joseph is sorry only for himself. He is sick and sore, his bones are bruised, he does not know the way to Egypt. He picks up an old grievance and once again warns (the first time was when he discovered Mary's pregnancy) young men against marriage.

Even in Chester, we get a little of this character development, not with Joseph in the scene of the flight, which is properly enough placed between Herod's command and the actual slaughter, but in the soldiers, who are bluff and loyal, but not at all pleased with their orders. They are perfectly willing to take on the stiffest champion in Christendom, even Samson, but "to slay a shitten-arsed shrew" of a baby, that is scarcely proper work for knights. So with the shepherds; Chester's characterization yields only to that in the two Towneley plays. In Ludus, on the other hand, there is scarcely any of this. The shepherds merely perform the roles assigned to them by the Gospel of Luke and the soldiers never become more than the instruments of a cruel king.

It would be certainly pushing speculation too far to assume that these two methods of development, the one emphasizing the exciting telling of a story, the other the interpretation of the story in terms of human character, are to be accounted for by the methods of staging or the guild politics behind the sponsorship of the plays. It is substantially the same phenomenon as we see in the two precursors of Shakespeare, Kyd, the specialist in plot, and Marlowe, the specialist in character. And perhaps the explanation is the same: difference in talents of the authors.

Be that as it may, the most memorable features of York and Towneley are the human insights. It almost looks as though the York and Towneley dramatists (and there were many) are ever on the lookout for an opportunity for some shrewd analysis of character, that they always view action as being understandable in terms of the individuals involved in it. For example, in the common York-Towneley play of Jesus and the doctors, the author sketches an unforgettable picture of a poor and humble Joseph, faced with having to enter the august presence of the gentry, in the persons of the doctors, and shrinking back from the prospect, until his wife pushes him into the hall. Or there is Cain in the play of the murder of Abel. In both Towneley and York plays—and they are by different hands—Cain is a rude farmer, who does not want to be bothered by all this theological nonsense of sacrifice, who is concerned over the loss of a tenth of his crop (which was not too good anyway), and who finally murders his brother as a sort of unreasonable protest against the hardships of existence. In almost every play in both cycles we have touches of this sort.

Against them, we can put the exciting tableaux which are the specialty of Ludus. The woman taken in adultery is a good sample. In none of the other cycles is the inherent excitement of this episode developed. It is lacking in Towneley, and only reported in York; Chester, here following scripture closely, begins the scene only after the apprehension of the woman. Ludus builds up the episode by starting with a sermon by Jesus on mercy and forgiveness. A scribe and a pharisee are plotting against this Jesus, who represents a threat to the strict Mosaic law they profess.

With the two points of contrast established, the scene gets under way. Enter "Accusator." He knows "a right good sport," he tells the pharisee and the scribe. "A fair young quean" has taken a "tall man"* as a lover. They are together at this very moment. Here is a chance to uphold the law of Moses and to trap Jesus. The three men close in on their quarry. As they break in the chamber, the young man rushes out "without his doublet, his stockings unlaced, and holding his breeches in his hand." When Accusator tries to stop him, he cries that any man who gets in his way will get "a dagger put in his crop." His bravado gets him off with only a curse; none of the men dare stop him. But the woman is left behind—a stroke of irony—and the three accuse her. Neither pleas nor offers of a bribe will satisfy them. They prepare to stone her, as the Law commands. Jesus enters and, without a word, begins writing. As each sees his sin written in the sand, he sneaks off. Jesus and the woman are left alone.

We note that the Ludus treatment of the woman taken in adultery is well motivated on at least two levels. The whole cycle is dedicated to exemplifying the meaning of Christianity, and certainly this episode makes clear the contrast between the mercy and forgiveness of the Christian dispensation and the severity of the old law. The dramatist opens with Jesus' promising forgiveness and ends with His forgiving an adultress. Added to this anagogical explanation is a more immediate one: the scribe and the pharisee seize on the case of the woman precisely because they think it is an opportunity to trap Jesus. Both of these motivations are implicit in the scriptural story, of course; the play merely phrases them in dramatic form.

No cycle has a monopoly on such devices. They appear here in one cycle, there in another, but sufficiently in all to show that the authors knew something of mechanics of the dramatic form. For instance, in all but Ludus, the motivation of Judas, which is fundamentally greed, is reinforced by pride. He was done out of a profit of thirty pence when Magdalen wasted her ointment on Jesus. As a business man he has not only lost money but has also been humiliated. So his betrayal not only restores his loss but also avenges him on the cause of his loss, Jesus.

The temptation in the desert is motivated in York and Ludus by Satan's uncertainty whether Jesus is the messiah or just the son of a carpenter. Ludus particularly emphasizes this motif, which has a long history in Christian theology, by making the whole manner of Jesus' birth, including

* Tall in the slang meaning of "brave," "personable," "admirable."

the marriage of Joseph and Mary, merely a means of deceiving Satan. In the temptation in the desert Satan finds out the real nature of Jesus. Later on, in York and Ludus, Satan tries to thwart the plot of Annas and Caiaphas by appearing to Percula, Pilate's wife, with a warning against killing this just man. The authors of the cycle plays did not, of course, invent these motifs; but they had the dramatic sense to use them.

Their artistry appears to good advantage when we analyze their use of such constructional devices as exposition, preparation, foreshortening, unity, and contrast. If we are to understand the action represented before us on the stage we must have certain information. Who are these people? What are they doing? What is their relationship to one another? We must know the answers to these questions, and fairly soon, or the action will be meaningless.

Some of the material can be conveyed by prologues, interpreters, narrators and the like. Half a century ago these devices were regarded as crude, and the playwright had to put his exposition into the mouths of his characters while they were playing the story. The contemporary theater, and even more the cinema and television, have gone back to the crude contrivances of the Elizabethan and the medieval stages, so that we no longer have to apologize for the opening soliloquy or the prologue when it appears in Towneley and York, which prefer often to put the exposition into fairly long opening soliloquy by one of the chief characters of the play, God in the creation, Noah in the deluge, and Pilate in several plays on the passion. Ludus and Chester sometimes do that, but more often have a formal prologue, called Expositor in several of the Chester plays, who stands somewhat outside the action, introduces it, and often interprets it. Ludus precedes several of its episodes by a formal prologue, called Contemplation.

In no cycle is this device used exclusively. It is always combined with other methods of exposition. Characters identify themselves by the costumes they wear and by the props they carry. The man with the scepter and crown is obviously the king or ruler, Pharoah, perhaps, or Herod. This sort of exposition was much more available to the writers of the cycles than it is today, for the Christian artistic effort of centuries had heaped up a vast supply of iconographical symbols, by which any reasonably alert Christian could instantly identify scores of personages of the Old and New Testaments.

We also have many excellent samples of characters identifying and describing themselves by their speech and action or by the speeches and actions of others: the shepherds in Towneley and Chester are obviously shepherds because they talk about sheep. In the Dublin Abraham and Isaac we have a chain of such identifications. God sends an angel to command Abraham to sacrifice his only son Isaac. The man to whom the angel speaks must be Abraham. He soon goes to his home, knocks on the door, and asks who is within. "No one but I and my son," a woman replies. If we have any doubts who she is, they are dispelled when she addresses Abraham as "my lord" and "my fere." The little boy must be the only son, Isaac, and she must be Sarah, else why would she be so concerned that he not get wet or fall off his horse? All this is, of course, obvious, and I should not belabor it, were not the impression still extant that the dramaturgy of the cycles is crude.

Actually, it differs less from contemporary practice than the architecture of Chartres differs from that of Radio City. Both are soundly constructed—perhaps one should reserve judgment on Radio City for a couple of centuries—but they are differently constructed of different materials.

The architects of the Chester cycle, like those of Chartres, knew their business. They knew, for instance, the importance of building up an entrance, or preparing the audience before it meets an important character in the drama. In the Adoration of the Magi, the three Magi have been brought together by their common quest of the newborn king of the Jews, foretold long ago by their prophets. After exchanging greetings and discovering their common purpose, they prepare to follow their star to the end of the journey. But lo, the star has disappeared. As they search about, they come upon "Explorator," a native in these parts. Will he help them? Yes, if they will tell him their wishes. They seek the newborn king of the Jews. Explorator is alarmed. "Hold your peace, Sirs," he warns, "I pray you."

> For if King Herod heard you so say
> mad
> He would go wood, by my fay,
> And fly out of his skin.

And so the rage of Herod when he learns the mission of the Magi does not come without warning.

The dramatist who handles historical or quasi-historical material often finds it diffuse. There is often too long a time between cause and effect, crime and punishment. Zola, for instance, died some months after Dreyfus' vindication, but this will not do in a cinema version of the Dreyfus case. So the scenarist rearranges history, and Zola dies the night before Dreyfus' restoration to rank in the French army, and as the ceremony breaks up the newsboys are selling the extras about Zola's death.

The cycle plays furnish many samples of this sort of foreshortening, all the more remarkable because it is divine history they are rearranging. In Ludus and Chester, Herod's death follows immediately after the slaughter of the innocents. In Ludus, the soldiers report that all the male infants are now dead. Relieved of a terrible fear, Herod decides to celebrate his "victory" with a banquet. He invites the knights and commands his seneschal to prepare "the best meats and the worthiest wines," even though the latter cost a thousand pounds a pint. As they sit down to rejoice themselves, Death appears. His presence is unnoticed and his speech unheard by the revellers. A knight boasts how "the boys sprawled at my spear's end." Herod has no doubt that his rival is now dead. He orders the minstrels to "blow up a merry fit." At the first note of the trumpets Death strikes Herod and the two knights, and they die.

Chester has a similar, though less spectacular, handling of the scene. The soldiers inadvertently kill Herod's own son, and he dies, possibly of grief, soon after. Chester completes the episode with the return of the Holy Family from Egypt. Immediately following, Chester accomplishes an even more noteworthy telescoping of material by combining the presentation in the temple, which according to the account in Luke was after the requirement of the Law (sixty-six days), and Jesus' disputation with the doctors, which, again according to Luke, occurred in Jesus' twelfth year.

The Towneley handling of the passion abounds in these omissions and abbreviations. In order to focus attention on Pilate, for instance, it entirely omits the trial before Herod, covering the omission only by a reference when the soldiers hustle Jesus before Pilate. The incidents of Peter's denial and Judas' suicide are likewise cut out. The gain in tempo and intensity undoubtedly supports the wisdom of the author, editor, or director responsible. The same is perhaps true of the curious combination of Jehovah's appearance to Moses in the burning bush and the delivery of the ten commandments in Ludus.

The whole problem posed by the vastness of time covered by the cycles—in fact they cover the whole of time—and the multiplicity and diffuseness of incidents is handled with admirable skill. The result could be sprawling, but it rarely is. The reason is that the dramatists found many ways of unifying their material. Their purpose was one way. They did not attempt to cover the whole of the Old Testament, but only a selected few foreshadowings and prophecies of the central incident, the redemption of mankind on the cross. This doctrinal purpose provided them with many ready-made unifying themes.

Towneley is most interesting in this regard. Summaries of preceding action abound, always with the emphasis on the scheme of salvation. Thus, God reviews man's creation, temptation, and fall as a prologue to the play of the Deluge, because it was man's sin that required the deluge as punishment. The Abraham and Isaac play is preceded by a similar summary, this time by Abraham, and there is another, by God again, as a prologue to the Annunciation. Here it serves as an introduction to the beginning of man's redemption, and it is reinforced with one of those parallels with which the devotional literature of the Middle Ages abounds. As there were three things in the fall, God says, a man (Adam), a maid (Eve), and a tree (of knowledge); so there will be three things in the redemption, a man (Jesus), a maid (Mary), and a tree (the cross).

The prophet play (and in Ludus the Tree of Jesse) serves the same function of tying together the Old Testament and the New Testament plays. Often the prophecies are repeated by the shepherds. The prophecies of Simeon and Anna in the Presentation in the Temple have a similar effect. Chester adds still another device: all three Magi identify themselves as "of Balaam's blood" and adduce his prophecy as the original cause of their search.

Similarly, the accusations of Jesus by Annas, Caiaphas, and their followers are, except in Towneley, which lacks any plays on the public ministry, summaries of the miracles dramatized earlier. Ludus is particularly notable for the unity which it attains in the play of the public ministry which precedes the passion plays. It has several scenes devoted to meetings and plots by the Jewish leaders interspersed with the episodes of the entry into Jerusalem, healing the blind man, and the Last Supper. In fact, the motif of the plotting Jews has been introduced in the episode of the woman taken in adultery.

After the passion, each cycle provides one or more recapitulations of the sufferings of Jesus and the reason for them, the redemption of mankind. The Towneley Jesus immediately after His resurrection makes such a summary, the famous "Charter of Christ." In all the cycles, Luke and Cleophas tell the story to the Stranger whom they meet on the way to Emmaus. In all the cycles but Ludus, we have a final repetition of this theme in the Doomsday play. Jesus pleads his sufferings as a justification for the judgment he is about to pronounce.

The over-all organization of the four extant cycles is remarkably similar. Each cycle has two peaks of dramatic intensity, the nativity and the passion. The Old Testament plays are all pointed toward the nativity, which fulfills the prophecies and amends the sins dramatized in the Old Testament series. A series of plays develops the implications of the nativity, the adorations of the shepherds and the Magi, the flight into Egypt, the presentation in the Temple, the disputation with the doctors. Then with the baptism by John we begin to build up to a new peak in the passion. The series of resurrection plays point back to the passion and develop its implications. Finally, all strands are gathered together in the doomsday play. Despite individual variations in material and despite the differences in tone and emphasis, this is the anatomy of the cycle play.

If an art form is to escape dullness it must establish some opposition to its unity. Critics call this contrapuntal effect contrast, tension, or, especially in the drama, struggle and suspense. It is doubtless true that because of the theological implications of its material, medieval scriptural drama could not become true tragedy. But it does not follow to any but the excessively theory-ridden aesthetician that effects of contrast and tension and even suspense are beyond the cycle plays. Scriptural story and theological dogma were not to them the strait jackets they usually become in contemporary efforts to dramatize religious subjects.

In fact, every cycle abundantly illustrates contrast and suspense. One such illustration is the episode of the healing of the blind man as it is exploited in Chester. Here it is a complete struggle between two opposed theological principles, the strictness of literal Mosaic law and the wideness of Christian toleration and mercy. Chelidonius and his parents are simple, honest people, involved in a struggle which they do not entirely understand. Chelidonius only knows that whereas he has been blind from birth, he now sees, and it is Jesus who wrought this miracle. He tells his story to his righteous neighbors and again to the Pharisees. No amount of grilling will shake him.

His parents, despite their fear and distrust of the Pharisees, heed the summons to the court of inquiry. They refuse to say whether Jesus is a sinner or a prophet. Let the Pharisees inquire into such matters. All they know is that their son Chelidonius, blind since his birth, now sees. And so all three of them stand up against the Pharisees, who use every argument to impugn their veracity.

Among the Pharisees themselves there is disagreement. First Pharisee is certain that Jesus is a sinner. He violates the sabbath, ergo he is a sinner, ergo he can do no good deed, ergo Chelidonius must be lying. Second Pharisee is not so sure. Chelidonius has been healed. No sinner could work such a wonder. Though he appears to waver and presents a united front with his colleague against the family of Chelidonius, he has to admit that "whence this is, we never knew." We hear no more of Second Pharisee—presumably he goes off shaking his head in doubt.

But the struggle goes on. Jesus enters and asks Chelidonius whether he believes in the Son of God. "Who is he?" "Thou hast seen him with thine eye." Chelidonius then believes. Outraged, First Jew calls on the crowd to stone Jesus, who remonstrates that he has done many good deeds for the people. Is He to be repaid with stoning? First Jew, mollified, proposes to let Jesus go this time, but no more talk about being God. The crowd, however, persist in their determination to stone Jesus, and He disappears. There is no resolution of the conflict, only a post-ponement, for the play is building up to the climax of the passion.

Another sort of excitement is provided by the sudden changes of tone and mood. All the deluge plays except Ludus illustrate this device. Noah and his wife are having a violent quarrel. She refuses to get on the ark. The pleas of her husband and her family are to no avail. She will not budge. Noah has to resort to violence, and presently a fist-fight is in progress. Then within a few lines they all board the ark and Mrs. Noah is assisting her husband with the navigation. In Chester they even sing a hymn. Critics who have called this crude dramatic construction have missed the point. If we suppose some terrifying natural interruption to the quarrel, a monstrous peal of thunder or the roar of a high wind, the scene is not only playable, it becomes a theatrical triumph.

Chapter VIII. THE LITERARY ART OF THE CYCLES

A RAPID DESCRIPTION of the dramatic structure of the cycles often makes it appear as though every detail or development not found in the bare scriptural narrative is an invention of the authors. This, of course, is not true. The cycle plays are not works of invention, imagination, or fancy—such categories are of recent discovery in literary criticism. The cycle plays are traditional in content and partially so in form, and the authors never attempted more than selection, arrangement, or interpretation of what their heritage gave them. Hence any true appraisal of their work must include some inventory and description of their sources.

Literary scholars are apt to use the word *source* in a highly restricted sense, to mean only the written word in books and records. These are perhaps the easiest sources to discover and the most amenable to discussion, but they are quite incapable to explain such a phenomenon as the Towneley Plays. Written sources are important, of course, but more important are the graphic and plastic arts, social customs and attitudes, folklore and folkways. One of the strengths of the English cycle plays is that they are built out of the totality of experience of the medieval communities which supported them.

The written sources, literary and documentary, are probably the easiest to describe and fix. Though none of the cycles, with the possible exception of parts of Ludus, is a learned production, their authors were literate men, and literacy in the fourteenth and fifteenth centuries was rarely confined to the mother tongue. Usually, anyone who could read or write at all, could read and write both English and Latin, and often French as well. So we can suppose that the authors of the cycles had some hold on the international language of Western Europe and that its documentary resources were open to them in some measure. We must not, however, conceive of the cycle dramatist as engaging in considerable research, the way a modern historical novelist does. Probably none of them had the resources of a Thomas Aquinas, or even of a Geoffrey Chaucer.

The literary sources of the cycles are, so far as we can ascertain them, mainly simple rather than recondite. Generally the authors preferred popular compilations and abridgments in the vernacular to the ultimate works in Latin, not so much because they could not read the Latin as because it was less available, and even more important, because a popular work in English had already performed part of the author's task of adapting his material to a lay audience.

The most obvious of the literary sources is the liturgy of the Church, which lay close at hand to any cleric, as we must suppose most of the authors were. Liturgy is the genesis of the drama, and the framework of a third to a half of the plays in any cycle is provided by the liturgical drama. We have already seen how the cycle plays used this material. But the use of liturgy was not confined to such parts of the cycle, the nativity and Easter plays, for instance, as had precedents in the liturgical drama. Even after the liturgy had ceased to generate drama within itself, it was a store house for dramatists. Every one of the cycles contains numerous psalms, hymns, and liturgical observances. Often liturgical material is translated, as in the visitation scene in Ludus, where Mary and Elizabeth recite the Magnificat, Mary saying two lines at a time in Latin, Elizabeth following with the English translation. Elsewhere only the paraphrase of the Magnificat is used.

On occasion, it is not the words but the actions of the liturgy that appear. At the end of the Digby *Slaughter of the Innocents* the virgins of the Temple form a procession bearing candles. This piece of business is borrowed from the liturgy of the Feast of the Purification (February 2), or Candlemas. Perhaps it is designed to connect the play with that feast.* It is quite probable that in the actual presentation of the plays on the visitation, and on other suitable episodes, a large requisition was laid on the liturgy, which does not appear in the texts.

I have even detected one burlesque of the liturgy. When the Pharoah of the common York-Towneley play on the exodus hears that the Israelites have escaped he says a prayer: "Heave up your hearts aye to Mahound,/He will be near us in our need." This is surely a parody of the *sursum corda* of the preface of the mass:

v. Lift up your hearts.
r. We have lifted them up unto the Lord.

It is impossible to separate the Bible from the liturgy, for much of the liturgy comes from the Bible. Obviously the Bible, both directly and through the liturgy, is the most important single source of the cycles. But "the Bible" does not mean just the plain text. By the time of the cycle plays the text of the Old Testament had been explained, refined, and sometimes distorted by fifteen or sixteen hundred years of commentary, for Old Testament exegesis starts before the New Testament was written; and a somewhat shorter but equally intensive labor on the New Testament was available to the dramatists. The result is that Scripture as understood by the commentators, and by the Christian

---

* Though the play itself is called, in the prologue, a St. Anne's Day play.

Church generally, is a vastly different thing from the bare text, so different as to deceive the unexpert.

A simple example will suffice. In all five cycle treatments of the fall of man, as in *Paradise Lost* and all other Christian literature I have encountered, Satan is the tempter. Yet this is not literal scripture. Genesis says only that the *serpent* persuaded Eve and she ate of the fruit and gave it to Adam, who also ate. Nowhere in either Testament is there a clear statement that Satan motivated or possessed the serpent, though several New Testament texts imply as much. For several hundred years all Christians have so understood Genesis.

Scriptural exegesis, patristic and scholastic, is thus necessary to understand the cycles. Even the choice of subjects, particularly from the Old Testament, is dictated largely by the typological significance. The murder of Cain, the deluge, Abraham and Isaac, the exodus—all these are types of some element of Christian theology. Much of this commentary we have lost, and must learn to apprehend the true significance of the cycles.

The sacrifice of Isaac is a revealing illustration. It is one of the types of the sacrifice of the Cross. Generations of exegetes had developed every detail of the story. Even the sheep that is substituted for Isaac is a type of Christ, the paschal lamb. The Chester treatment of the Abraham story goes even further by beginning with Abraham's reception by Melchizedek, the priest-king who offered Abraham bread and wine. Expositor tells us the significance of this action: the bread and wine is a type of the clean sacrifice of the New Law, the Eucharist and the mass, which replace the bloody sacrifices of the Old Law. Protestant exegetes, beginning with Calvin, naturally rejected this interpretation, and it is probably familiar to few of my readers, yet every educated priest or layman of the Middle Ages knew it, for it is alluded to in the canon of the mass.

To the scriptural commentary must be added as another important ultimate source the body of devotional, often fantastic, material labelled rather confusingly the "New Testament Apocrypha." No medieval author mistook these works for scripture or gave to them any special authority. But they were useful material for dramatists. The gospel of Pseudo-Matthew, for instance, gives an account of the parentage, birth, and upbringing of Mary, on which is founded several episodes of the Ludus, the story of the midwives in all the cycles except Towneley and York, and much else. The Gospel of Nichodemus describes how the banners bowed when Jesus entered the court of Pilate and is the ultimate source of this scene in York. Another group of apocrypha furnish the basis for the plays on the assumption in Ludus and York. Even Towneley which uses the least apocryphal material of any of the cycles uses

Pseudo-Matthew when it makes Joseph describe Mary's needlework in the Temple: "Mary wrought purple, the others none,/But other colors sere." And just one sentence in Towneley provides us with a clue to the understanding of its characterization of Pilate. In the prologue to the *Play of the Talents*, Pilate says "King Atus gat me of Pila."

The story here alluded to occurs in the apocryphal legends of Pilate, which make Pilate the bastard son of King Atus and a miller's daughter, Pila (whence his name Pil-atus). The legends set forth the whole history of Pilate from the time he killed a king's son to his execution by the Emperor for his part in the crucifixion. The Wakefield Master apparently knew this legendary material, and it may well be the reason for the unusual characterization of Pilate in Towneley, where he is the most thoroughgoing villain to be found in medieval drama. The Pilate legend, too, helps us understand the action of *Talents*. Pilate wanted the seamless coat of Jesus, was willing to cheat a common soldier out of it, because it was a magical coat which protected its wearer from all harm. The Emperor had to strip Pilate before sentencing him.

When the Chester Expositor cites Gregory the Great in one play and Augustine in another, when we see in Ludus a theological motif developed by Chrysostom, when York lays the Gospel of Nichodemus under requisition and Towneley the Pilate legends, we must not suppose that the authors were savants assembling all this material for themselves. They got it second or third hand from a comparatively few encyclopedic works such as the *Cursor Mundi*, an English poem almost 24,000 lines long of the early fourteenth century. Itself based on a variety of sources, the chief of which is Peter Comestor's *Scholastic History*, it "overrunneth nearly all," as the author boasts in explanation of the title. Both in structure and contents it is just the sort of thing the authors of the cycles would find useful. It could furnish most of the apocryphal material, a quantity of summarized commentary, and, of course, the scriptural narrative itself.

Another such work was the *Golden Legend* of the Dominican friar, Jacobus a Voragine. Organized according to the calendar of feast days, it could have provided much of the stuff we find in the Ludus plays about the Virgin, and the Pilate legend of Towneley as well. Large sections of it were Englished by John Mirk about 1400 and it was raided by numerous authors throughout the fourteenth and fifteenth centuries. Two collections of sermon materials drawing on both the scriptures and the lives of the saints are the *Northern Homily Cycle* (in the northern dialect) and the *Southern Legendary* (in the southern dialect). Both abound in material useful to the dramatists, and the narrative of the passion of the *Northern Homily Cycle* almost certainly influenced York and Towneley. There was also a version of *Gospel of Nichodemus* in the northern dialect which may well be the immediate source for such scenes as the bowing of the banners in York.

Of special importance is the *Meditations on the Passion* of St. Bonaventure.* There are five different English translations in a total of twenty-six manuscripts. With its unforgettable pictures of thorns piercing the brain, pieces of flesh being torn from Jesus' body, and nails driven into quivering flesh, its account of the passion inspired dozens of visual representations and must have been the core of hundreds of Franciscan sermons. Its burning fervor found its way into the encyclopedic works we have been considering, and it certainly underlies the violence and horror of the passion in all the cycles.

A dramatic source other than the widespread liturgical plays has been proposed for one of the cycles. Several scholars have argued that the Old French *Mistère du Viel Testament* lies behind the Chester plays. Not only the presence of parallels, which might be explained as commonplaces, but also similarity in material and structure lends color to the supposition. Certainty is hard to achieve in such matters, because, for one thing, the form of the *Mistère* which we know is that printed about 1500, which is doubtless much different from the form it had in the fourteenth century, when the Chester cycle came into being.

Nevertheless, close studies such as that of Professor Baugh make it likely that Chester, probably in its earliest stage, was influenced by the *Mistère* and perhaps by other French plays as well. Chester, for instance, is the only English cycle with a scene between the Emperor Octavian (i.e. Augustus) and the Sibyl, which appears not only in the *Mistère* but in several other French plays. Chester's borrowings from French religious drama are unusual. No other piece of English dramatic writing, with the exception of *Everyman*, which may be a translation, seems beholden to any continental drama in the vernacular, as distinguished from the liturgical drama in Latin.

On the other hand, there are many bonds of influence between and among the English cycles themselves. We have already noted that six of the Towneley plays are borrowed outright from York and changed but little. Other borrowings are also manifest, that of the Brome Abraham and Isaac from Chester, that of the York shepherds play from the Shrewsbury Fragments. Textual scholars have multiplied instances of this sort of thing. It ought not to surprise us, for it is merely the common medieval habit of reusing old materials when possible, the same economy that led the Norman builders of Colchester castle to use

---

* Older scholars label this work "Pseudo-Bonaventure," but it is now firmly established as an authentic work, though the rest of the *Meditations on the Life of Christ*, of which it often forms a part, is by other hands.

quantities of the old Roman brick which they found lying about the site.

Another application of the same principle leads to the employment of a great number of cliches and commonplaces which floated about in the medieval literary atmosphere. Two of them we have already noted: the theme of old age in Noah and Joseph in all the cycles; and the shrewish wife of the Noah plays. Anyone at all familiar with the literature of the Middle Ages will instantly recognize these stereotypes. They appear in Chaucer, in Langland, and in a dozen other authors, and they have been traced back to Horace and Juvenal and Propertius, who doubtless took them from Greek poets, and they in turn from Egyptians or Babylonians.

Modern critics tend to condemn stock characters and situations; modern scholars often think they have sufficiently explained the conventional when they have traced its ancestry. Both critics and scholars miss the point. Dramatists of all ages, Shakespeare among them, have found stock characters and situations useful. Audiences expect and accept them. They save time, and there is always the delight in recognition. One also suspects that the chief reason for the longevity of such themes as the old husband and the young wife or the shrewish woman is that, in all climes and ages, old men will marry young women and middle-aged women do often develop sharp tongues. Stock characters and situations are ubiquitous simply because they correspond to ubiquitous experience.

The important critical question is whether a stock character comes alive. Noah's wife certainly does. Each author seems to have been inspired by the very stockness of the character to do his best by way of making her credible. So in each play she is endowed with different expressions of her shrewishness, and not infrequently we are led to sympathize with her just as much as with her husband. In Towneley she wants to know where Noah has been—wives sometimes have good reasons for curiosity about their husbands' whereabouts—accuses him of laziness, calls his attention to the exhausted state of the family larder. The Mrs. Noah of York justifies her attitude by saying that Noah has been secretive, he spends most of his time away from home and does not tell her what he is doing. In Chester she cannot bear being separated from her friends. All of these are reasonable attitudes. A stock character Mrs. Noah certainly is, but she is also true to life.

Equally striking is the application of the stereotyped January-and-May theme to Joseph and Mary. Consider the problem of the dramatist: the clarification of the relationship between Mary and Joseph. He has been away from home for a considerable time and returns to find his wife pregnant. Why not explain this in terms of a literary cliche? The minute the Towneley Joseph says, "It is ill coupled of youth and eld," the audience makes the identification. It is the situation familiar in dozens of stories, like the one Chaucer used for his *Miller's Tale*. Likely, too, the stories arose out of experience, which must have been not uncommon in a society in which knights were frequently away from home long periods of time, and the trading merchants of the cities as well.

This method of using the literary cliches which floated around in the cultural atmosphere appears also in the learning incorporated in the cycles. Though considerable in bulk, it is generally of the most commonplace variety, simplified and vulgarized to reach the uneducated layman. The casual reader may wonder why, for instance, scholastic theology and philosophy contributed so little to the drama. Occasionally one finds a dim echo of the logic of the schools, as when the Chester Pilate puts together into a disjunctive Jesus' statements about his power: "Ergo a king thou art or was." But mainly the plays seem to owe no direct debt to the schools.

This is, of course, what we should expect. Formal learning is hard to manage on the stage. A closer inspection, however, will show that almost the whole corpus of Christian theology, as developed through twelve centuries, is involved or explicit. Typological, mystical, moral exegeses and applications of the scriptures confront us at every turn. Symbols and allegories abound, and one could make an anthology of topics eventually traceable to all the great fathers and doctors of the church. All, however, is digested and assimilated; it does not come to us in its original form, but in that proper to the popular manuals of instruction, like the one John Mirk prepared for parish priests, and to the sermons of the itinerant friar preaching at the town cross. The one great exception is Ludus, the most learned of the cycles. Here when Jesus disputes with the doctors in the temple he does not, as in other cycles, recite with simple explanations the ten commandments. Instead he asserts the doctrine of the trinity, which he exemplifies by the famous analogy of the sun, which, though one, has three effects, splendor, heat, and light. He follows this mystery by another, the virgin birth, which was necessary to deceive the devil. Well might the doctors be amazed at this child!

Dom Timothy Fry, a theologian as well as a literary scholar, found this theme, which he calls the "abuse of power theory," one of the important structural elements of Ludus. Briefly stated this very subtle proof of the necessity of the virgin birth is that man by original sin was delivered into Satan's power, but this power did not include Christ, who was born without original sin. The manner of His birth had to be such as would deceive Satan into thinking that He was a man subject to the effects of original sin. The virgin birth accomplishes this deception.

Satan then supposes that he has power over Jesus, procures his death and thus overreaches himself. He has abused his power and hence forfeited it, so that man is now free of Satan's domination. This rather sophisticated explanation of the mechanics of salvation naturally appealed to such minds as St. Augustine and St. Cyril of Alexandria, but it is rather unexpected in a popular art form. Perhaps it is indicative that, though York hints at the same theory in the temptation play, there is no further development, as in Ludus.

Ludus is exceptional in this respect. The dominant principle of selection and presentation of material in the cycles is constantly to establish connections between scriptural story and the personal experience of the audience. Both history and dogma have to be fitted out in familiar garments. This process we may call "artistic anachronism."

It takes many forms. Characters like Pharoah, Herod, and Pilate swear by Mahound. On the other hand, the Towneley Second Shepherd salutes his fellows like an orthodox Christian:

> He save you and me, overthwart and endlong,*
> That hung on a tree, I say you no wrong,
>   Christ save us.

Yet these are Jewish shepherds waiting the good news of Christ's birth! Stranger still, the Chester messenger who announces the entrance of the Emperor Octavian prays that "the Lord that died on Good Friday," may save all the company. In Ludus Satan offers Jesus not only such lands and cities as Jerusalem, Galilee, and Zebulon, but also Spain, Italy, France, Normandy, Paris. The Towneley Herod promises to make his counsellor Pope, and before the Last Supper Jesus explains to his apostles that "the feast of Easter" draws near.

Some of this anachronism is unconscious, imputable to ignorance; some is for comic effect, as when the Towneley Second Shepherd wakes from a nightmare—he dreamed he was in England! But educated men in the Middle Ages were not so ill informed as to think that Mahommed was born before the Exodus. Underneath the anachronism we see a pattern and a purpose. The whole attempt of the cycle plays is to dress the great mysteries and the great stories of religion in a garb familiar to their audiences. That is why Caiaphas and Annas and Moses' father-in-law Jethro, the high priest of Midian, become bishops.

It is also why Pilate worships Mahound. Pilate is a pagan, therefore a non-Christian. The non-Christians most familiar to Western Europeans of the time were the followers of Mahommed, who were thought to worship an idol called Mahound. The dramatic point is that Pilate was a pagan, moreover a villainous one engaged in persecuting the great

* I.e., everywhere and all the time.

Christian, Christ himself, and the point is indisputably made when Pilate swears by Mahound, however unhistorical such an action may be. The authors may well have known that the Emperor Octavian and Pilate worshipped Jupiter, Mars, Minerva and the whole Roman pantheon. But these names were unknown to many in the audience, and they carried no connotation of villainy or error to any. The stage is no place for showing off one's erudition. Herod naturally swears by Mahound because he is a villain.

The characters of the cycle plays from Adam to the damned souls of the doomsday plays are more than a little the sort of folk you would meet in contemporary York, or Chester, or London. The shepherds are watching their flocks not in the Judaean hills, but just outside Wakefield. Cain is a Yorkshire plowman, Pilate a venal sergeant of the law, Annas and Caiaphas strong-arm ecclesiastics, very much like Bishop Hugh Dispenser, who slaughtered the revolting peasants in 1381. And why would the Emperor order a census? Obviously because he wanted to collect a head tax.* The audience would know what that meant, for the Kings of England collected them with annoying frequency. So Mary and Joseph take along their ox, for at the end of the journey there will be a tax, and to raise the money they will have to sell something, just as the common folk of England did.

The one source of the cycles that penetrates and controls all others is this feeling for life. No matter how removed from the experience of a fourteenth-century burgher a theme or episode may seem to be, it is invariably interpreted into some kind of conformity. This consistent interpretation produces two noteworthy results: it keeps the cycles from being overpowered by the miraculous and it provides constant social commentary.

It was, of course, neither desirable nor possible to suppress the miraculous completely, for that would falsify the very essence of Christianity. Anyway, the miraculous was to the fourteenth century a part of experience, for belief is a part of experience. But the miraculous must not be pushed too far, as it often is in the longer continental passion plays, which are cluttered up with a mass of extraneous and mainly decorative elements that obscure the basic issues. York falls into this trap in one scene, the bowing of the banners, where the whole drama of the trial before Pilate stops and marks time while this bit of apocrypha is played. Ludus could easily have become as sprawling as the French *Passion d'Arnoul Grèban*, but for the constant effort to balance the miraculous with the everyday.

* The Vulgate text of Luke 2:1-2 says nothing about a tax: "An edict went forth from Caesar Augustus that the whole world should be registered (*discriberetur*)," not "taxed," as in the Authorized Version.

For instance, Ludus chooses to dramatize the apocryphal incident of the trial of Joseph and Mary. In the original source, this is completely fantastic. When Mary's pregnancy becomes obvious, the scribe Annas accuses Joseph of having defiled a Temple Virgin. Before the priest who hears the accusation, both Mary and Joseph protest their innocence, Mary that she has known no man, Joseph that he has not touched her. The priest gives them the "water of the conviction of the Lord" to drink; if they have sinned the water will make their sin manifest. Both drink, and both are vindicated.

Ludus keeps this framework, which it probably got from an intermediate source, but at the same time it humanizes and localizes it. The setting is an ecclesiastical court, before which three detractors appear to lodge a complaint against Joseph and Mary. The Summoner, Den, is sent to fetch the accused. Like Chaucer's summoner, Den is not above using his position for private gain. He will take a bribe; in fact, Joseph and Mary had better give him one if they don't want trouble. None offered, he takes them to the bishop, commenting on their foolishness and offering Joseph a bit of advice on how to handle such a wife. Den's venality and cynicism has exactly the effect of bringing the fantasy of the original down to earth.

There is an overtone of social criticism in this scene from Ludus, but sometimes the effect of this sort of interpretation is merely a homely touch which humanizes some episode of sacred history, as in the Towneley play of the visit of Mary to her cousin Elizabeth. Scripture and convention require that the high point of this play be Mary's hymn of praise, the Magnificat. But the author preludes this with some conversational courtesies between the two women. Mary inquires after Elizabeth's health. It is as good as a woman of Elizabeth's age can expect. Then Mary makes a polite remark about Elizabeth's approaching motherhood, and Elizabeth naturally asks about Mary's welfare and then:

> And Joachim, thy father, at home
> And Anna, my niece, and thy dame
> How stands it with him and her?

What more natural than for an elder relative to ask about the old folks?

York provides a companion piece, emphasizing municipal rather than domestic courtesy and showing a remarkably keen awareness of bourgeois sensibilities. According to the account in Luke and Matthew of the entry into Jerusalem, Jesus first sent two disciples to get an ass colt in a nearby village, instructing them to say to the owners that "the Lord hath need of him." This seemed to the York author a bit vague in its handling of property rights. So when Peter and Phillip untie the animal, Phillip assures Peter (and the audience) that the colt is common town property and hence they do not need the permission of any owner to use it. The Janitor, apparently a town official, asks the two apostles why they make so bold as to use the beast "without livery."* Phillip replies that his master has need of the animal. Who is he? Jesus of Nazareth. This satisfies the Janitor perfectly. Jesus is a great prophet: "take the beast with heart full free."

But as a municipal servant, or official, he has another duty to perform. It is not every day when the city is visited by a great prophet like Jesus. So he hastens to tell the burghers, who thereupon hold a little meeting. They have all heard of Jesus' miracles and teachings. It would be a great blot on their civic reputation if they did not receive him worthily. Get branches, strew flowers in the street, let the children lead the procession singing. And so when Jesus enters, Jerusalem is ready with a suitable welcome, the same sort, we imagine, that York gave to Richard II and Henry IV.

Another sort of assimilation of material to contemporary social pattern appears in the use of French. Chester is particularly notable among the cycles. Many of its kings and potentates speak a little French, the Emperor Octavian, Herod, and Pilate. This may be, as some of the older scholars thought, a holdover from a stage when the whole play, except for Latin liturgical remnants, was (like *Adam*) in French, but the language is retained because of its suitability to the portrayal of upper class characters. It serves somewhat the same purpose as Shakespeare's use of blank verse when Hamlet is speaking to his peers but prose when he is speaking to the grave diggers, but with the added advantage that it corresponds to contemporary social custom. French was commonly the upper-class language of fourteenth-century England, and the practice probably died slowly in the fifteenth century.

So when a messenger begins to speak French in the Coventry nativity play we know at once that we are going to see high society, in fact Herod and his court. Even in Towneley and York the high-born characters, Pilate for instance, interlard their conversation with French phrases. "Bene beneuew, bewscher," says the York Pilate to his son, *bien venu, beau sire*. The Chester Magi ring a change on this sociolinguistic phenomenon, they express themselves at Herod's court in a mixture of French and Latin:

> Infant queramus de graund parent
> Et roy de caeli et terrae.

* Probably meaning that they are apparently not servants of some lord or members of some guild and so privileged to use the town property.

"We seek an infant of great parentage and the king of heaven and earth." But of course they are foreigners from distant lands and cannot be expected to employ the language of Herod's court.

One can hardly refrain from calling attention to the remarkable coincidence, certainly by pure accident, that the linguistic usage of the Chester Play precisely parallels the actual situation in Judaea, where the educated and cosmopolitan upper classes used Greek, the common folk Aramaic, and, to make the comparison complete, there was also a dead language used by scholars and in the church, Hebrew.

This is the portrayal of classes above the majority of the audience and the producers of the cycles. They were craftsmen, and when the occasion arose they naturally translated the bare scriptural narrative into the operations of a particular craft. The building of the ark, for instance, they saw in terms of the shipwright's, or the carpenter's, skills. Chester and York both develop the scene in this manner. In Chester each of Noah's sons comes to work with a tool, Shem with the best axe in town, Ham with a hatchet, and Japhet with a hammer to knock in the pins that hold the planking to the ribs. Noah makes a mast of a tree "tied with gables* that will last." He provides the ship—for the ark contrary to the scriptural description is always regarded as a ship—with a "sail yard for each blast," with a topcastle and a bowsprit, with cords and ropes.

The York Noah apparently knows less about the construction and outfitting of a ship. He first asks God for instruction, which he gets in some detail: square the tree trunks and do not get them askew; cut the squared lumber into boards and "wands," apparently meaning slats or shims; do not make the boards too thin; lay the joints close together; nail the boards well so they will not pull loose. Noah is an apt apprentice and is soon explaining the processes to the audience. He tries the boards with a line to see that they are straight. He makes sure they are all of the same thickness, planing them down when necessary. Then he pins them together at the joints with a "gin," sticks them to ribs with "cement," and uses good new nails to hold them.

The ship built, it must be navigated. The Chester Noah takes the helm as they cast off. In Towneley Mrs. Noah tries to help out with the navigation. She finds the "seven stars," probably Ursa Major (not the Pleiades), whose pointers locate north. But Noah feels incompetent to manage the craft in such high seas and calls on God, the best steersman of all. He then turns over the helm to his wife and takes a sounding, as does also the York Noah. The scriptural information that the water stood fifteen cubits over the high hills (Genesis 7:19-20) is thus conveyed. The Towneley Noah takes another sounding a little later and

*I.e., "cables."

discovers that the waters have "waned a great deal." The third sounding shows that the ship is aground and hence the passage safely made.

How seriously one should take such material is always a puzzle. Certainly if one approaches any medieval art form without a sense of humor, he will miss much and distort all, for humor is a basic ingredient of the medieval world view. Even in the most solemn products, a treatise on doctrinal theology, the scribe is likely to fall to doodling and by prolonging the loops of the l's and h's into fish, produce an effect utterly at variance with the spirit of the text. In an apparently straightforward drawing of a lecture room with the august Doctor of Civil Law expounding Justinian, we will notice that down in a corner one of the students is sound asleep.

Never perhaps was the essential incongruity of life so strongly felt. Like much of the world's great humor, *Don Quixote* for example, the comic in the cycles is apt to be ambivalent. Towneley specializes in the high comic which changes into the high tragic before your very eyes. In the slaughter of the innocents a soldier approaches one of the mothers, sword in hand to slay her infant. Follows this exchange:

1 SOLDIER. Dame, think it not ill,
   Thy knave if I kill
1 MOTHER. What, thief, against my will?

Does the author want the audience to laugh, to weep, or to cry out in anger?

The whole play of *Talents* displays this ambivalence. Its position, between the crucifixion and the harrowing of hell is one of great solemnity. Yet the spectacle of the Procurator of Judaea, a Roman officer of high rank, playing dice with common soldiers for the possession of a coat is essentially ridiculous. Yet the coat is of great value—it is a magic coat which protects its wearer against all harm. Shall we therefore take the action seriously? After Pilate has bluffed one of the soldiers out of his winnings in a game of chance, the soldiers launch into a homily on the evils of gambling. Is this plain moralization or is it burlesque? Whichever it may be, it certainly is irony below irony, a sort of bottomless pool of irony.

The possibility of burlesque is always present, for it is of the very nature of the medieval spirit to burlesque the things it held most sacred. In five of the six shepherds' plays (omitting only Ludus), the shepherds leave gifts for the babe, a horn spoon that holds a hundred peas, an old stocking, a little spruce box, a bob of cherries. In one sense the effect is one of pathos: these poor men have nothing else to give. But the genesis of this motif is certainly the parallel between the curious offerings of the shepherds and the gorgeous ones of the Magi—gold, frankincense, and myrrh. And in that sense, it is surely burlesque.

The Towneley development of this motif in the Second Shepherds' Play skirts the blasphemous, at least by modern standards. When the shepherds visit Mak's hovel in search of their stolen sheep, the Wakefield Master is actually burlesquing the adoration of the Infant Jesus which follows. The parallel is complete: the slatternly Gill, who births a bairn a year, and the Virgin Mother; the shifty Mak and the saintly Joseph; the long-nosed sheep in the cradle and the Son of God in the manger, even the gifts of the shepherds, for the discovery of Mak's deception is made by one of them as he tries to leave a gift for Mak's "bairn."

One of the most daring burlesques in Towneley comes at a point where we would expect it even less than at the nativity, in the crucifixion. In the religious allegory of the time Jesus is sometimes represented as a knight going out to joust with Satan. *Piers Plowman*, for instance, uses this idea as a point of departure:

"Is this Jesus the Jouster," quoth I, "that Jews did to death?"

Towneley turns this allegory upside down and inside out by putting it in the mouths of the torturers preparing to nail Jesus to the cross. You say you are a king, jeers a torturer. Then you must joust in a tournament. The others take it up. The cross is Jesus' palfrey. It will take skill to ride that steed. They will help him mount:

> Stand near, fellows, and let see
> How we can horse our king so free.

So that he will not fall, they will bind him fast to his mount—with nails!

I always find this point hard to make to my students, most of whom have conventional modern attitudes towards the sacred. They cannot understand how an "age of faith" could parody the most awesome mysteries of religion, how the adulterous cult of courtly love could have its "ten commandments of St. Venus," how slapstick and reverence can stand cheek by jowl. The truth is that medieval artists could do such things precisely because their belief was unshakeable. If you believe, as Dante did, in the papacy, you can put the pope in hell. And hence these sudden forays into burlesque, mixing the sublime and the vulgar, which abound in Towneley, York, and Chester, and are occasionally implicit even in Ludus.

Even where there is no burlesque, the spirit of irony dominates.

Chester, which is perhaps the calmest and apparently the least lively of the cycles, is forever practising Chaucer's favorite trick of pulling the reader's leg. A characteristic sample comes in the building of the ark. After the men have organized the work with axe and hatchet and hammer, hewing and fitting the boards, Mrs. Noah proposes to do her bit. Women, she says, are weak to undertake any great work; so she will carry the timber! Mrs. Shem provides a "hackstock," a sort of chopping block on which the men can hew the beams. Mrs. Ham collects the pitch for caulking the boat, and Mrs. Japhet gathers chips for the fire, presumably to melt the pitch. She will also use it in the only properly feminine task of the lot, getting dinner.

The humor of the cycles is all pretty much of a piece. Farcical situations, such as we have in the blanket-tossing episode of the *Second Shepherds' Play*, and purposefully comic characters, like Watkin of the Digby *Slaughter*, though found, are not the most characteristic elements. The wry comment of an underling on the affairs of his betters, the exploitation of the incongruous, the unexpected development of a situation which has the shock value of the unorthodox resolution of a chord—these are the tricks with which the cycles are forever puzzling and delighting the careful reader.

The humor of the cycles is at the other end of the scale from that of the high comedies of Restoration. The point of view of the cycles is most often that of the yeoman or the small burgher of the towns, the group which provided the major share of the audience and also bore most of the cost. The material dramatized naturally deals a great deal with kings and potentates, but they are always viewed from beneath. The product is thus often satiric. One feels a constant criticism of the leaders of the state, the church, and the social organization generally. It is hard to discover a good ruler in the cycles. Pharoah, Herod, Pilate—they are all villains or close to it. The Magi are kings, to be sure, but we never see them ruling or judging; in fact they are not presented as equal in power, though perhaps they are in dignity, to Herod.

The satire on state, church, and society which we find in the cycles is fairly typical of medieval satire in general. It is rarely directed at institutions or beliefs. Although the revolt against the established church which Wyclif initiated occurred at the formative period of the cycles, it is hardly alluded to. Tutivillus, the devilish prosecuting attorney of the Towneley judgment play, calls himself a "master lollard," but it is doubtful if the word carries any more meaning than "worthless fellow." The possibility of popular insurrection is alluded to in the Coventry episode of the slaughter of the innocents: one of the soldiers objects that the killing of so many infants is likely to provoke a rising.

In a century and a half which produced such events as the Hundred

Years War, the deposition of Richard II, the Wars of the Roses, and several peasant uprisings, notably the Peasants' Revolt of 1381 and Jack Cade's of 1450, so few topical allusions would appear remarkable, but they are equally few in Chaucer, and even the ones in John Gower and *Piers Plowman* are rather well covered. The fact of the matter is that medieval satire is not very topical. The view that the ills we bear are the results of institutions, ideologies, or even scientific discoveries is strictly modern.

Medieval man was sure that the cause of evil is original sin. On this he could be quite specific, enumerating the vices to which each condition of man was specially vulnerable, seeing in every region and time applications of the general rule that man is naturally prone to sin, providing the sharpest illustration of this proneness in a Herod or an Annas. Apparently, too, there was an implicit belief that the higher the man, the worse the sin. Consequently medieval satire is at the same time tremendously general and utterly specific. One other quality is evident also: medieval satire spared no one, emperor or serf.

What we find in the cycles is a constant calling attention to the vices of the great. Chester uses Herod, for instance, as an illustration of flattery. When Herod asks his "chief of clergy" to look up the prophecies of Christ, the eminent doctor finds it expedient to soften Herod up for the bad news. No prophet, the doctor assures the king, would write anything "your heart to cold," or to deny his right. Further apologies follow:

> I beseech your Royal Magesty
> With patience of your benignity
> To hear the truth and pardon me
> Their sayings to declare.

The doctor's position is a hapless one. All his preparation serves no purpose. At the very first prophecy, Herod breaks out in a frenzy of denunciation of "that old villard Jacob, all doted for age." And the further the doctor goes, the madder Herod gets.

Most of the satire in the cycles is in little touches like this. In offering to take a bribe Den, the summoner of the Ludus *Trial of Joseph and Mary*, symbolizes the venality of the law. The reiteration in all the cycles of the charge that Jesus is an enemy of the law is a contrivance by which the dramatists transfer to the Pharisees, Annas and Caiaphas, and Pilate the general hatred of the law and all its works, an attitude violently expressed when the revolting peasants of 1381 burned charters wholesale and killed every judge, lawyer, and juror who fell into their hands. The characterizations of tyrants—one fourth of all the plays in Towneley are built around tyrants—have a similar purpose, to dress evil in a guise which the audience already detested.

Perhaps the most thorough social satire is in the Towneley *Second Shepherds'*. Almost all critics have commented on it, but many have missed its most striking qualities, its combination of so many conventional themes of satire and the fact that it is so hard to localize in time—it seems equally pertinent to any period between 1350 and 1500, or perhaps beyond.

There is protest against taxes, which bear unduly on the poor:

> We are so crippled hamyd
> Fortaxed and oppressed ramyd
> We are made hand-tamyd tamed
> By these gentlery men.

This is joined to the winner-and-waster theme, the division of society into the men that create wealth and those that destroy it:

> These men that are lord feast; they cause the plow tarry.
> That men say is for the best—we find it contrary.
> Thus are husbands farmers oppressed, in point to miscarry.

Unreasonable feudal services, which were perhaps commoner in the North than in the South, come in for dishonorable mention:

> There shall come a swain, proud as a po. peacock
> He must borrow my wain, my plow also.

There is no use denying these forced loans of time and equipment:

> If I should forgang it withhold
> I were better be hangyd hanged
> Than once say him nay.

For, and this is the heart of the matter, these extortioners are always in the service of some great Lord, who invariably backs them up:

> He can make purveyance requisition
> With boast and bragaunce bragging
> And all is through maintenance
> Of men that are greater.

132

The "maintenance" of which the shepherd complains was viewed by both moralists and legislators as one of the chief evils of the age. It was simply the practice of the powerful to hang together and to back up their subordinates, by legal means if possible, by force if necessary. The outcry against it was shared by commoner and lesser noble.

One is naturally tempted to see in the shepherd's words a sort of program for revolution, but he specifically disavows any such intention. He is merely blowing off steam:

> It does me good, as I walk thus by my own,
> Of this world for to talk, in manner of moan

So he will get back to his sheep.

One of the most important source materials of the cycles has been both overemphasized and underemphasized by scholars and critics. This is folklore and its progeny in folk tale, folk custom, and folk wisdom.* Some have seen Germanic and Celtic folklore as the sole fountain and origin of medieval drama, as though there were no such thing as a Christian tradition or liturgical drama. Others have ignored the very real levy the cycles and their liturgical predecessors made on folk materials, even regarding the St. George plays as nothing more than degenerate miracle plays.

A true assessment of the contribution of each tradition, Christian and pre-Christian, is extraordinarily difficult. The very Bible itself, as the great Frazer showed, abounds in folk lore. The Christian tradition developing from the Bible picked up bits and pieces of the myth and ritual of nearly every race and sect in the Roman empire, and some beyond. Even the smaller task of distinguishing Germanic and Celtic elements from all the rest is formidable, if not impossible, because Germanic myth, known to us chiefly in its Old Norse form, so often parallels Celtic, Graeco-Roman, and Semitic. All seem to have one ultimate source.**

What we can do is to suggest by a few examples the size of the cycle's debt to the folklore and folk custom which was pretty certainly alive during the formative stage of the cycles (some of it still is) and which is pretty surely Germanic or Celtic. Mr. John Spiers has analyzed the Towneley cycle from this point of view, and much of what he has to say about Towneley is true of the other cycles as well. The ritual significance of most of the material had, of course, been lost by the time of the cycles; it lived on as story, game, or custom.

One of the archetypal patterns of folk ritual is the seasonal drama of the dying god and the resurrected god, which is of course the regular

---

* I am purposely ignoring the distinctions between folk story and popular literature, proverb and proverbial saying, and the like. Folklorists will be able to categorize my material; others have no need for categories to perceive my meaning.

** For instance, the Cain-Abel story is paralleled by that of Romulus and Remus.

succession of winter and spring. A variant of the resurrected god is the newborn god. Both versions are inherent in the Christian tradition. We can, however, detect some elements in the nativity plays not wholly explicable in terms of Christian tradition.

One is the emphasis on cold, storm, flood, and destruction which we notice in all the nativity plays. The pagan festival of Yule which preceded the Christian nativity season celebrated the death of an old god, that is, the coming of winter. The rituals of the festival emphasized cold and death. It was a funeral ceremony, attended, as often in pagan rituals, with boisterous games. These became attached to the feast of the nativity—the feast of fools, the boy bishop, and the rest—and the Church warred against them for centuries. An allusion in *Gawain and the Green Knight* makes it probable they were still extant in fourteenth-century England. And we find remnants of them in the two Towneley shepherds' plays and the one in Chester.

Many details suggest that the writers of these plays raided folk customs for material. The comic meal of the shepherds, which is pulled out of a bag, suggests the magic cauldron of Welsh folklore or the cornucopia of the Romans. The Mak story, which is extraordinarily widespread, as numerous analogues prove, seems concocted of ritual and mythic elements. Mak himself, like Shakespeare's Autolychus, derives probably from the Germanic God Loki, the Celtic Curoi, or the Roman Mercury, all three of whom are vagrants, shape-shifters, brawlers, and thieves. Mak is definitely a magical person: he performs an incantation which keeps the shepherds asleep while he steals the sheep. Mak's punishment, being tossed in a blanket, is a survival of the mock-killing of the old god. The wrestling match in Chester, in which a Mak-like figure called Trowle* throws the shepherds one after another, has similar antecedents.

The old god reappears in the tyrants, especially Herod, who fears the newborn god, tries to kill him, and eventually dies himself. These activities are likely remnants of an old ritual play which coincides with the scriptural narrative. A proof of Herod's double or multiple ancestry is in his serio-comic rages. He is the familiar folk figure of the "sinister clown," and his boasting and ranting, shared by Pilate and Pharoah, has its antecedents in the berserks and flyting contests so common in early Scandinavian story.

Another pattern derived from folk custom, and ultimately from ritual, appears in the buffeting and scourging scenes of the passion. The cruel soldiers who strike Jesus and then ask him to prophesy who struck the blow are, one suspects, playing such medieval games as "hot cockles" or the still extant "blind man's buff," which have their obscure origins in some orgiastic cruelty connected with the killing of the old god. Several

* The name inevitably suggests *troll*.

German passion plays point out the game pattern of this buffeting by assigning the soldiers a counting-out rime, of the one-two-buckle-my-shoe variety. Yet another game is suggested in the scene in which the soldiers dice for Jesus' garments. Glutton's confession in *Piers Plowman* gives a vivid, though not entirely clear, description of an ale-house game in which contestants wagered clothes.

Finally, there are the devils that play so large a part in the harrowing of hell and the doomsday plays. These certainly have little scriptural warrant, and they cannot with confidence be derived from the demons of Hellenistic syncretism. Their ancestry is patently in the dwarfs, bogies, gnomes, trolls, omadhauns, and hob-goblins with which Germanic and Celtic mythology peopled the underworld. To be sure, the Christian tradition had absorbed these spirits long before the cycles were put together. The cycle dramatists who wrote devils into their plays may have been quite unconscious of their origin,* but that is precisely why they are so significant. The most important of all sources is the one of which the author is least conscious, the beliefs he shares with his community. It is of the very nature of folklore that it is preserved by people who are totally unconscious of its origin. The very concept of folklore arises only when the scholars begin to explore it; and when they begin to analyze its appearances in art they inevitably falsify its nature and use.

Possibly no element in the cycles has been more intensively studied than the versification, especially stanza form. Scholars have sought the clue to problems of authorship in stanza form, on such suppositions as that varieties of stanzas correlate with differences of authorship, that simpler stanzas belong to an earlier stage of composition than more complex ones, that irregularities in versification point to interpolations, cuts, and rewritings in the plays. Nearly eighty years of intensive study of certain elements of versification has produced some work important for the critical judgment of the poetic achievements of the cycles— some but not much.

The cycles are verse drama, and an over-all estimate of their worth necessitates attention to the vehicle they use. Yet no aspect of medieval drama is more obscure or difficult to analyze. It is not that we lack facts, but that we lack the tools to deal with the facts. A cursory reading of the cycles is likely to lead only to an endorsement of Marlowe's famous characterization of his immediate predecessors: "the jigging veins of riming mother wits."

The most pertinent fact about the verse of the cycles is that the bulk of it was written in the worst of all centuries of English verse, the fifteenth. After Chaucer and Langland, the technique of English verse

---

* Or they may not have been so unconscious as we sometimes suppose. Chaucer knew quite well the origin of fairies, witness his *Wife of Bath's Tale*.

went to pieces, because the English language was shifting sand. Consider what happened to the sounds of the language: The final *e* ceased being pronounced. The long vowels one after another shifted position and some of them broke into diphthongs. Open vowels became closed. A number of consonant sounds (*gh*, initial *k* and *g*, before *n, l* in many words) muted. English literature still bears some of the scars of this wholesale carnage. In order to read Chaucer in the original we have to go through a period of training scarcely shorter or less arduous than that required to acquire a proper French accent. If we do not, we lose the rhythm, many of the rimes, and virtually all of the intricate and subtle sound effects, which are a main constituent of good verse.

The case is more serious with the cycles than with Chaucer, who wrote the sort of English that ultimately became standard, whereas the cycles are all in provincial dialects. Chaucer's syllabic verse has also become standard; the alliterative tradition which profoundly affected some of the cycle dramatists has been almost wholly lost. Moreover, the labors of scholars, working with over eighty manuscripts of the *Canterbury Tales*, have given us a trustworthy text, something we lack for the cycles. And the text of Chaucer was always a much more stable thing than any theatrical text can be, for the requirements of repeated production result in constant rewriting and cutting. This is undoubtedly one cause of the mangling of stanzaic form and meter which is so common in the cycles.

Until a great deal more work is done by the scholars on the texts of the cycles, on versification, and on linguistic problems, we cannot hope for a thorough critical evaluation of the poetic achievements of the cycles. However, enough is visible in the texts as they presently stand to make a few observations.

All the cycles are written in verse, and nearly all this verse is stanzaic. Anything except the directions and scriptural tags which looks like prose or which seems to lack stanzaic or metrical form can probably be accounted for by one of the several disintegrating elements we have reviewed, phonetic change, textual corruption, the effects of continued production. This is not to say that all the verse in the cycles was originally good; it is hard to see how some of it could ever have been anything above mediocre. But it is possible to see that some of the authors were better than competent, they wrote the best verse to be found in the fifteenth century.

With the exception of Chester, all the cycles display an extreme variety of stanza and metrical forms, sometimes several in the same play. Chester has only a few departures from a simple eight-line stanza. Towneley is a welter of forms, some of them with internal rimes, intricate interlacings, and extreme variations in line length. York is little better, and it has in addition to syllabic verse some definitely alliterative meter, which, to add complications, has been rimed and marked off into something like stanzas. Ludus is the most puzzling of the lot, in that its stanzas sometimes seem to be utterly without metrical pattern. It also exhibits the only use of which I know in all dramatic literature of a two-foot line for ordinary dialogue:

> Lord in throne
> Maketh no moan.
> Queans gin groan
> In world about.

This is one of Herod's soldiers speaking as he goes about the bloody business of killing babies.

One could gather many examples of this sort of clash between metrical and dramatic effect, but it is not characteristic even of Ludus, where often the very irregularity of the scansion combined with the frequent riming on unaccented syllables makes it easy to read a whole passage as prose. In general, the authors found it possible to do what the play demanded despite the verse forms which they used. A few of them exhibited great skill in fitting the verse to the tempo and mood of the dramatic situation.

The eight-line stanza of Chester, for instance, has considerable limitations as a dramatic vehicle. It is not suitable for rapid fire dialogue, and speeches in Chester tend to stretch out to the full eight lines of the stanza. Occasionally as in *Abraham and Isaac* the stanzas break up to produce a more fluid interchange of speeches, and in the shepherds' play the author has departed considerably from the stanza. Its general effect, however, is one of quietness and some lack of movement.

But if Chester's eight-line stanza has limitations for dialogue, it has great possibilities for lyric, and the best poetic effects in Chester are of this sort. Time and again the stanza becomes sweetly melodic:

> I, Ezechiel, sothly see
> A gate in God's house on high;
> Closed it was, no man came nigh.
>   Then told an angel me:
> "This gate shall no man open, I wis,
> For God will come and go by this;
> For himself it reserved is;
>   None shall come there but he."

In the midst of the most prosy passages one is apt to come on a line memorable for its evocative simplicity. For instance, the enumeration of the animals that entered the ark is not a notable performance. The pictures dominate the scene, and the verse is supposed to be only accompaniment:

> Here are cocks, kites, crows,
> Rooks, ravens, many rows,

and so on. But among these mere names is one line that would do credit to Blake or the Wordsworth of the Dorothy-poems:

> Redshanks running through the lakes.

At the opposite extreme is the nine-line stanza of the Wakefield Master, in which several of the Towneley plays are wholly or partially written. It is one of the most complicated in the cycles. The four line *front* of the stanza is hexameter with internal rime,* followed by a short line of usually one foot, then three riming trimeter lines, and finally another short line, usually two feet, riming with the fifth line. One would suppose it to be about as unwieldy a pattern as a dramatist could tie himself to. Yet the Master uses its most notable feature, its gathering speed, to build up tension, particularly in scenes of violent conflict. Annas and Caiaphas are quarreling over what to do with Jesus. Caiaphas is for direct action, Annas for a more discreet and judicial approach:

ANNAS. We may by our law / examine him first**

CAIAPHAS. But I give him a blow / my heart will brist [burst]

ANNAS. Abide to ye his purpose know. / [till]

CAIAPHAS. Nay, but I shall out thrist [thrust]
Both his een on a row. / [eyes] [together]

ANNAS. Sir, ye will not, I trist [trust]
Be so vengeable
But let me oppose him.

CAIAPHAS. I pray you, and sloes him. [slay]

ANNAS. Sir, we may not lose him, [loose]
But we were damnable.

As used by the Master, this unique stanza is admirably fitted to scenes of rapid and violent action, to the trials before Annas and Pilate, to the Noah play with its fight between Noah and his wife, to the two shepherds' plays. With its frequent anapestic substitution and feminine rimes,

* At least the manuscript writes it so; one can also make it eight lines of trimeter, riming alternately.
** Is *first* a copyist's mistake for *frist* demanded by the rime?

it is a good medium for insult and counter-insult. Perhaps it lacks solemnity, and the Master seems to have felt this, for in the two trial plays, Jesus speaks but a few lines. The nine-line stanza does not appear in plays in which Jesus has a large speaking part.

The old alliterative meter of *Beowulf*, which underwent a considerable revival in the fourteenth century, appears in several York plays. As differentiated from the use of alliteration for adornment, common in English verse of all periods, the alliterative meter is distinguished by freedom from syllable counting; or perhaps, more exactly, it uses pauses and several degrees of stress, instead of a strict division of syllables into accented and unaccented, as syllabic meter does. The line customarily has four beats, three of them, and sometimes all four, falling on syllables which carry the alliteration. Even when rimed and marked off into stanzas, as in York, the alliterative meter has some of the freedom and flexibility of blank verse. It can be enormously varied. The opening speech of God in the creation play illustrates the form:

> I am grácious and gréat, Gód withouten begínning,
> I am máker unmáde, all míght is in mé,
> I am lífe and wáy, unto wéalth wínning,
> I am fóremost and fírst; as I bíd shall it bé.

With this alliterative meter York frequently joins a syllabic one, which, according to Professor Reese, who has made an exhaustive study of the versification of York, is designed to change the mood. Thus in the *Second Accusation before Pilate*, Annas and Caiphas finally convince Pilate that Jesus menaces Roman power and must be executed. Pilate, who has been under terrific pressure by Annas and Caiphas and their followers, bursts out angrily:

> mad   wizard
> What! Weenis that wode warlowe overwin us thus lightly?
> A beggar of Bedlam, born as a bastard,
> Now, by Lucifer, loath I that lad, I leave him not lightly.

The strong beats, the insistent alliteration of these lines make them rush and roar. It is the bolt of lightning out of the dark clouds.

Soon, however, Judas enters. He is not angry, even at himself. His mood is of complete desolation, he has betrayed his Master, repaid kindness and love with treachery. So the meter changes. The alliteration holds over as a binding element, but a quieter syllabic meter and the Burns stanza are the structural elements:

> pence?
> The purse with his spens about I bore.
> trusted
> There was none trowed so well as I

trusted
Of me he trist, no man more,
And I betrayed him traitorly
plot
With a false train
blameless
Sakless I sold his blessed body
Unto Jews to be slain.

One of the qualities of verse not affected by phonetic change is imagery, and it is the imagery more than any other one element that distinguishes the true poet from the merely capable craftsman. Medieval verse is not so rich in imagery as that of the Elizabethans or the metaphysicals, possibly because it is more often didactic or narrative. Nevertheless, we can find plentiful evidence that some of the cycle dramatists had mastered this tool of the poet, and knew how to construct and link images.

Chester, as we should suspect, often provides delicate visual images. One in the Antichrist play is a good sample. Elijah is speaking of Antichrist's imminent fall:

And as the flower now springs,
hangs?
Falleth, fadeth, and hings,
So thy joy now it reigns,
That shall from thee be raft.

The fading flower as a symbol of mortality or impermanence is of course a commonplace, but Shakespeare and Herrick did not reject it therefore. In Chester it is not used for ornament alone. The end of the world is approaching as Elijah speaks, and the flower image is almost a motif in the three last plays of the Chester cycle. Antichrist boasts, with some unconscious irony, that he has created all things on earth, even "the flowers fresh that fair can spring," and the Saved Emperor at doomsday says that Christ has restored "My flesh, that fallen was as the flower." There is a tissue of such images, always used as a contrast of the evanescent with the eternal.

The Wakefield Master and some of the York playwrights specialize in another sort of images, earthy and often anticlimactic, as befits their satiric purpose. Tutivillus in the Towneley judgment play describes the proud courtier in similies taken from the sights of daily life:

buttocks
His luddocks they look like walk-mill clogs,
bristled
His head is like a stook, hurled as hog's.

140

The clogs worn by the "walkers" as they fulled the cloth, the haystacks of the field, the hog's bristles—these are typical of the concrete, usually deprecatory, images of perhaps the greatest satirist of his times.

One of the York playwrights uses an image well calculated to appeal to a people whose chief source of wealth was the wool trade. Pilate asks his butler to help him into bed. When the butler exclaims at Pilate's weight, he replies, "Ya, I have wet me with wine." The allusion is to the old trick of wetting wool before selling it so as to increase the weight.

A complete study of the poetic qualities of the cycles must wait for better texts, for the more thorough application of our increased knowledge of Middle English linguistics, and, above all, for fundamental work in prosody, particularly that of the alliterative meter. Until that time, however, we can recognize that not all the unknown versifiers whose efforts gave us the scriptural drama of Medieval England were incompetent hacks.

Chapter IX. THE DRAMA OF THE INDIVIDUAL CHRISTIAN: THE MORALITY

UNLIKE THE CRAFT CYCLES and the other scriptural drama, the morality play had no long history of development. As a dramatic form it springs into existence, pretty much completely developed, in the fourteenth century. Nothing that would explain the type can be found in the liturgical or the transitional drama, though all its elements are found elsewhere, in non-dramatic forms.

The only precedents for the extant morality plays, all but one of which come from fifteenth century, are the Pater Noster Plays, which composed a part of the dramatic activity of several towns which produced cycles. A treatise defending translation of the Bible into English written by Wyclif or one of his disciples, probably in the early 1380's, mentions that the friars teach the Lord's Prayer in English, "as men seen in the play of York." Records show the existence of a Guild of the Lord's Prayer in York in 1389, and there are accounts of presentations of a play at various times in the fifteenth century. One record from 1399 speaks of a "Play of Sloth." Beverley also had such a play in 1469, and the fact that there were seven stations and eight pageants, one each for Pride, Lust, Sloth, Gluttony, Envy, Avarice, Wrath, and "Vicious," shows that its structure was based on the scheme of the seven deadly sins. Lincoln, too, had such a play, with performances in 1398, 1411, 1425, 1456, and 1521.

Nothing but the records are preserved of any of these Pater Noster Plays. But scholars, with the notable exception of Professor Craig, have seen in them the ancestor of the extant morality plays. The connection is in the medieval exegesis of the Lord's Prayer. It is commonly divided into seven petitions, in which St. Augustine had seen the seven-fold operation of the Holy Ghost. The mid-twelfth century Hugo of St. Victor, whose devotional writings achieved enormous popularity, pushed the interpretation further by seeing in the seven petitions the seven virtues opposed to the seven deadly sins. Dramatize this conception by having seven characters to represent the virtues, another seven for the vices; add a figure to represent mankind or his soul—this is a common understanding of "Vicious" in the Beverley play—and arrange some sort of contest in which the sins and virtues fight over mankind's soul, and you have a morality play. If you remember that vice is always more appealing in the theater than virtue (in the pulpit too, for that matter), you have a satisfactory explanation of the course in which the later morality play developed.

The earliest extant morality play is a fragment called, by its modern editors, *The Pride of Life*. Perhaps a better title would be *The King of Life*. The text is written in the blank spaces of a roll containing the accounts of the canons of Christ Church, Dublin, for the years 1333-46. The manuscript was written by two scribes who spoke different dialects. Brandl, an early editor, supposed that this text is the copy of a copy of the original, which he supposed, partly on the evidence of language and partly on that of place names, to have been written in the South of England before 1400.

The staging of the play is of the station-and-place variety, as is true of most extant moralities. The King of Life has a tent, which could apparently be opened or closed, and the Bishop has some sort of locale, possibly a platform. A messenger runs back and forth between the two places.

The play begins with a prologue, somewhat resembling the banns of the craft cycles. The speaker of the prologue asks the attention of the audience, suggests that all pray for good weather—the performance was outdoors—introduces the chief characters, announces the theme that Death spares no one, knight, nor Caesar, nor king, and summarizes the action.

A boasting speech by the King of Life* opens the action. He brags of his power and possessions, altogether in the manner of the Herods, Pilates, and Pharoahs of the cycles. Two retainers, Strength and Health, encourage him by promising to uphold his power and royalty against all challengers. The Queen of Life, however, is fearful. Let the King remember that all must die and therefore make his peace with God and the Church. The King scorns this advice. You are hoping that I will die, he jibes, so that you can get a new husband. The more the Queen urges the instability and treachery of the world, the more obdurate the King becomes.

The Queen sends the messenger, Solace, to get the Bishop, whose preaching, she hopes, may avail more than hers. The Bishop arrives and delivers a long sermon on the evils of the times: meed (i.e. graft) is a judge, oaths are false, love is become lechery, the rich are ruthless, and so on. This is apparently addressed primarily to the audience. Turning to the King, the Bishop reiterates the inevitability of death and recommends to the King deeds of charity, which will insure his eternal life.

The King will hear none of this. The Bishop is a babbler, let him go home and learn to preach better. So arrogant is the King in his pride that he sends Solace on a mission to proclaim his might from east to

* An exact translation of the speech tag of the manuscript, *rex vivus*, is "the living king," but the text itself several times calls him "king of life."

west and thus see whether Death dares enter the lists against him. Solace departs to cry these banns:

> I am sent for to inquire
> About, far and near
> <small>raise up</small>
> If any man dare war arear
> <small>warrior</small>
> Against such a bachelor.

The King of Life fears no one, even though he were King of Death, in all his hardiness. He will seethe heart's blood of any who strive against him.

At this point the play breaks off. From the prologue we can pretty well guess what came later. The King of Life and the King of Death fight, and the King of Life is overthrown. When the King of Life's body suffers, his soul awakens. Probably the play here used a well-known motif of the debate of the body and the soul, in which the soul accuses the body of having brought it to eternal damnation and the body replies that the soul did not exercise its duty of commanding the body and hence is justly punished. Then, if one is to believe the prologue, the Virgin Mary intervened and rescued the King of Life (or his soul) from hell. If this is what happened, *The Pride of Life* is unique among the moralities. Man is always saved, but not through the intercession of the Virgin.*

The Pride of Life, even in its fragmentary form, is a sufficient illustration of one of the great morality themes, the coming of Death, and of one of the types of morality, the partial. For like scriptural drama, the morality play can be either partial, as in a nativity play, or full-scope, as in the cycles. The most often played and best loved of the English moralities, *Everyman*, concentrates all its attention on the coming of Death. *The Castle of Perseverance*, on the other hand, takes its hero, Mankind, from birth to death and judgment. In so doing, it uses several other themes. The conflict between the powers of good and evil for Mankind's soul is dramatized in the promptings of the good and bad angels, in the seductions of various vices, and in the attack on the castle by the vices, whose charge is repelled by the virtues. Action, as in the cycles, is on three levels, a mundane one, where Mankind lives; an infernal one, concretized in the stage of Belial, and a celestial one, represented in the parliament of heaven, where the four daughters of God debate whether Mankind is to be saved or damned.

With no more than this summary one can see what is wrong with the

---

* Salvation through the intercession of the Virgin is common in another dramatic form, the Miracle of Our Lady, which, though popular in France and the low countries, is unrepresented in the extant corpus of English medieval drama.

definition of the morality play as one in which the action is performed by personified abstractions. The clue to its real nature is found in the fact that one of the cycles, Ludus, uses the same theme of the parliament of heaven. In Ludus Truth and Righteousness, Mercy and Peace debate what is to be done with the race of men; in the *Castle* they are concerned with only one individual, Mankind, who is no abstraction, but a dramatic individual capable of generalized application. The difference is the difference between the John Q. Public of the cartoonists in democratic lands and the "masses" of communist propagandists. Or it is the difference between the justification of the ways of God to men which Milton attempted in *Paradise Lost* and the one he attempted in *Samson Agonistes*.

Given the existence of the cycles, which showed the plan of salvation for the race, it was almost inevitable that some author would try to show the plan as it existed for the individual Christian. The specific form which the attempt took, the morality play, is explained by the literary materials which its authors used, certain religious obsessions of the late Middle Ages, and a psychological analysis of human conduct which had been developing for nearly two millenia.

The materials for such a dramatic form lay close at hand. The seven deadly sins probably had their origin in the seven planetary deities of Babylon. They appear in Christian literature before the end of the Classical period, in the *Psychomachia* ("battle over the soul") of the Christian Latin poet, Prudentius (d. *ca.* 405). Here the seven deadlies engage in epic battle with their opposite virtues, who rout the sins by pelting them with roses, the symbol of the passion. Well-known to the literate, the seven sins were introduced to all conditions of men by the preaching of the mendicants, who found in them a convenient scheme for the analysis of moral action.

The Dominican Peraldus systematized and popularized the sins in a *Summary of the Vices and Virtues* (before 1250), which was adapted in French by Friar Laurent, begot an enormous progeny, of which Chaucer's *Parsons Tale* is an example, and served a multitude of authors as a framework for narrative, as in Gower's *Confessio Amantis* ("confession of the lover"), or moral allegory, as in *Piers Plowmen*. Still another classification, which could be used in conjunction with the seven deadlies, was the "three enemies," the World, the Flesh, and the Devil, which seems to have been a favorite of the Cistercians.

The scholarly bishop of Lincoln, Robert Grosseteste, wrote in the mid-thirteenth century a *Castle of Love* in which the Virgin's body is symbolized by a castle, defended by four forts (the cardinal virtues of Prudence, Temperance, Fortitude, and Justice) and seven barbicans (the virtues). Grosseteste also used the theme of the Parliament of Heaven, in which Truth and Justice procure punishment for the King's errant thrall, Adam, but the King's son offers to ransom him. Originally written in French, the *Castle of Love* was translated three times before 1400, and there are several extant manuscripts. A large portion of it also got into the encyclopedic *Cursor Mundi*.

One of the great favorites of the thirteenth and fourteenth centuries was the French *Romance of the Rose*, begun by Guillaume de Lorris (d. *ca.* 1237) and completed in the 1270's in a totally different spirit by Jean de Meung (or Clopinel). It is perhaps the most influential literary work of the two centuries, translated, among others, by Chaucer, adapted, and raided by numerous authors all over western Europe. Its subject is love. A lover wishes to pluck a rose in a garden. Access to the garden, which is of course the lady's favor, is alternately invited and repelled by numerous personages, Fair Welcome, Danger, Largesse, Slander, Pity, and the like, who are obviously personifications of the moods of the lover and his lady, the attitudes of her family and friends, the conditions of courtship.

The allegory is erotic, of course, but it did not remain to modern psychoanalysts to discover the intimate connection between sexual love and religious zeal. Most of the medieval mystics knew it, witness such works as St. Bernard of Claivaux's sermons on the Song of Solomon, and any competent literary craftsmen could easily translate erotic allegory into moral or religious, or vice versa.

In the fourteenth century another French poet, De Guilleville, penned a *Pilgrimage of Human Life*, and another *Pilgrimage of the Soul*, which were read and admired beyond their poetic deserts. The indefatigable and prolix Lydgate translated these *Pilgrimages*, which represented the moral issues of life in linear terms as a journey from place to place, in the manner of *Pilgrim's Progress*. Nothing in de Guilleville's works seems to have passed over directly to the moralities, beyond possibly the plan of portraying allegorically the entire life of a representative man.

This, too, was something of the plan of *Piers Plowmen*, the latter part of which is the lives of three personages, Do-Well, Do-Better, and Do-Best, which represent three states of life, each more perfect than the last. The familiar morality themes of the seven deadlies, the attack on the castle, the coming of death (or more accurately Old Age, which amounts to the same thing) appear in *Piers*. In fact, whole sections of the later part, especially in the C-text, look as though they had been lifted bodily from a morality play—only chronology insists that it must have been the other way round.

So there was no dearth of material for the writers of the moralities to work on.

Social attitudes existed, too, and religious needs to which the moralities ministered. The latter part of the Middle Ages witnessed a turning of religious sensibility inward, away from institutional forms. The mendicant friars with their emphasis on preaching and confession were but one manifestation of this increasing interest in individual salvation. It produced quantities of devotional works in the vernacular and for the layman, and where in the fourteenth century the manuscript of such a work was likely to be owned by a church, monastery, or priory, in the fifteenth the owner was often a burgess or a knight—not the magnates of the land but commoner folk. Mystics flourished, and these were no longer as earlier always monks. Richard Rolle of Hampole (d. 1349) was never even in orders; Margery Kemp (d. after 1438) was a married woman.

Sometimes this new enthusiasm by the laity took perverted forms, flagellation, ecstatic dancing, nudism, though these are all continental phenomena. One of the commonest forms, and the most important for the morality play, was the cult of death, which might be either mild or severe and which was as prominent in England as on the continent. This had always been latent in Christianity with its catacombs, charnelhouses, and saints' relics, but it seems to have reached greater intensity in the fifteenth century. Traditional literary forms were the treatise on the "art of dying well," including detailed instructions and formulas for preparing for the inevitable hour; and "the four last things," a sounding of the meaning of death, judgment, heaven, and hell.

The plastic and graphic arts abound in realistic portrayals of the physical effects of death. Mortuary monuments show grinning skulls and fleshless cadavers, or half rotten bodies eaten by worms, as in the late Wakeman cenotaph in Tewkesbury Abbey. One favorite motif, often represented in art but apparently also sometimes dramatized, is the "dance of death," in which Death, a skeleton, plays his fiddle as Emperor and commoner move to his tune. Sometimes a preacher pictures forth the horrors of death as the skeleton summons, one after another, sometimes as many as forty figures representing all conditions of man- and woman-kind. The Dance of Death has often been connected with the morality play. It certainly grew out of the same social psychology.

Not only allegory itself but that variety of it which uses a cast of characters consisting of senses, moods, faculties of the intellect, social attitudes, and the like received tremendous support from the learning of the schools. In fact, it is hardly possible for such a form as the morality play to have arisen except after the intense philosophical inquiry into the cognitive process that characterizes thirteenth-century scholasticism. Starting with the Socratic command, "Know thyself," the Victorines, especially Richard of St. Victor (d. 1173), built up a system, expressed in allegorical structures, by which man could rise from sense cognition to spiritual contemplation. The Story of Jacob, his wives, concubines, and children served Richard's purpose well. Leah is the active life, Rachel

THE DRAMA OF MEDIEVAL ENGLAND

the contemplative. The various intermediate states between sense knowledge and the contemplation of the divine are the children, ending with Benjamin, the highest state of contemplation.

The philosophers then took over the problem and the great debate over universals raged, especially at the University of Paris. What is the reality of Truth? Is Truth the reality, from which a particular true proposition derives its being? The realists, beginning with Anselm, so affirmed. Or is the particular true proposition the basis of the reality of Truth? Those who held such a view were the conceptualists, of whom St. Thomas Aquinas was the greatest. Or, finally, is the only reality of Truth its existence as a word, a controlled emission of breath? Nominalists such as Rocellinus and, in part, William Ockham, saw it that way. This debate over universals occupied the energy of the keenest minds in Western Christendom for over a century.

No party won final victory, but the world was enriched by a searching analysis of the nature of knowledge and the nature of action, with their interactions. Such an analysis necessarily multiplied terms like "common sense," "active intellect," "will," "appetite," all designed to describe and delimit the phenomena of such commonplace actions as a person eating an egg. How does he know it is an egg which he eats? And why does he choose an egg instead of a bit of beef? Because it is Friday, when flesh is forbidden? If so, is it the knowledge that the day is Friday or the will to keep a commandment of the Church dominant?

There is essentially nothing esoteric about this philosophical analysis. It produced a great quantity of abstract, or more exactly "conceptual" terms. But so did Freud's analysis of human personality. I have never been able to see that "appetite" is any more "metaphysical" than "the id." In fact, the two concepts are remarkably similar, and so are "reason" and "superego."

So scholastic philosophy furnished the dramatists of the morality plays a method of analyzing and portraying moral behavior, precisely the sort of service Freud has performed for modern novelists. The morality play is a popular and sometimes naive presentation of certain parts of scholastic philosophy. Its position on universals is that of the realists. In the *Castle of Perseverance* the cast of characters is mostly universals: Mankind, Humility, Pride. The title of still another morality, *Mind, Will, and Understanding* (also called *Wisdom*) sufficiently suggests its dependence on scholastic psychology. The morality play also adopts the voluntaristic position, which frequently accompanies the realistic one. It emphasizes, along with St. Bonaventure and the Franciscan school, the centrality of the will, instead of the intellect, as Aquinas had preferred.

The one complete morality play in English, which combines nearly all the typical themes and in which the attitudes and dramatic purposes of the uncorrupted morality can be seen, is the *Castle of Perseverance*. Coming to us in a sort of manuscript anthology of moralities called the *Macro Plays* from an early owner, it is usually dated about 1425. One scholar, Smart, would prefer a date twenty years earlier. Its dialect is that of Norfolk or Lincolnshire, and an allusion to the "gallows of Canwick" and several similarities to Ludus suggest the area about Lincoln as its probable home. It is a long play, over thirty-six hundred lines, with a cast of thirty-six players, according to the manuscript, though one, Vainglory, has no speaking part in the play as we have it.

A special interest of the play is its staging, which is indicated by a plat in the manuscript itself. In the center stood the castle, no doubt a small and flimsy structure. The place is surrounded by a ditch or moat, if possible, filled with water, or by some sort of barrier. A recent student, Richard Southern, believes that the ditch was to restrict the view of the play to those who paid admission. The excavated earth, he believes, was piled inside the circle and served as sitting room for some of the spectators, in the manner of a small stadium. On all sides of the castle is the "place," the open area in which most of the action occurs. Five scaffolds are furnished for the ranking personages of the piece. In addition, specific directions are given for Belial's appearance in the assault on the castle and for the costuming of the Four Daughters of God.

The *Castle of Perseverance* begins, like Ludus, with a prologue by two vexillatores (banner bearers), who sketch the action and, again as in Ludus, promise a performance "on the green" at undern (nine a.m.) "this day sevennight."* The action begins with the World, Belial (or the Devil), and the Flesh each boasting of his power and promising to entice Mankind to his destruction.

Next we see Mankind, newly born, naked, and helpless. A Good Angel and a Bad Angel have been assigned him. He prays for grace to follow Good Angel, who then exhorts him to serve Jesus. Bad Angel advises him to serve rather World and thereby get rich. The two angels then debate. To Good Angel's plea that Mankind always remember his end, Bad Angel retorts that there will be time enough for that when he is sixty. Mankind decides to follow Bad Angel.

The scene then shifts to the platform of World, who brags of his power to make his followers kings and to give precious goods. Enter Mankind led by Bad Angel, who presents him to World's courtiers, Pleasure, Folly, and Vainglory. Backbiter, World's courier, promises to turn Mankind over to the seven deadly sins, and World gives him "seisin" of all the world, sea and sound, park and palace, lawn and land. Good Angel predicts ruin for Mankind, but his concern goes unheeded by the victim.

* A matinee in the original sense of the word!

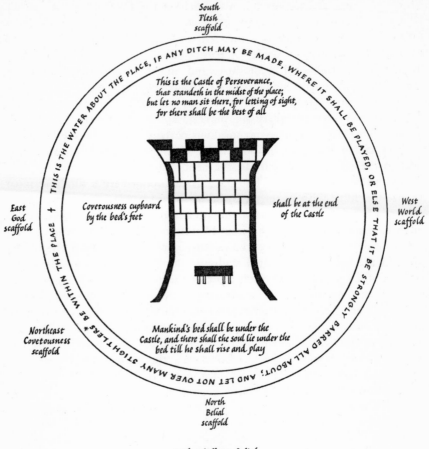

South
Flesh
scaffold

THIS IS THE WATER ABOUT THE PLACE, IF ANY DITCH MAY BE MADE, WHERE IT SHALL BE PLAYED, OR ELSE THAT IT BE STRONGLY BARRED ALL ABOUT; AND LET NOT OVER MANY STIGHTLERS* BE WITHIN THE PLACE +

This is the Castle of Perseverance,
that standeth in the midst of the place;
but let no man sit there, for letting of sight,
for there shall be the best of all

East
God
scaffold

Covetousness cupboard
by the bed's feet

shall be at the end
of the Castle

West
World
scaffold

Northeast
Covetousness
scaffold

Mankind's bed shall be under the
Castle, and there shall the soul lie under the
bed till he shall rise and play

North
Belial
scaffold

He that shall play Belial,
look that he have gun-powder
burning in pipes in his hands
and in his ears, and in his arse,
when he goeth to battle

The iiij daughters shall be clad in mantles,
Mercy in white, Righteousness in red altogether, Truth in sad green, and Peace in black;
and they shall play in the place all together till they bring up the soul.

Backbiter puts Mankind in the care of Covetousness, who promises
him great wealth if he will give himself over to extortion, symony and
jury bribing, pay no wages to his servants or tithes to the church, give
no alms, and buy and sell by false weight. When Mankind accepts these
conditions, Covetousness introduces him to the six other deadly sins.

* "Stightlers" seem to correspond to ushers; their main function was apparently to
keep order, perhaps also to collect admission fees.

Three of these, Pride, Wrath, and Envy are servants to Belial, three, Gluttony, Lechery, and Sloth, to Flesh. Covetousness himself is a follower of World. Each of the Deadlies gives Mankind a piece of advice, Pride that he wear only the newest fashions of clothes, Wrath that he spill blood, Lust to go to bed with her, Sloth to sleep through mass.

Good Angel again mourns Mankind's unhappy condition and gets Shrift to help save him. Shrift at first has little success. Mankind is in no hurry; he can wait until Good Friday for confession. However, when Shrift calls on Penitence, Mankind becomes more pliable. Penitence is able to induce sorrow in Mankind's heart and Shrift then hears his confession and absolves him. Mankind asks protection against the further attacks of the seven deadlies and their masters.

So Shrift and Penitence lead Mankind into the Castle, where he will be safe. A missing leaf robs us of the scene of his reception. At the end of the hiatus Charity is exhorting him. Abstinence, Chastity, Industry, Generosity, and Meekness follow. These are the Seven Virtues opposite the Seven Deadlies.* They were apparently represented as women in the play, as they usually are in literature and the plastic arts.

But of course the Three Enemies and the Seven Deadlies do not give up easily. Bad Angel has seen Mankind's entrance into the castle and at once dispatches Flibbertigibbit, a devil, and Backbiter, to inform World, Belial, and Flesh. Each of these abuses and punishes his subordinates who have lost Mankind. These promise to recapture Mankind, Covetousness being especially confident.

The Three Enemies with their followers then attack the castle. Bad Angel urges them on, while Mankind prays and Good Angel summons the Seven Virtues to the defense. The battle is a series of boasts by the Deadlies, followed by rebuttals by the Virtues, followed by single combat. The Virtues probably use roses as weapons, and one by one the Deadlies cry out in pain and run from the battle. Only Covetousness remains, and he uses guile instead of force. Instead of attacking his opposite, Generosity, he asks Mankind for a parlay, which, despite Generosity's strenuous objections, Mankind grants.

Once Covetousness gets Mankind talking, the game is won. Mankind complains that he waxes hoar and cold, his back begins to bow and bend. Covetousness has the remedy: marks and pounds, lands and people, houses and homes. Wealth is the cure for the ills of age. Mankind protests that he doesn't want to leave his friends, the Virtues, but Covetousness overcomes his objections. The Good Angel cannot keep Mankind from leaving the Castle and joining Covetousness.

* Patience, the opposite of Wrath, is missing in this scene, but appears later.

All the Virtues mourn Mankind's defection, but, as Meekness points out, he has free will and no one can blame them for his use of it. Good Angel grieves that Mankind puts his faith in "Pennyman," and World rejoices. Covetousness gives Mankind a thousand marks, warning him not to lend it or give it in alms to the poor. Mankind will bury it and see a neighbor hang before he parts with any of it.

Mankind's new defection is promptly followed by the entrance of Death with his boy. All dread him, Death says. He was well known in the great pestilence, but some now forget him. He will abase the proud. Mankind will learn a new lesson. Mankind cries out for help when he sees his grisly summoner. First he appeals to World, who says he is powerless against death and predicts that Mankind will suffer for his outrages. World then calls his servant to turn Mankind out of his hall and seize his property. Mankind cannot even leave his goods to his wife and children. They will all go to a stranger called "I wot never who." In his agony Mankind exhorts all men to be warned by his example, and he prays to God for grace, else Hell will certainly be his portion. Then he dies.

But the play is not over—in fact this is the part for which all the rest is preparation. For as he dies, from beneath the bed comes Soul. Immediately he begins to reproach the body: "Thou didst brew a bitter bale." Now Soul will have to suffer for it. Another missing leaf probably contained the body's reply, which in many versions of the debate of the body and the soul is that it was the soul's duty to control the body. This is missing. What follows is instead a debate between Good Angel and Bad Angel—hardly a debate, however, since Good Angel knows no defense for Mankind. He has sold himself to Covetousness and must pay the penalty, unless Mercy succors him. Soul appeals to Mercy, and Bad Angel carries him off to Hell, gleefully describing the pains he must there endure.

But Mankind has appealed to Mercy, and his appeal must be heard. Mercy therefore summons her sisters, Truth, Justice (or Righteousness), and Peace. These are the four daughters of God and their deliberation is the Parliament of Heaven, which we have seen before in Ludus. Mercy and Peace plead for Mankind, adducing the sufferings of Christ on the cross; Truth and Justice oppose this contention: let every man bear his own guilt. Peace suggests that they appeal to the Judgment of God the Father, and they go to his platform.

Here Truth and Justice repeat their indictment of Mankind, Mercy and Peace eloquently offering the sufferings of Christ as reparation for Mankind's sins. The Father "sitting on his throne" renders his judgment for Mercy and Peace: "My mercy, Mankind, give I thee / Come sit at my right hand." The Father then reviews the "Great Judgment" which is to come when king and kaiser, knight and champion, pope and patriarch will render account for their lives. He will ask all whether they have fed the hungry, given drink to the thirsty, clothed the naked. Let all take warning and "think on your last ending." The rubric calls for a "Te Deum" to end the play.

The *Castle of Perseverance* is an extraordinarily even piece. The author seems always in control of his medium and his material, and the unity of mood and tone seems a matter of choice. Partly this is an effect of the versification which, though never brilliant, is always competent. A thirteen-line stanza, somewhat similar in organization to that of the Towneley Master though radically different in effect, is the dominant form, supplemented by a few quatrains, nine-line stanzas, and eight-line stanzas of two foot lines, similar to those found in one scene of Ludus. Alliteration is extremely frequent, but never structural.

The dramatic possibilities of these stanzaic forms are not exploited as in Towneley and York. The author has an annoying habit of making each speech two stanzas long, when one would often suffice. He never divides a stanza between two or more speakers, as the Master so often does. Thus rapid dialogue is not to be found in the *Castle*. One can excuse the author, however. He was writing about 1425, or even earlier, and thus his work is before the present form of both Towneley and York (before those of Chester and Ludus, too, for that matter). Perhaps his technique is somewhat primitive.

But it is also possible that he does not desire the effects which the more advanced technique of dialogue produce. Certainly they would destroy the somber, almost funereal, evenness of his play. The moral and doctrinal points would not be made so clearly, and the essential message might be blunted. Perhaps for the same reason he eschews humor. One of his characters, Backbiter, World's messenger, could easily have been developed as a comic. His antecedent, Solace, in *Pride of Life* is a merry fellow, and many of the messengers of the cycles are similarly characterized. Certainly such a possibility must have been within the dramatic experience of the author, and he almost as certainly avoided it.

One must not imagine that he is without resources. He has a great deal of understanding of dramatic structure. For instance, the appearances of Good Angel and Bad Angel are carefully spotted to give a continuity to the story and to compose a motif throughout. The description of Belial as he goes to the assault on the castle shows that spectacular effects are not alien to him, and the specification of the colors of the garments worn by the Four Daughters shows that he understood symbolic costuming.

In fact, even a careful reading of the play hardly does it justice. It must be reconstructed by a knowledge of the immense treasure of symbolism which pictorial art had developed for the virtues and the vices. And we must not miss the pageantry and color of the processions from scaffold to scaffold.

Critics have occasionally found the allegory confused in places. Sir E. K. Chambers, for instance, finds it hard to distinguish between Lust (Voluptas) and Lust (Luxuria). But this may as easily be subtlety as confusion. As they appear in the play Voluptas, which I render "pleasure" rather than "lust," appears to be the attitude of mind that sees the world as a place to have as much fun as one can, whereas Luxuria, properly translated as "lust," is confined to sexual indulgence. And so Voluptas, Pleasure, appears first, is a servant to World, and with Folly sets up the temptation of Mankind by the specific sins, Lust among them.

Another example of acute analysis appears in the handling of Mankind's repentance. Good Angel, disturbed by Mankind's waywardness, calls on Shrift. Confession is the way back to grace for the Christian who has lost it. But Shrift has no success. Mankind tells him that Good Friday is soon enough for confession. Shrift then calls in Penitentia, which must surely represent not the sacrament of penance, but the state of mind, penitence. Penitence is able to induce a feeling of remorse in Mankind, who then is ready for the ministrations of Shrift. The point the author is making is that Mankind is no heathen, but a nominal Christian, who makes his Easter duty (hence the reference to confession on Good Friday), but whose heart is given over to the world nevertheless. Shrift is to him merely a mechanical process, and that is not good enough for real moral regeneration. Shrift is impotent until penitence, real sorrow for one's sins, does its work. Then Mankind enters the Castle.

The author has made an interesting change in the usual pattern of the seven deadlies which also tells us something about his attitude towards his times. This is the dominance of Covetousness in the whole play. Ordinarily, Covetousness is only one of the seven. If any one is given preeminence, it is Pride. Yet in the *Castle* Covetousness plays a role certainly equal to Belial and Flesh. He has a platform to himself, alone among the sins. It is, of course, widely recognized that Covetousness is the old man's sin, and there is nothing strange that, when Mankind is old, he should yield to Covetousness even after he has repelled the attacks of the other six. But in this play Covetousness is equally prominent in Mankind's youth. Clearly the author is saying that Covetousness is the sin of the age—and many moralists and satirists agreed with him.

The Castle of Perseverance is the only full-scope, cradle-to-grave morality in English. There are remnants of what may have been another in the degenerate *Mankind*, which precedes *The Castle* in the Macro manuscript. As it has come down to us, only a few of the structural elements of the morality remain, these overlaid with low comedy, dance and vulgar song. In its present state the piece is probably to be dated from a reference to a King Edward, who must be Edward IV, which would have little point until Edward's final consolidation of his power in the 1470's. One scene in the play has several references to persons and places: Master Huntington of Sanston, William Thurlay of Hanston, Pichard of Trumpington, and the like. Those places which have been positively identified all come from either the area about Cambridge or that about King's Lynn. Scholars have therefore concluded that the form of *Mankind* we have was played by a touring company of professionals who made a circuit in Cambridgeshire and another in northwestern Norfolk, or perhaps the two areas are the termini of a continuous circuit.

It is impossible and useless to summarize the action of *Mankind*, but a quick review of the underlying morality plot establishes the genre of the piece. Mercy, a man, opens with the usual speech of pious exhortation. Mischief and his followers, New Guise, Now-a-days, and Nought, try to interrupt, but Mercy gets rid of them before Mankind, apparently newly born, enters and asks Mercy for guidance. Mercy gives him a great deal of good advice, especially warning him against the vices New Guise, Now-a-days, and Nought and the devil Titivillus.*

Mercy then leaves Mankind to spade up his fields and sow his corn. Immediately the vices beset him and he drives them off with his spade. They complain to Mischief of the blows they have received. Mischief summons the aid of Titivillus, who has a net to ensnare Mankind and can go invisible. Titivillus then puts a board in the ground where Mankind is digging. Mankind finds the labor so frustrating and the prospects of a good crop so slight that he gets discouraged. When Titivillus makes him dream that Mercy has been hanged for horse theft, Mankind gives up and joins Mischief and his company. As Mischief asks him to swear that he will seduce all good wives of the country when their husbands are away, will rob, steal, and kill, will go to the ale house instead of to matins and mass, Mankind each time replies, "I will, sir."

Mercy, who has not been hanged at all, learns what has happened and mourns Mankind's inconstancy. He prays to Mary to pity the fickle creature and aid Mercy to rescue him. Mischief brings Mankind to Mercy, apparently to gloat over his conquest. Mankind perceives his folly, but, despairing, calls for a rope. Mercy scares off Mischief and his henchmen, who are eager to help Mankind hang himself. Eventually Mercy talks Mankind out of his despair. The piece ends rather ambigu-

---

* Here a rather different character from the Tutivillus of the Towneley *Judgment*.

ously. Mercy has a long speech on avoiding the temptations of the World, the Devil, and the Flesh, and apparently Mankind is saved.

From this outline it is easy to see that *Mankind* was originally a serious morality, probably a cradle-to-grave one—the cradle part is still there, but the grave has disappeared. Even so, the remnant contains much interesting material. The plot apparently differed signally from that of the *Castle*, where Mankind falls into sin early, and without considerable motivation, is rescued, and then falls again. In *Mankind* the sequence is more natural: Mankind tries to live virtuously until overcome by the frustrations and disappointments of life.

The emphasis on labor in *Mankind* is notable. Mankind immediately embraces a life of productive work, digging in his field. As long as he sticks to his business, he is safe from temptation. Only when Titivillus is able to frustrate Mankind's industry by putting the board in the ground, does he weaken. Then he loses confidence in Mercy and falls into sin. Titivillus' methods—putting a board in the ground and sending a dream that Mercy has been hanged for horse stealing—may seem trivial to us, but the truth symbolized is none the less apparent. If these two instances are representative of the original *Mankind*, it may well have had some of the earthy pungency of *Piers Plowman*, whose finest effects are created by just such homely details.

But *Mankind* passed under corrupting masters. A company of strolling players took it up and, keeping only a part of the morality plot and hardly any of the seriousness of tone, built up the entertainment value and dropped most of the edification. They made Mercy a sort of straightman, whose pompous "English Latin" got cheap laughs when burlesqued by Mischief and his followers. They added dance and music which are quite extraneous to the action. They made the piece into a sort of mummer's play suitable for the Christmas season, when scatalogical songs (*Mankind* has about as bad a sample as has ever been written down) seem to have been customary. Most of all, they seized every chance for irrelevant low comedy, so that the tone of the piece is now that of the burlesque theater or the lower sort of music hall.

The reason for all this change is clear. This was a professional company, making a living (probably scant) from the pennies and groats of rustic audiences. To them the high point of the play was the entrance of Titivillus. From off stage he roars "I come with my legs under me." Then the play stops and New Guise, Now-a-days, and Nought take up a collection. The audience will have to pay to see Titivillus' "abominable presence." Now-a-days announces that Titivillus "loveth no groats, or pence or twopence," but rather "red royals."* However, New Guise corrects him, any who cannot pay the one may pay "tother."

* A gold coin worth 10 shillings, first coined in 1465.

The company was a small one, probably only six, for the script calls for seven parts, of which two, Mischief and Titivillus, can be doubled. The manuscript does not indicate any scenic effects, and none are demanded by the action. Props are of the simplest, a spade, a board, a net for Titivillus, and they could easily be carried by the company, or even borrowed on the spot. In one scene Mischief asks the hostler for a football, which may be evidence that the play was performed in an inn yard. "The good man of this house," with whom New Guise begins the collection must then have been Mine Host.

All of this is of utmost importance to the historian of the theater, but the price we have paid for the information may well have been the loss of a play as fine or finer than *The Castle of Perseverance*.

Immediately following *Mankind* in the Macro manuscript is another moral play, more than half of which is also found in another manuscript anthology of fifteenth-century dramatic pieces, the Digby collection. Untitled in either manuscript, it has been called *Wisdom* by some scholars, *Mind, Will and Understanding* by others. It contains no certain allusions by which it can be dated; most guesses are the period around 1460. Some allusions to London legal practices ("the Holborn Quest") have led Professor Craig to argue for a London home for the piece. Others prefer East Anglia.

As a dramatic work it is unique among the moral plays of the fifteenth century. Combining the seriousness, though not the scope of the *Castle of Perseverance* with some of the entertainment value of *Mankind*, it differs from both in the thoroughness and erudition of its analysis of human personality, the bones of which are provided by scholastic psychology and the flesh by contemporary social conditions. Its author was considerably more learned than those of comparable pieces, or at least he used more of his learning. This circumstance has led some to speculate that *Wisdom* was not aimed at a general audience but at a special one, probably well educated. It may therefore be a fifteenth-century predecessor of a genre common in the next century, the school play written for and performed by the students of a public school, a college, or an inn of court. In the fifteenth century such a play might be performed in a monastery, a convent of friars, a cathedral school, or possibly in one of the Oxford or Cambridge colleges.

Though this is unproved and unprovable speculation, it does explain some of the unique features of *Wisdom*, the heavy use of scholastic psychology for one. The play opens with the usual self introduction of Wisdom, a character who combines the intellectual abstraction with its realization in the Flesh, Christ. Next we see Soul, who desires Wisdom as its lover. Wisdom then enunciates one of the fundamental principles of medieval mysticism, that self knowledge (meaning the knowledge of

157

the nature and operation of the human soul) leads to the knowledge of God. The twelfth-century Victorines had proclaimed this doctrine, and it was popularized by such fourteenth-century English mystics as Rolle of Hampole and Walter Hilton.

In the ensuing dialogue Soul asks and Wisdom answers questions about the soul. It has two parts, the rational and the sensual, and these two parts are symbolized by the white dress and the black mantle worn by Soul. The sensual part of the soul is ministered to by the five wits, represented by five virgins dressed in white. The soul has three "mights" or powers: mind, will and understanding, which then become the chief personages of the rest of the play. This trinity of powers corresponds to the trinity of persons in the Godhead and to the three theological virtues, faith, hope, and charity.

Against this intellectual background, we must view the action of the play. Lucifer appears, first in his proper form to explain his office and his intent to seduce Mind, Will, and Understanding. Then he changes to the guise of a "gallant." His temptation is extremely shrewd. His first approach is to Mind, and it is not understandable except as a dramatization of the debate over the active and the contemplative states of life. Lucifer does not make the mistake of urging complete abandonment to the world. Instead, he urges a sort of compromise between the active and the contemplative states, the "mixed" state in which one uses the spiritual strength gained by contemplation to assume leadership in the world. This position was espoused by St. Bonaventure and indeed is part of the ideal of the mendicant friars. It also appears in *Piers Plowman*, where Do Best, the mixed life, represents a higher state than Do Well, the active life, or Do Bet, the contemplative.

But, of course, Lucifer perverts the argument for the mixed life into an appeal for the total acceptance of the world. In the intellectual approach characteristic of the play, this becomes an exhortation to Mind to let the five wits spread abroad, in other words, to be guided solely by the senses. He follows this up by urging Will to do what he wants instead of deferring to Reason.

The results are what Lucifer desires. Each of the powers gives himself over to the world. Mind espouses "maintenance," the peculiarly late-medieval vice of using violence and coercion to gain one's ends. Will becomes a lecher, and Understanding a perverter of the law. These decisions are dramatized in a sort of ballet, in which Mind in the character of Maintenance leads Indignation, Sturdiness,* Malice, Hastiness, Vengeance, and Discord in a dance. Understanding as Perjury leads a "Holborn Quest" of six jurors, Wrong, Slight, Doubleness, Falseness, Ravine, and Deceit. Will has become Lust and his dancers are all women, Recklessness, Idleness,

* "Being tough" would perhaps be an adequate modern translation of this word.

158

Surfeit, Greediness, Spouse-breach or Adultery, and "gentle" Fornication. Obviously what the author intends is three groups with seven sins in each, a sort of trinity of seven deadlies.

At this point in the play the dramatic structure almost disintegrates. The author is not able to put his scheme to work as a plan of dramatic action. He has stated it, and can do little more. Instead of symbolic action, such as the attack on the Castle, he can only rely on talk. Mind, Will, and Understanding say that they will go to their places of business, Understanding to the law courts at Westminster, Mind to the Parvise of St. Paul's, Will to the stews. Will proposes a dinner to cost three nobles (one pound); Understanding is willing to spend only nine shillings. Will is laying plans to seduce his "cousin" Jenet, whose husband is a churl, and Understanding offers to assist by terrorizing the husband out of his jealousy, while Mind offers to get him imprisoned.

The fundamental plot of *Wisdom* is the same as that of *Mankind:* temptation and sin followed by repentance and salvation. So at this point Wisdom intervenes, rebukes Mind, Will, and Understanding, and displays to them Soul, now foully disfigured. Six small boys "in the likeness of devils" run out from under Soul's mantle and then run back again. Mind, Will, and Understanding acknowledge their sins and seek forgiveness, Soul asks for mercy, and the devils scamper off. Wisdom urges true contrition and Soul, Mind, Will, and Understanding leave to go to confession, Soul singing a mournful verse from Lamentations "as it is sung in passion week." The time required for the confession is filled by a lecture by Wisdom on the "nine points" most pleasing to God. Soul and the three Powers reenter in their original costumes (the restoration of the soul to grace through confession) and the four of them take turns with Wisdom in expounding the moral and doctrinal meaning of the events just represented.

Besides the elaborate allegory, *Wisdom* has other interesting features. Its versification is, for the mid-fifteenth century, more than competent. The author has frequently divided verses among speakers, in some places six changes of speaker in eight lines, so that the dialogue has, in the scenes of sinful life, considerable rapidity. The indictment of maintenance and perversion of the law has a topical pertinence, for we know from records that these vices were rampant. To audiences of the time the speeches of Mind and Understanding in their roles of Maintenance and Perjury probably had a sharpness which we miss.

Nevertheless, one can hardly call the play a success. The psychological allegory is hardly realized in dramatic form, and the mystical experience which the play tries to portray never becomes clear. Probably the author wanted skill in theatrical composition. Anyway, drama hardly seems the proper vehicle for the development of such purely conceptual entities.

Perhaps the best comment is that of Lenin, who, after witnessing an attempt to put Marxist economics on the stage, remarked that he could do it better in a pamphlet. But these criticisms are perhaps beside the point if the piece was intended for the lecture hall rather than for the theater.

The morality play best known and most widely performed in modern times is *Everyman*. In the last seventy years it has been produced professionally many times, sometimes on extensive tours, and its amateur productions by school and church groups must number in the tens of thousands. Required reading in most school and university syllabi, it is certainly the most widely known piece of early drama, regarded by many as typical of the achievements of English drama before the Elizabethan era.

Yet *Everyman* is decidedly atypical. For over half a century scholars have been debating whether it was of English origin or was a translation of a Dutch work called *Elckerlijk*. One is certainly a translation of the other. The question of priority has probably been decided by Professor De Vocht, who amasses a great quantity of evidence to show that, whereas the Dutch is frequently confused, inaccurate, or meaningless, the English is always clear. On the principle that unskillful translation is likely to produce just the features we find in the Dutch version, he argues that the English must be the original.

There is no proof that *Everyman* was ever performed as a stage play before the nineteenth century. The play is known to us in four undated early printings, two of them only fragments. The title of a somewhat later printing calls it a "treatise . . . in the manner of a moral play," as though the publisher did not think of the work as a stage play at all. Moreover, indications of staging, costuming, and action, so noticeable in the late fifteenth-century theatrical works, are totally absent from *Everyman*.

Nevertheless, it is eminently stage-worthy—it has triumphantly survived the severest test of all, amateur production—and if it ever was actually staged, it must have been highly moving. Totally lacking in the spectacular quality of most English works contemporary to it, its effectiveness lies, like that of the *Castle of Perseverance*, in its high serious tone, unmarred by comic interlude, meretricious amusement, or extraneous sensationalism. In essence its plot is the simplest of the morality plots, the coming of Death, expressed even more tersely than in the *Pride of Life*.

At God's command, Death comes to summon Everyman, who finds himself deserted by all on whom he has depended, by Fellowship, by Kindred, and by Goods. Only Good Deeds is willing to accompany him on the great journey, but Good Deeds is too weak to rise off the ground. Good Deeds, however, has a sister, Knowledge, who will "go with thee and be thy guide / In thy most need to go by thy side." Knowledge leads Everyman to Confession, who gives him a scourge to mortify his flesh. When Everyman scourges himself, Good Deeds gains strength and rises up to accompany him. Discretion, Strength, Beauty, and Five Wits join the company. Everyman makes his will, leaving half his fortune to charity and the other half in "bequest" apparently to satisfy his just debts and perhaps to repay those whom he has defrauded. Discretion advises Everyman to receive the last sacraments. So prepared, Everyman and his company set out. As they near their destination, the grave, one by one Discretion, Strength, Beauty, and Five Wits leave Everyman. Knowledge is the last to go, and Everyman takes only Good Deeds with him into the grave. An Angel announces Everyman's salvation and in the epilogue Doctor points the moral:

> He that hath his account whole and sound
> High in heaven he shall be crowned.

Everyman is unique in at least two respects. It is the only morality in English that uses the pilgrimage motif, so common in non-dramatic moral literature of the later Middle Ages. The whole action is conceived as a journey. God commands Death that he show Everyman that "a pilgrimage he must on him take," and Death sees Everyman first "walking." Everyman later weeps that he has "no manner company / To help me in my journey." It is for company on a journey that he begs Fellowship, Kindred, and Goods. Good Deeds cannot walk until after Everyman has confessed. Knowledge promises to be his guide. The final journey is to the grave, and Strength, Discretion, and Beauty turn off before the end of the road. Even Knowledge's farewell is the kind one gives a friend at the railway depot. There can be no doubt that the author conceives his work as an account of a journey or pilgrimage. This, rather than the dance of death advocated by many critics, is the basic structure of the play.

Even more unusual is the moral theology of *Everyman*. The emphasis is nearly all on "good deeds," what the theologian would call "works," instead of on mercy, or grace. This fact emerges in a comparison between *Everyman* and *The Castle* or even the degenerate *Mankind*, where Mercy has to rescue mankind from the results of his folly. Wisdom, that is Christ, performs this function in *Wisdom*. Sir E. K. Chambers noted this peculiarity and tentatively explained it as due to "a Protestant temper rather than a Catholic one." This is uncharacteristically wide of the mark. No variety of Christianity holds that man can do anything of his own motion; he is born in original sin, and only grace can rescue him. Protestant Christianity has usually emphasized grace even more than Catholic.

An explanation is to be found in the ultimate source of *Everyman*, which turns out not to be Christian at all. It has long been recognized that *Everyman* derives from one of the "apologues" in *Barlaam and Joasaphat*, an eighth-century work in Greek, usually ascribed to St. John Damascene.

The main story of *Barlaam and Joasaphat* is a Christianized version of the life of Buddha. This is well known, but until lately the origin of the apologues was unknown though presumed to be "eastern."

Lately a Japanese scholar, Professor Genji Takahashi, has provided the authentic original source for the plot of *Everyman*. It is a collection of parables ascribed to Buddha, the Miscellaneous Agama, No. 101. In the Buddhist version a man has four wives, three favored ones, the fourth an unloved drudge. The Messenger of Death summons him to a journey and he asks the three wives to accompany him. All refuse, but the fourth will go with him to the very end, "whether it be death or life, pain or joy." Buddha then explains that the wives are man's body, his wealth, his kindred and friends, and, the fourth, his intention. This last alone goes with him to the end. And the spiritual exegesis is in terms of Karma and Nirvana. In a theology which emphasizes reincarnation, this parable makes sense. A man cannot take wealth or beauty into the next life with him, but his deeds, which in a moral system are always really his intentions, are what determine whether he will be reborn into a higher or lower stage of existence.

In spite of a thorough attempt to Christianize the story, *Everyman* still strikes perceptive scholars as being out of line with other moralities. The Christian coloring does not hide the essential purpose of the parable as Buddha or one of his followers originally told it. This explanation will doubtless come as a shock to all the church dramatic societies which have performed the piece almost as a work meritorious unto salvation. But the phenomenon has happened often in the history of literature. No amount of Christian reinterpretation can disguise the fact that Shakespeare's *Hamlet* depends fundamentally on the heathen Germanic duty of the blood feud.

Chapter X.   ROMANTIC DRAMA: SAINTS' PLAYS AND MIRACLES

EXTRAORDINARILY FEW SAMPLES of the popular saints' play remain, only two in fact. Perhaps one should add to *The Conversion of St. Paul* and *Mary Magdalen*, both found in the Digby collection, the several plays on St. Anne and the early life of the Virgin which have been assimilated into Ludus, and also the assumption plays of both Ludus and York, all of which are essentially saints' plays.

But even this larger number is an inadequate representation of what once existed. There are accounts of saints' plays from Basingbourne, Bethersden (Kent), Braintree (Essex), Canterbury, Coventry, Hereford, Lincoln, London, and Shrewsbury. The elaborate Creed Play of York may have been such. The saints celebrated in these recorded plays are a varied lot. Women seem especially favored: St. Catherine, St. Clara, St. Christina, SS Feliciana and Sabina, St. Margaret, and St. Susan (which may be Susanna and the Elders from one of the apocryphal sections of Daniel). Saints George, Thomas à Becket (at Canterbury as we should expect), Andrew, Swithin, Lawrence, and Placidus all had one or more plays devoted to them. The Cornish had a play about one of their favorites, St. Meriasek, still extant in the ancient Cornish tongue. The Aberdeen Corpus Christi procession had pageants, which may or may not have been plays, about Saints Bestian, Lawrence, Stewin, Martin, Nicholas, John (which one is not stated), and George.

Of the two saints' plays contained in the Digby collection, one, *The Conversion of St. Paul*, is entirely based on Scripture, the other, *Magdalen*, partially so. *The Conversion* also has liturgical precedent. It is, however, rather improbable that the liturgical play which we have is the exact source of the Digby piece, though the two are remarkably similar in content. Of the scriptural scenes of *Magdalen*, the raising of Lazarus has forerunners both in the liturgical and in the vernacular cycles, and the visitation of the sepulchre carries us back to the very origin of medieval drama. These scenes, however, are only a small part of the total play.

Both plays are of the late fifteenth century. They were probably not written more than twenty years before the date given by the scribe for the manuscript, 1512. Both seem to belong to the East Midland area. About the conditions of their performance, whether by some town guild, either religious or occupational, or by some semi-professional company, we know nothing, nor do we have any firm ground for speculation.

The Conversion of St. Paul follows the scriptural story rather closely. After a prologue by "Poeta," Saul, dressed as an "adventurous knight,"*

---

* I.e., a knight errant prepared for a mission.

introduces himself as a foe of the Christians. He asks and receives letters from the "bishops," Annas and Caiaphas, and departs with two knights for Damascus. Follows an unconnected passage of low comedy between a servant and a stable boy. In the next scene Saul on the road to Damascus sees a vision and hears the voice of Christ, "Why dost thou me pursue?" Struck blind, he is led to the city by the knights.

God then appears in a vision to Ananias and commands him to meet Saul in "the street called Straight." His fears calmed by God's assurance, Ananias meets Saul. The Holy Ghost appears, but does not speak. Saul repents his persecution of the Christians, his sight is restored, and he asks for baptism. Next we see the knights reporting Saul's defection to the bishops, who at first refuse to believe the story, then swear vengeance on him. In a scene apparently added later, Belial tells how he sent Saul to persecute Christians. The diabolic messenger Mercury enters to report Saul's conversion. Belial will inspire the bishops to contrive Saul's death.

Saul preaches a sermon against the seven deadly sins. A servant of the bishops commands him to appear before them. He is apparently going. We cut back to the bishops, who condemn the absent apostle to death. An angel appears to him to warn him to leave Damacus. He says he will escape over the wall in a basket. Here the play ends with an apologetic epilogue beseeching the audience to forgive the play's lack of "intelligence" of rhetoric.

The play, as a dramatic piece, needs some apology. Historically, it has some interest. The themes and devices mainly derive from the cycle plays. Saul's initial speech is of a sort with the rantings of Herod and Pilate though moderated. The devil scene comes from the harrowing of hell. Emphasis on the spectacular of the sort noted in Ludus appears in the thunder and lightning of the vision on the road to Damascus and the "fiery flame and tempest" of the devil scene. The staging is apparently a bit different from what we know elsewhere. Stage directions divide the play into several scenes, with Poeta announcing the coming scene in some such words as these:

> Finally of this station we make a conclusion
> Beseeching this audience to follow and succeed
> With all your diligence this general procession.

Evidentally the audience was expected to move from one station to another, somewhat like spectators following a golf-match.

The Digby *Mary Magdalen*, though longer and altogether more elaborate, is constructed in much the same manner. Following the life of Magdalen as it is found in *The Golden Legend* or in the several English works derived from it, *Magdalen* tells a rather sprawling story of adventure and miracle, partly scriptural but mostly legendary. The play contains nearly every element of technique available to the late fifteenth-century dramatist. Some scenes go back to the liturgical Easter play, some are developed on the pattern of the craft cycles, some parallel the moralities. The cast is tremendous, over sixty characters in all, but many parts could be doubled or tripled.

The play opens with several introductory speeches by the Emperor Tiberius; by Cyrus, the father of Magdalen; by Herod; and by Pilate. Tiberius sends letters to Herod and Pilate to suppress the Christians. These potentates receive them and give requisite orders with much scurrying from court to court. Cyrus announces himself as the father of Magdalen, Lazarus, and Martha. When he dies he intends to divide his property among his children, "the Castle of Magdalen" to Mary, Jerusalem to Lazarus, Bethany to Martha.

After Cyrus dies and Mary inherits Magdalen, a morality episode tells the plot of World, Flesh, and Devil, with their followers, the seven deadly sins, against Mary's chastity. Lechery, here a woman, undertakes the task. She calls on Mary and, finding her grieving for her father, suggests some innocent relaxation. Mary assents and Lechery takes her to a tavern. Here she meets Curiosity, a handsome young gallant dressed in the latest fashion, who makes love to her and at length seduces her. A Bad Angel reports the success of the mission to World, Flesh, and Devil.

We next see Mary waiting for her lovers in the arbor of Simon the Leper. A good angel appears to her, apparently in her sleep, and urges her to repent her sins. Just then Jesus comes to visit Simon. Overcome with remorse, Magdalen washes His feet with her tears and anoints them. Jesus tells Simon the parable of the two debtors (Luke 7:41-44) and forgives Mary. Seven devils who have possessed her flee from her to the sound of thunder. In hell these and the Bad Angel report their failure and are flogged.

Next comes the death and raising of Lazarus, presented pretty much as in the cycles. It is not as spectacular as in some versions, probably because it has more miracles and wonders with which to compete. After the Lazarus episode, the play forecasts the main plot by introducing the King of Marseilles. A devil then reports that Christ has harrowed hell. The following scenes are the visitation of the tomb by the three Marys, their announcement of the resurrection to Peter and John, and the meeting between Magdalen and Jesus disguised as a gardener.

Here we shift again to the King of Marseilles, who is making a sacrifice to his god, Mahound. A comic scene between the priest and his boy is a pattern for several others that follow. The boy reads a burlesque "lection of Mahound" in dog Latin:

> Slaundri stroumppum, corbolcorum,
> Snyguer, snaggoer werwolfforum
> Standgarda lamba befettorum.

A scene in which Pilate sends the news of the resurrection to the Emperor, who orders it entered in the chronicles, and another in which Jesus, now apparently ascended, sends the angel Raphael to Mary with a command to go to Marseilles, prepare us for the ensuing action. The next scene opens with a comic interlude between a shipman and his boy.* Enter Mary seeking passage to Marseilles.

The stage properties evidently included a practicable ship, for Magdalen embarks and disembarks before the King's palace in Marseilles. Here she preaches before the King, who goes to his temple to consult his god about the message. The god, the priest tells the King, will not speak while a Christian is present. Mary prays, and the idol quakes, the temple bursts out in flame, and the priest "sinks," apparently through a trap door. The King is now willing to accept Christianity if his childless wife will bear a son. At Mary's prayer, the King and Queen have dreams which determine them to become Christians. When the Queen finds herself with child, the King decides to go to Judaea to be baptized by Peter.

The Queen insists on accompanying him. The two take passage on the same ship that brought Magdalen to Marseilles. A storm arises at sea, the Queen is delivered of her child, and then apparently dies. The sailors insist that the body be thrown overboard, but finally agree to leave the apparently dead Queen and her infant on a rock in the midst of the sea. When they make port, the King searches out Peter and is baptized, returning home by the same ship. The inevitable miracle ensues: the Queen is found alive on the rock and the child as well. All return happily to Marseilles. Finding Mary preaching to the people, they kneel before her in gratitude. She announces that she must leave to spend the rest of her life as a hermit in the wilderness.

The last scenes of the play, though as full of the wondrous as the rest, are somewhat anti-climactic. Angels feed Mary; Jesus appears to foretell her approaching death and salvation, a priest visits her, bringing the eucharist, which she receives and dies. The priest buries her, and the play closes with a *Te deum* and a short apologetic epilogue.

This sprawling play is hardly memorable dramatic art. Characterization, the interplay of character and situation, the purposeful selection of incident to embody theme, of these it has scarcely any. Its contribution is rather to technique. The story is radically romantic—saints' lives are often called the romances of the church. Its architecture fits its story: variety of incident and character, action which crosses and recrosses the Mediterranean, time covering thirty or forty years, staging which strives for the representational in a practicable ship (probably a sort of pageant wagon on wheels to ply back and forth across the stage).

* One imagines that all these master-and-boy scenes were done by the same pair of comics.

Obviously, we are well embarked on the road to the romantic drama of the Elizabethan age, the sort Shakespeare gives us in *Pericles* and *The Winter's Tale*. Scholars like Sidney ridiculed those rambling concoctions in which "two young princes fall in love; after many traverses she is got with child, delivered of a fair boy, he is lost, groweth a man, falleth in love, and is ready to get another child—all this in two hours space." But the English theater-goer held to his taste; and the critics were never able to foist on the English theater, except for one brief period in the late seventeenth century, the supposedly Aristotelean unities. And it was in plays like the Digby *Mary Magdalen* that the technique of the romantic drama was worked out.

Modern scholars have been much occupied with the mixture of forms in *Mary Magdalen*. Elements from the liturgical and the craft drama mix with those of the moral play, and slapstick stands cheek by jowl with spectacle. But, of course, these categories exist only in the mind of the scholar. In the late fifteenth century, when the piece was composed, the building material of a playwright included all this stuff, so why not mix it? The critic of contemporary cinema may recognize that the western, Old Vienna, and the American Civil War are subjects which are each embodied in a characteristic cinematic genre, but the script writer and the director may refuse to recognize such partitions. I once saw a picture which combined six or seven such genres, together with such eccentric developments as a Chinese physician who spoke perfect Edinburgh Scots. In the last scene the lovers, one an ex-Confederate officer turned bandit and the other a Viennese ballet dancer, set out from Old San Francisco for Virginia in a droshky piloted by Russian serfs!

The Conversion of St. Paul and *Mary Magdalen* are the two surviving independent saints' plays. Two other pieces, one only a fragment, belong to a type often subsumed together with the saints' play under the heading of "miracle plays." In fact, *Duk Moraud* and the *Croxton Play of the Sacrament* have little in common with *The Conversion* and *Magdalen*. The first apparently uses a plot common in the French "Miracles of Our Lady" —the conversion of a sinner after a life of crime; the second makes the same kind of use of the spectacular and the miraculous as *Magdalen*.

Duk Moraud has the additional interest of being considerably earlier than the other pieces we have been considering, earlier even than the craft cycles in the forms now extant. It is a fragment containing, like the Shrewsbury fragments, a single actor's part.

It comes to us in a long, narrow roll of parchment cut from a legal document containing court records of the thirteenth century from Norfolk and Suffolk. The play itself is usually dated in the fourteenth century, probably the middle or the latter half.

Though the extant text has nothing but the speeches of Duke Moraud, with no stage directions or even cues, the action of the play was restored by its editor, Dr. Heuser, from other versions of the same story, an unlovely account of incest and murder. The play as we have it begins with the routine threatening and boasting speech in which Moraud magnifies his power. His wife then proclaims her intention of leaving for a while, apparently to go on some sort of journey. Moraud says good-bye and promises to behave himself.

The wife gone, he makes love to his daughter, who yields to his entreaties, probably quite willingly, since there is no evidence of either moral or physical resistance—one speech accomplishes the seduction. The wife returns, discovers the sin, and is apparently going to make it public. Moraud laments that he can never be happy until she is slain, and the daughter does the deed. Moraud rejoices. Somewhat later the daughter bears a child. Moraud is again fearful of exposure, until the daughter kills the child. Moraud is again merry.

The church bell rings. Moraud determines to go to church, "some good deed to work." At church he repents and confesses his crimes to the priest. When he urges the daughter to follow his example, she kills him. As he dies, he prays Jesus to forgive her. That is the end of Moraud's part and of the fragment. Whether it was the end of the play, we cannot know, except that if it was, *Duk Moraud* is unique in the religious and semi-religious drama of the period in presenting a crime both unrepented and unpunished. A closely related version closes with the daughter's suicide. On the other hand, the conventional formula for this sort of work is the conversion of some great sinner through some holy work, often devotion to a saint or the Virgin. If *Duk Moraud* followed this pattern, the daughter was the main character, and what we have of the play may well be little more than an introduction.

The second of the extant miracle plays is usually called *The Croxton Play of the Sacrament*. The first part of the title comes from the banns preceding the play proper, which promise a performance "at Croxton on Monday." In the Trinity College (Dublin) manuscript which contains it, the piece is headed "The Play of the Conversion of Sir Jonathas the Jew by Miracle of the Blessed Sacrament," an amply descriptive title. The hand in which the play is written is of the late fifteenth century and the text itself describes the miracle on which it is based as having been "done in the forest of Aragon, in the famous city of Eraclea in the year of our Lord MCCCCLXI." The manuscript closes with a list of players and the statement "IX may play it at ease"—perhaps a proof of professional performance by a touring company.

The date of the miracle, of course, we cannot take seriously, for it is actually the old theme of ritual profanation, versions of which are known from the end of the thirteenth century. But 1461 is certainly the date before which the play could not have been written. Croxton ought to be a help in locating the provenance of the piece, but it is not. There are too many Croxtons in the Midland area, to which linguistically the play must belong. Other place names in the play ("Babwell Mill") point to a Croxton in the vicinity of Thetford, Norfolk, though one in Cambridgeshire is also possible.

The play is a crude affair. After the banns, the chief characters introduce themselves: Aristorius, a wealthy Christian merchant whose ships make the ports of the world; the parish Priest; Jonathas, a Jewish merchant and his four servants, Jason, Jasdon, Malchus, and Masphat. When the priest leaves to say his evensong, Aristorius and Jonathas meet to transact business. Jonathas wants to prove the Christians wrong in worshipping a "cake," the sacrament of course, and is willing to pay one hundred pounds for a host, so that he can prove it nothing but bread. After some hesitation, Aristorius agrees to get Jonathas one. When the priest finishes evensong and leaves the church, apparently unguarded, Aristorius secretly enters and purloins the host.

Once Jonathas has possession of it, he calls his servants to witness a disproof of Christian belief. He calls on them all to plunge their daggers into the wafer. Here comes the first miracle: the host bleeds. Undismayed, Jonathas picks it up to cast it into boiling oil. But the host adheres to his hand, he cannot let go and runs about madly. The servants nail the host to a post and they try to pull him loose from it. Instead, his hand separates from the arm.

At this point the author inserts a comic interlude between Master Brundich of Brabant, an itinerant quack, and his boy, Colle, who cries his master's skill in medicine and solicits patients. This is the standard doctor of folk drama, familiar to us as the ointment merchant in the German resurrection plays and also in the St. George plays. In the Croxton play his introduction is totally unmotivated and serves no dramatic purpose, since Jonathas does not use his ministrations, instead ordering his servants to drive the imposter away.

The action then resumes. One of the servants pulls out the nails that hold the host (and Jonathas' hand) to the post, and, holding it in a cloth, casts it into the cauldron of oil. As the oil boils it turns to blood. Next the Jews put the host in an oven. The last and most spectacular miracle follows when the oven bursts, blood runs out the cracks, and an image of Jesus with bleeding wounds appears. Jesus then speaks to the Jews: Why do they persecute him anew? At last convinced, Jonathas asks forgiveness and all are converted. Jesus commands Jonathas to put his arm into the cauldron and, lo, it is rejoined to the hand.

Jonathas then goes to the Bishop to confess his wrong and ask forgiveness and baptism. When the Bishop enters his house the image changes back into bread. The Bishop carries the sacrament back to the church, and the Jews form a procession behind him. As it approaches, the priest asks Aristorius the meaning of this marvel, Jews following the Bishop in solemn procession. Aristorius understands what has happened and tells the priest how he stole the sacrament. Then Aristorius publicly asks forgiveness of the Bishop. The priest, too, admits his laxness in not guarding the sacrament better. The Bishop forgives both and preaches a sermon, emphasizing particularly the duty of priests to keep their "pyxes locked," and guard the key to God's temple. The Jews are baptized, and the play ends with a *Te deum.*

Despite its lack of artistry, the Croxton play has some interesting features. For one, it is the nearest thing to topical propaganda found in the drama of the fifteenth century. Its didactic purpose is rather narrow: a demonstration of the doctrine of transubstantiation. Miss Cutts, who has investigated the play's background, finds miracles involving the host extremely popular after 1382, doubtless as a counterblast to Wyclif and his followers, who attacked the dogma of the real presence. Literary popularity was reinforced by pictorial representations. Miss Cutts finds the incident of the stabbing of the host depicted in an illuminated gospel lectionary of 1408 and a wall painting, now destroyed, in a Lincolnshire church dating from the middle of the century. Wyclif's teachings retained influence over a considerable body of followers almost to the beginning of the sixteenth century, especially in East Anglia. The probable provenance of the play in this area is significant.

Dramatically, the play has little significance, except possibly as testimony to the hold of the dramatic form on the people—the popularity of a product is frequently proved by the number of cheap imitations—and its adaptability to propaganda, a use to which it was increasingly put in the Tudor age.

Chapter XI. EPILOGUE

AMONG THE ACHIEVEMENTS of English dramatic writing up to about 1500, one achievement is lacking. We have no considerable body of secular plays from medieval England, as we have from France. One possible and one certain piece make up the extant secular drama of Medieval England.

A fragmentary thirteenth-century *Interlude of the Clerk and the Girl* may be part of a play, but it may also be part of a non-dramatic narrative poem. It incorporates a theme well known in the verse of the wandering scholars. A clerk woos a Maid Malkin and, repulsed by the girl, seeks the assistance of an older woman, called "Mome Elvis." From the latter part of the fifteenth century comes a play of Robin Hood and the Sheriff of Nottingham, which may well be the one played by Sir John Paston's servant, who had also, according to Sir John's letter, a play of St. George in his repertory.

Sir E. K. Chambers found records of a play on Eglemour and Degrebell given at St. Albans in 1444 and one on a "knight cleped Florence" at Bermondsley. Sir Eglemour and Sir Florence are both known as heroes of romance, and these were undoubtedly secular pieces. One cannot be quite so sure about a play of King Robert of Sicily given at Lincoln in 1453 and at Chester somewhat later. Robert of Sicily could also be treated in the manner of a miracle play.

Although this is a meager record, we cannot, when we remember how unrepresentative the total of religious drama is of what actually existed, dismiss secular drama as virtually unpractised in England before 1500. Professor Wickham has collected several records of performances which may well have been drama. These come in a variety of categories, tournaments and *pas d'armes*, which were sometimes preceded by an allegory in which "shepherds" or "wild men" appeared; coronations and royal entries, like the one described by Richard Maidstone in 1393, which certainly had tableaux vivants involving personification; mummings and disguisings; and all manner of social pastimes, performed certainly in court and probably seeping downward at least to the nobility, and probably to the gentry and the wealthier burgesses; a series of folk games, on May day, during the Christmas season, and at various other times—all these are on the fringes of drama.

They all involve impersonation of some sort. Any which told stories would qualify as drama. With so many spectacles, with the well-known medieval habit of telling or implying a story in all artistic products, even in such unlikely media as stone, it seems unlikely that none of these quasi-dramatic forms ever crossed the boundary into drama.

What we lack, of course, to make the likelihood a certainty, is texts. There is a good reason why these would be lacking. The tournaments, royal entries, courtly pastimes were ephemeral—any text would be made for the unique performance and would stand small chance of survival. Folk material is committed to memory, not paper. The folk plays we have, many of them certainly going back to medieval origins, were not written down until antiquaries became interested in folk lore and local customs. This did not happen until the seventeenth and eighteenth centuries. The fact that we have one fifteenth-century text of a Robin Hood play ought to be taken as proof that there were many such plays in the later Middle Ages.

Nevertheless, when we have allowed for the existence of a considerable quantity of secular drama, we still have no evidence of sophisticated secular pieces like the uproarious French farce, *Patelin*, or the Spanish *Celestina*, both of them safely datable before 1500. Such things were to come in the Tudor era, but in this kind of drama England was, not uncharacteristically, half a century behind the continent.

When secular plays did come, a few years before 1500,* their authors and actors built on the solid foundations laid by their medieval predecessors. Well into the Elizabethan age the pattern of the morality play dominated the theater, extended and adapted as it was to a variety of purposes, religious controversy, social satire, political propaganda, and even the dramatization of history. That most Elizabethan of genres, the chronicle play, had as its first representative *King John* written by the ex-Carmelite John Bale on the model of a morality: the vices Sedition, Private Wealth, and Dissimulation find names and local habitations as Stephen Langton, Cardinal Pandulph, and Raymond of Toulouse, and King John himself is a sort of Mankind, now leaning towards vice, now towards virtue, which are papal and anti-papal policy, respectively.

The student of the greatest products of Elizabethan drama, the tragedies of Shakespeare, recognizes at every hand carry-overs from the dramatic experience of half a millenium that preceded them. The effects of the cycle play and the morality on the very structure of a play like *Hamlet* are profound. One only has to read a tragedy of Sophocles or of Racine to appreciate the indebtedness of Shakespeare to his predecessors in the religious drama of the fifteenth century, which, of course, was still performed in Shakespeare's youth.

The pushing forward of the story in several lines, which cross and separate and interweave, the complicated plot with its several sets of characters which this management makes possible, the swift transfer of

---

* Henry Medwall's *Fulgens and Lucrece*, though not printed before 1513, is dated by its editors, F. S. Boas and A. W. Reed, in 1497. Another work of Medwall's, *Nature*, a sort of secular morality, was written probably after the turn of the century.

the action from place to place, the fluidity of time—these characteristics can never be explained or justified by anything the classical drama of Greece or Rome produced. Yet they are the very essence of Shakespeare's dramatic craftsmanship. Can anyone imagine the action of *Macbeth* taking place entirely in Glamis Castle or within a space of a few hours? Who with only the experience of the Greeks and their imitators as model would think of putting on the stage the "very casques that did affright the air" of Agincourt?

Or if these more serious structural elements fail to convince, what of those low comedy scenes, that series of grave-diggers and porters, and fools that enhance or mar the finest tragic efforts? One looks in vain for anything like them in Sophocles or Euripides, but finds them in abundance in the cycles and moralities, often used purposelessly and tastelessly. But when a genius like the Wakefield Master writes low comedy into the solemn adoration of the shepherds, then we recognize the kinship.

The stage used by Shakespeare and his contemporaries is a logical extension of that used by the liturgical dramatists and the moralities. Historically, its form may well be derived from the inn yard, but the use to which the playwrights put such a playing space, the way they blocked their action on it, follows exactly the example of their medieval predecessors. In fact, the Elizabethans found ready-made a stage on which armies could march and fight, kings and cardinals enter in solemn procession, or, as different exigencies demanded, a man could have a quiet talk with his wife in their bedroom, or a tortured soul pour out his meditations on the futility of life. Every such scene found in the works of Shakespeare or his fellows can be paralleled in the cycle plays or the moralities.

The most important of the contributions of the medieval drama to the Elizabethan lies, unfortunately, beyond the ken of the literary historian, who must perforce be confined to documentary remains. This is the continuity of a professional craft of the theater, the tradition of actors, directors, and producers, hardly ever reduced to writing, but ever maintaining itself as a living entity. When James Burbage and John Brains opened the first permanent professional playhouse in England in 1576, they did not have to recruit and train a corps of actors. One had existed in England for over a century, in the form of the strolling players who presented *Mankind* to rural audiences for groats and pence, equally in the form of actors renowned enough to be summoned all the way from London to play in the York cycle and good enough to merit a payment of four shillings for playing Pilate at Coventry.

We can only guess and imagine what this means. Even today the

173

theater has traditions handed down through generations, often in the same family, since the late seventeenth century—a certain series of gestures, for instance, still used in Brutus' speech to the Roman citizens after the assassination of Caesar. This is the way the professional theater has always maintained its traditions: old actors coach the younger ones. One imagines that many of the actors that came to occupy the stages of the Theater or the Fortune or the Globe were sons of fathers who had played at Coventry or York or Chester in the last days of their cycles, perhaps had even themselves got their start in such a manner. And they may have had grandfathers and greatgrandfathers who were similarly occupied. Or if the relationship was in craft rather than by blood, it was just as strong.

The Elizabethan theatrical company was a closely knit family, actors, writers, directors living and working together. What would be more natural, when producing a play calling for a royal entrance, than the director's calling on the experience of one of the older actors who remembered how they did it when Herod came on in the Chester passion play? This is the most probable road by which the collective dramatic experience accumulated by five centuries of religious drama penetrated the secular theater.

But, of course, the unknown playwrights, actors, and producers of the cycles and the moralities did not know they were making straight the road for Marlowe, Shakespeare, and Jonson. That was not their intention, and it should not be our criterion for judging their work. Enough has already been said in this brief account to make it clear that they created a vital dramatic literature which, even in the fragmentary state it has come down to us, can stand on its own excellence.

In at least one way they outdid the Elizabethans, or any other group of dramatists who have ever lived, except perhaps the tragedians and comedians of Athens. The Elizabethan theater was largely confined to London. Companies sometimes went on tour—generally when the plague closed the theaters of the capital—but the plays were written in London, produced in London, and seen mainly by Londoners. In more modern times the theater has normally centered in the large cities, London, New York, Paris. The product of the cinema industry is widely dispersed, its audience being virtually international, but the manufacture is extremely centralized.

The medieval drama is as near a true national effort as the history of dramatic literature affords, or, if one thinks of the liturgical drama, international, for the Middle Ages had the advantage over us in having a supra-national language in Latin. Even in the vernacular drama, there can have been few places in England more than thirty or forty miles distant from a town where plays of some sort or other were regularly given. In as social an art as the dramatic this fact is of enormous significance. It means that the medieval drama comes closer to expressing the totality of national consciousness than its successors.

One limitation we notice, not geographical, but social and economic. The drama of the fourteenth and fifteenth centuries, at least what remains of it, gave almost no expression to what we know from other sources were the dominant literary interests of the upper classes. Neither in the cycle plays nor in the moralities do we find any considerable use of the motifs of knightly romance, courtly love, or the ideals of chivalry. The reason is not that such material would not fit into the religious drama. Material as seemingly unsuited as social and political satire, for example, gets in. The reason is that the drama is the work of townsfolk, of the burgesses, and such ideals as that of courtly love found little place in their consciousness. The plight of the carpenter of Chaucer's *Miller's Tale*, the old man japed by the young wife, they could understand and they wrote such material into the Mary-and-Joseph scenes; but Launcelot and Guinevere left them cold.

With this exception almost everything else in the vivid life of the fourteenth and fifteenth centuries finds some expression. All is dominated, as we should expect, by religion, a circumstance which agrees with what we know of the social actualities of the period. This religion is, again as we should suspect, the religion of the parish church and the street-corner sermon of the mendicant friar, not of the doctor of divinity in the University. Though not simple, it is a popular religion, broad enough to comprehend all life and deep enough to set the world in order by establishing a grand scheme of history which explained all the diverse phenomena of the world.

This scheme in its universal form was the subject of the cycles, in its pertinence to the individual man, that of the moralities. And, of course, every viable society has some counterweight to its official ideology, some little corner in which the usual rules do not apply. The miracle plays, with their wild romance, occupy this corner in medieval drama.

The vitality of this creation of the late Middle Ages is sufficiently proved by its capacity to endure. The cycles themselves lasted two centuries or more, though with constant changes, and the morality as a form perhaps a century. The intrinsic stageworthiness of both genres has been amply demonstrated in the modern theater, where the plays themselves have found appreciative audiences and the dramaturgic resources of medieval playwrights have contributed greatly to the technique of the modern theater.

Beginning with amateur productions, motivated largely by historical interests, the revivals of medieval plays started with *Everyman* and the

Towneley *Second Shepherds' Play* and have now encompassed whole cycles. Both Chester and York have found admiring modern audiences. Originally planned for the Festival of Britain in 1951, the York plays, presented in an abbreviated version made by Dr. Purvis, proved so fascinating to both critics and the general public that they have become a fixture given every three years. In 1958 Mr. Martial Rose directed a performance of the Towneley cycle, in a still unpublished modernization, at the Bretton Hall School, near Wakefield. Professor Wickham has produced several parts of Ludus, and in 1960 the section dealing with the childhood of Mary and the nativity of Jesus was presented at St. Mary's College in Indiana, with direction by E. Martin Browne, who also directed the York cycle in its 1951 production. *The Castle of Perseverance*, which even academic critics have usually dismissed as dull, turned out to be stageworthy when played a decade ago by the Oxford University Dramatic Society.

The production at York is at least semi-professional, and *Everyman* has often been done in the professional theater, sometimes taken on tour. The chief clientele for the medieval drama, however, will always be the church dramatic society, the amateur theatrical group, and the school, and for the best of reasons: the plays were written for amateur production. None better have ever been written. Universality of theme and soundness of construction make them fool-proof. So much modern drama needs the services of the slick professional director and of seasoned actors to conceal its essential shallowness of meaning that anything less than a first class production is a fiasco. The cycle plays and some of the moralities, like folk story and popular ballad, have had all triviality and adventitiousness knocked out of them in their long history.

The greatest testimony to this basic soundness is the way the modern theater has returned to both theme and constructional technique of the medieval drama. Two of the greatest successes of the American theater have used the essential structure of the craft cycle, Marc Connelly's *The Green Pastures* and Thornton Wilder's *Skin of Our Teeth*. The former establishes its kinship with York and Chester in its material, the Bible seen through the eyes of Louisiana negroes, the latter in its attempt to dramatize the history of the human race. Both use liberally one of the main devices by which the cycle dramatists interpreted the meaning of sacred history, purposeful anachronism. When Mr. Wilder has a radio news bulletin announce the ice age, he is following precisely in the steps of the medieval playwright who made Annas and Caiaphas bishops.

In technique, the last quarter century or slightly more has seen a persistent effort to abolish the proscenium arch and to ignore the curtain. Drama has been taken outdoors whenever possible, as in the processional pageants on historical themes of Paul Green and his disciples. Even indoors the playwright uses the aisles or builds runways to carry the action into the audience. Often he tries to include the audience in the action, by having apparent members of it rise and step into the play. No longer content with the neat drawing-room comedy or tragedy, he attempts to open up the play both spatially and temporally. In all these devices, he is following the precedent of both the liturgical and the vernacular medieval drama. The theater-in-the-round is essentially a return to the fifteenth-century stage. It can hardly be accident that this new dramaturgy gains popularity exactly when the study of the medieval drama, starting with the antiquarians and passing to the academics, begins to overflow first into the amateur theater, and then into the professional.

The end of the old religious drama came in the sixteenth century, first to the moralities, which died a natural death, that is, they were modified to new uses and eventually absorbed into the professional drama of the Elizabethan age. For half a century or more the transitional morality lived an energetic, if not always artistically laudable, life as a vehicle for political and social satire and for religious polemic.

The cycle plays, of course, could not be so absorbed, though much of the dramatic tradition they build up was, as Professor Farnham demonstrated. They differed in one important respect from the moralities, and so they suffered a more sudden, though later, demise. The morality pattern could be used as well to attack the old church as to disseminate its doctrines and attitudes. In fact, in the period from 1535 to about 1560 or a little later, there are more Protestant moralities than Catholic. But the scriptural drama of the cycles was not so flexible. Such doctrines as transubstantiation, the veneration of saints and images, and the sacramental theory of grace are inextricably woven into the great cycles. They are not external adornment which could be removed or broken up the way the images were in Scots churches. They are the structure: remove them and the whole collapses.

Father Gardiner, who has made the most exhaustive study of the final days of the great cycles, is right in saying that the one immediate cause of their death was the opposition of the Protestant authorities in church and state. The York cycle was last given in 1569, the Chester in 1575. It was neither want of interest in the plays nor the rivalry of the professional theater that ended them. The dates of the last performances are significant, for this is exactly the period when the Elizabethan settlement was firmly established, Elizabeth's anti-papal foreign policy made explicit, and England become irrevocably Protestant. Nearer the center of Protestant sentiment, the home counties and the southeast, performances ceased sooner, probably in the late fifties in Norwich.

The last cycle to go was probably in the most out-of-the-way place, Kendal, where the old plays may have lasted until 1603.

It was not that Protestantism was necessarily or always opposed to the drama as a form, though among proto-Puritans there are evidences of this: the municipal authorities of London frowned on plays, wherefore the dramatic companies of Shakespeare's day usually found it safer to have their theaters across the Thames. But many Protestant leaders, both in England and on the continent wrote plays, John Bale being an eminent English example and Theodore de Bèze, Calvin's lieutenant and successor, a continental one. The sixteenth century produced dozens of scriptural plays, generally on Old Testament subjects, by Protestants.

The specific things in the old drama to which the Protestant reformers objected appear clearly in the command which the Diocesan Court of High Commission for York, an arm of the Privy Council of the realm, addressed to the officials of Wakefield under date of 27 May, 1576:

This day upon intelligence given to the said Commission that it is meant and purposed that in the town of Wakefield shall be played this year in Whitsun week next or thereabouts a play commonly called Corpus Christi Play, which hath been heretofore used there, wherein they are done t'understand that there be many things used which tend to the derogation of the majesty and glory of God, the profanation of the sacraments and the maintenance of superstition and idolatry, the said Commissioners decreed a letter to be written and sent to the bailiff, burgesses and other inhabitants of the said town of Wakefield that in the said play no pageant be used or set forth wherein the Majesty of God the Father, God the Son, or God the Holy Ghost, or the administration of either the sacraments of baptism or of the Lord's Supper be counterfeited or represented, or anything played which tend[s] to the maintenance of superstition and idolatry or which be contrary to the laws of God or of the realm.

And so the Towneley plays passed into literary history, for you cannot play them, or any other cycle, without representing the person of God on the stage or playing the institution of the Eucharist at the Last Supper. It was the whole rationale of the old drama to which the reformers objected.

Protestant opposition is then the chief immediate cause for the abandonment of the cycles. But the Protestant movement, especially in England, comprehends much more than a theology. It adopted many of the attitudes of humanists like Erasmus, who remained a good Catholic, and More, who became a martyr for the old church, both of whom strenuously opposed many practises that are written into the cycles.

It is testimony to the humanist opposition to the sort of drama represented by the cycles that it ceased in Italy before it did in England, being replaced by a religious drama on the classical model. In Spain, where humanism was not so strong, but where Protestantism was the feeblest of anywhere in Western Europe, a religious drama sprang up which was neither classical nor medieval, the *auto sacramental*. The trinity of great dramatists of the Golden Era, Tirso de Molina, Lope de Vega, and Calderon, all wrote numerous autos, using pretty much the same structure that they used in their secular plays.

In German speaking lands the old religious drama lasted into the seventeenth century in the hinterlands like Bavaria and the Tyrol. In France it succumbed earlier than in England to the combined assaults of a strong Protestant movement, a critical humanism, and the sensitivity of reform-minded Catholics embarrassed by the excesses of the old drama in the way of the uncontrolled invasion of comic elements and the over-elaboration of the legendary and the apocryphal.

It would therefore be fair to say that, even had not the official Protestant policy of the English government given the death blow to the cycles in the third quarter of the century, changing tastes, an altered social structure, and necessary religious reforms would either have led to their abondonment or changed them into something totally different.

They were the products of a definite social, political, and intellectual milieu. The vigorous life of the late medieval city, the relative freedom allowed the city in the political organization of the nation, the centrality of the church—all these are the roots of the medieval drama. Once they were cut, as they were in the sixteenth century, the tree must have withered.

THE MUSIC OF THE QUEM QUAERITIS

THE FOLLOWING TRANSPOSITION of the music of the Winchester Troper, (Oxford, Ms Bodl. 775) which beyond reasonable doubt was that of the first dramatic version of the trope, preserved in *Regularis concordia*, was made by Dr. W. L. Smoldon, through whose generosity it is reproduced here. The version given on pages 181-182 represents a slight correction of versions previously published by Dr. Smoldon.

Quem quae- ri- tis in se-
pul- chro, (o) Chri-sti- co- lae?
Ihe- sum Na- za- re- num cru- ci-
fi- xum, o cae- li- co- la.
Non est hic, sur- re- xit si- cut prae-di-
xe- rat; i- te, nun-ti- a- te qui-
a sur- re- xit, di- cen- tes:
Al- le- lu- ia, re- sur-re- xit Do- mi-
nus ho- di- e, le- o for-
tis, Chri-stus fi- li- us

De-i; De-o gra-ti- as, di-ci-te e- ia! Ve-ni-te et vi-de-te lo- cum u-bi po-si-tus e-rat Do-mi-nus; al- le- lu- ia, al- le- lu- ia. Ci-to e- un- tes, di- ci- te di-sci-pu- lis qui- a sur-re-xit Do-mi-nus; al- le- lu- ia, al- le- lu- ia. Sur-re- xit Do-mi- nus de se-pul-chro, qui pro no- bis pe-pen-dit in li- gno; al- le- lu- ia.

THE MUSIC OF THE QUEM QUAERITIS

The music of the liturgical drama receives increasing attention from musicologists. The two best treatments, both of which incorporate many scores transcribed into plainsong notation, are both by W. L. Smoldon: "Liturgical Music Drama," *Grove's Dictionary of Music and Musicians*, 5th ed., ed. Eric Blom (1954); "Liturgical Drama," *New Oxford History of Music*, Vol. II (1954). "The History of Music in Sound," a series of recordings prepared to illustrate the *New Oxford History of Music* (issued in the United States by RCA Victor and in Britain by HMV) contains in Album II, side 8, the quem quaeritis and some music from the Beauvais *Daniel*. The latter has been recorded in its entirety by the New York Pro Musica, Noah Greenberg director, Decca DL 9402.

SOME BOOKS ON MEDIEVAL DRAMA

CHAPTER I. The relationships between ritual and drama are developed in Herbert Weisinger, *Tragedy and the Paradox of the Fortunate Fall* (London, 1953). Extreme views on the origin of medieval drama in pagan ritual are found in Robert Stumpfl, *Kultspiele der Germanen als Ursprung des mittelalterlichen Dramas* (Berlin, 1936) and B. Hunningher, *The Origin of the Theater* (The Hague & Amsterdam, 1955).

CHAPTERS II-III. Latin texts of the pieces discussed are in Karl Young, *The Drama of the Mediaeval Church* (Oxford, 1933). English and Latin texts of the *Regularis Concordia* are in the edition of Thomas Symonds (Oxford, 1953), the quem quaeritis on pp. 49-50. English translations of some of the texts can be found in J. Q. Adams, *Chief Pre-Shakespearean Dramas* (Cambridge, Mass., 1924). Robert Schenkkan and Kai Jurgensen, *Fourteen Plays for the Church* (New Brunswick, N. J., 1948); and David Fay Robinson, *The Harvard Dramatic Club Miracle Plays* (New York and London, 1928) contain texts of several liturgical and continental pieces adapted for church dramatic societies. Discussions of the liturgical drama are found in Sir E. K. Chambers, *The Mediaeval Stage* (Oxford, 1903), with which compare his later *English Literature at the Close of the Middle Ages* (Oxford, 1947); and Hardin Craig, *English Religious Drama of the Middle Ages* (Oxford, 1955).

CHAPTER IV. The Shrewsbury Fragments are in Adams and in Osborne Waterhouse, *The Non-Cycle Mystery Plays*, Early English Text Society, extra series, 104 (London, 1909). Rossell Hope Robbins published one of the French-English fragments in *Modern Language Notes*, vol. 65 (1950), pp. 30-35; and J. P. Gilson the other in *Times Literary Supplement*, 26 May 1921, pp. 340-41, with discussion in the issues of 2 June, p. 356, and 9 June, p. 373. The French text of *Adam* is edited by Paul Studer as *Mystère d'Adam* (Manchester, 1918); an English translation by Edward Noble Stone appears in the *University of Washington Publications in Language and Literature*, vol. 4, no. 2 (Seattle, 1926). Only the French text of the Anglo-Norman *Resurrection* is available, edited by T. A. Jenkins and others, Anglo-Norman Texts, vol. 4 (Oxford, 1943).

CHAPTERS V-VI. Records of the craft plays are found in Chambers, *The Mediaeval Stage;* Craig, *English Religious Drama*, and his edition of the two Coventry Plays, Early English Text Society, extra series, 87 (London, 1902); and F. M. Salter, *Mediaeval Drama in Chester* (Toronto, 1955). The standard edition of the Chester Plays is by Herman Diemling, Early English Text Society, extra series, 62 and 115 (London, 1892, 1916); Maurice Hussey has modernized the cycle, *The Chester Mystery Plays* (London, 1957). Lucy Toulmin Smith's edition of the York Plays (Oxford, 1885) is still the only complete text, though the version prepared by Rev. J. S. Purvis for presentation at York is excellent for the general reader: *The York Cycle of Mystery Plays* (London, 1951). The Towneley Plays are edited by George England, Early English Text Society, extra series, 71 (London, 1897); and Ludus by K. S. Block, Early English Text Society, extra series, 120 (London, 1922). Waterhouse, *The Non-Cycle Mystery Plays,* edited the Norwich Grocers' Play, the Brome and Dublin Abraham and Isaac plays and the Newcastle Noah. The Digby *Slaughter of the Innocents* is in *The Digby Plays,* ed. F. J. Furnivall, Early English Text Society, extra series, 70 (London, 1896). Two recent paperbacks give generous representation to the cycles (including the Cornish in Cawley's): *Religious Drama,* vol. 2, ed. E. Martin Browne (New York: Meridian, 1958); and *Everyman and Medieval Miracle Plays,* ed. A. C. Cawley (New York: Dutton, 1959). Several anthologies and school texts, contain the Chester *Deluge* and the Towneley *Second Shepherds'.* There are also several anthologies of pieces from the cycles modernized for church dramatic groups: E. Martin Browne, *Religious Plays for Use in Churches* (London, 1932); Lynette Fessey, *Old English at Play* (London, 1944); Roger Sherman Loomis and Henry W. Wells, *Representative Medieval and Tudor Plays* (New York, 1942); Rev. Phillips Endecott Osgood, *Old Time Church Drama Adapted* (New York, 1928).

CHAPTER VII. Denis van Alsloot's paintings are reproduced with commentary by James Laver in *Isabella's Triumph,* Faber's Gallery, published by Faber and Faber. (London, n. d.) Dr. Hildburgh's "English Alabaster Carvings as Records of the Mediaeval Religious Drama" appears in *Archaeologia,* vol. 93 (1949), pp. 51-101. A valuable new study of staging is Glynne Wickham, *Early English Stages, 1300-1660,* Vol. I (London and New York, 1959).

CHAPTER VIII. The scholarly works cited in this chapter are Albert C. Baugh, "The Chester Plays and French Influence," *Schelling Anniversary Papers* (New York, 1923), pp. 35-63; John Spiers, "The Mystery Cycle: Some Towneley Plays," *Scrutiny,* vol. 18 (1951), pp. 86-117, 246-65; Dom Timothy Fry, O. S. B., "The Unity of the Ludus Coventriae," *Studies in Philology,* vol. 48 (1951), pp. 527-70; Jesse Byers Reese, "Alliterative Verse in the York Cycle," *Studies in Philology,* vol. 48 (1951), pp. 639-68.

CHAPTER IX. The text of *The Pride of Life* is in Waterhouse, *The Non-Cycle Mystery Plays;* those of *The Castle of Perseverance, Wisdom,* and *Mankind* in *The Macro Plays,* ed. F. J. Furnivall and Alfred W. Pollard, Early English Text Society, extra series, 91 (London, 1904). Richard Southern, *The Medieval Theatre in the Round* (London, 1957), is a detailed study of the staging of *The Castle of Perseverance. Everyman* is easy to find, being often reprinted in anthologies, school texts, and modernized acting versions. Professor Henry de Vocht's *Everyman: a Comparative Study of Texts and Sources* appears in *Materials for the Study of the Old English Drama,* vol. 20 (Louvain, 1947). For the source of *Everyman,* see Genji Takahashi, *A Study of Everyman* (Tokyo, 1953).

CHAPTER X. *The Conversion of St. Paul* and *Mary Magdalen* are in *The Digby Plays, Duk Moraud* in Adams' *Chief Pre-Shakespearean Dramas,* the Croxton *Play of the Sacrament* in Waterhouse. Miss Cutt's study appeared in *Modern Language Quarterly,* vol. 5 (1944), pp. 54-60.

CHAPTER XI. The text of the *Interlude of the Clerk and the Girl* is in Chambers' *Mediaeval Stage,* that of *Robin Hood and the Sheriff of Nottingham* in Adams. On the effects of the medieval drama on the Elizabethan see Professor Wickham's study and Willard Farnham, *The Medieval Heritage of Elizabethan Tragedy* (Berkeley, Calif., 1936), and on the last days of the cycle plays Harold C. Gardiner, S. J., *Mysteries' End,* Yale Studies in English, vol. 103 (New Haven, 1946), from which I quote the Wakefield document.